THE SECRET LANGUAGE
of the MIND

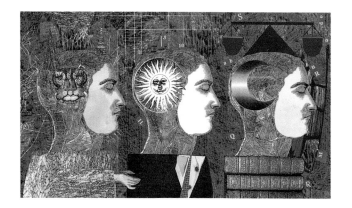

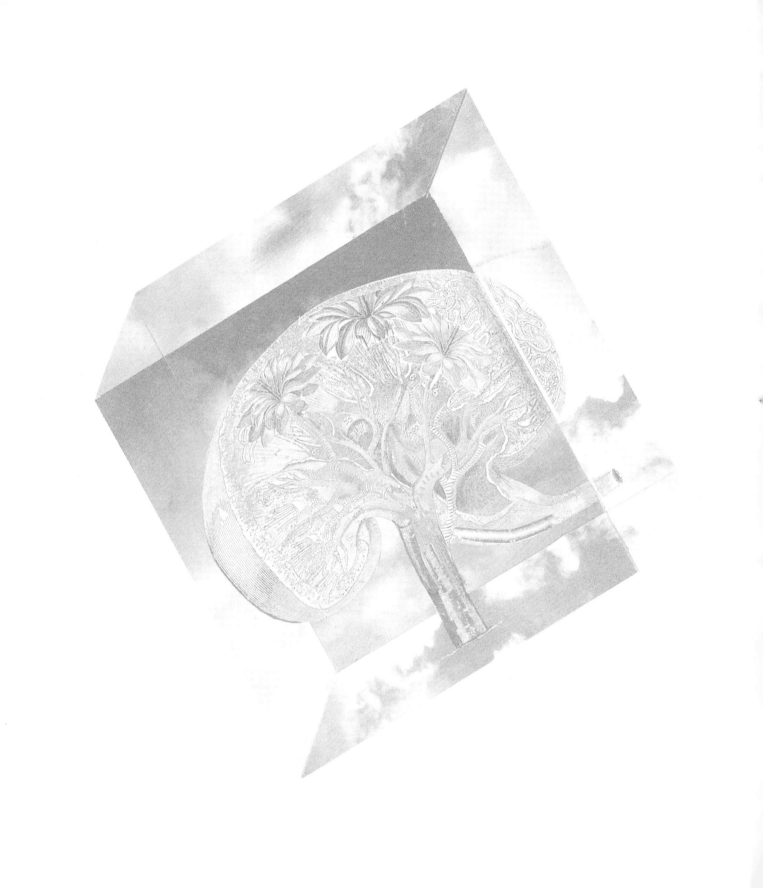

THE SECRET LANGUAGE
of the MIND

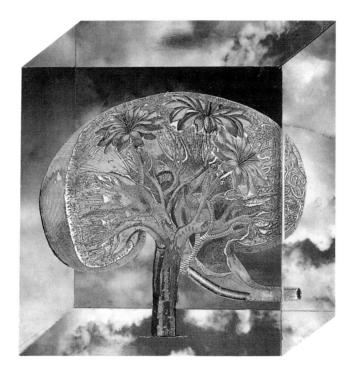

A VISUAL INQUIRY INTO THE
MYSTERIES OF CONSCIOUSNESS

DAVID COHEN

CHRONICLE BOOKS

SAN FRANCISCO

The Secret Language of the Mind
A Visual Inquiry into the Mysteries of Consciousness

First published in the United States in 1996 by Chronicle Books

Conceived, Edited and Designed by
Duncan Baird Publishers
Sixth Floor
Castle House
75–76 Wells Street
London W1P 3RE

Editors: *Stephanie Driver, Marek Walisiewicz*
Designers: *Paul Reid, Lucie Penn*
Commissioned Artwork: *Neil Packer, Matthew Richardson, Lorraine Harrison*
Commissioned Photography: *Claire Lazarus*
Picture Research: *Cecilia Weston-Baker*
Indexer: *Brian Amos*

Library of Congress Cataloging-in-Publication Data

Cohen, David. 1946-
    The secret language of the mind : a visual inquiry into the
mysteries of consciousness / by David Cohen.
        p.   cm.
    Includes bibliographical reference and index.
    ISBN 0-8118-1407-6. -- ISBN 0-8118-1431-9 (pbk.)
    1. Consciousness. 2. Perception. 3. Altered states of consciousness. 4. Mind and body. I. Title.
BF311.C5546 1996
153--dc20   96-10435
                                                                                                  CIP

Typeset in Berthold Walbaum
Colour reproduction by Colourscan, Singapore
Printed in Singapore

Distributed in Canada by
Raincoast Books
8680 Cambie Street
Vancouver, B.C. V6P 6M9

10 9 8 7 6 5 4 3 2 1

Chronicle Books
275 Fifth Street
San Francisco, CA 94103

The mind of man is this world's true dimension
And knowledge is the measure of the mind;
As the mind in her vast comprehension
Contains more worlds than all the world can find,
So knowledge doth itself far more extend
Than all the minds of men can comprehend.

from *A Treaty of Human Learning* (1633)
by Fulke Greville (1554–1628)

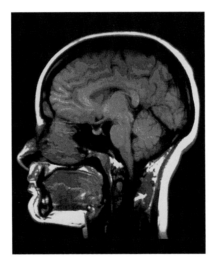

Unfathomable mind! now beacon, now sea.
Samuel Beckett

Contents

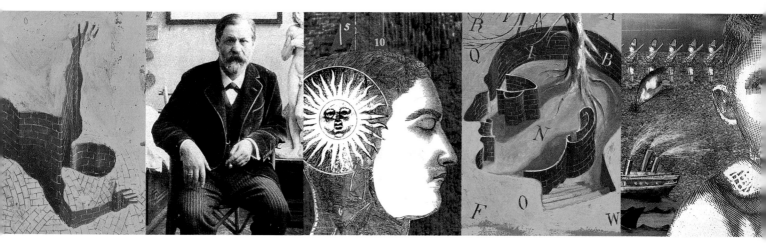

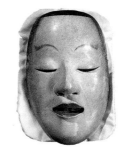

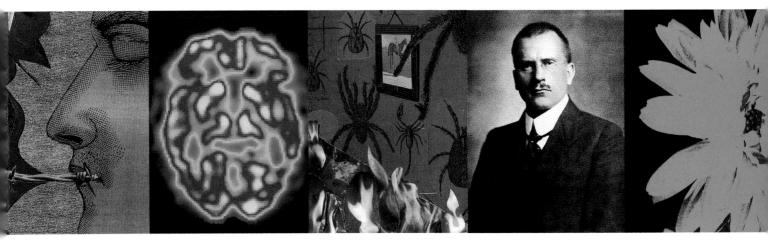

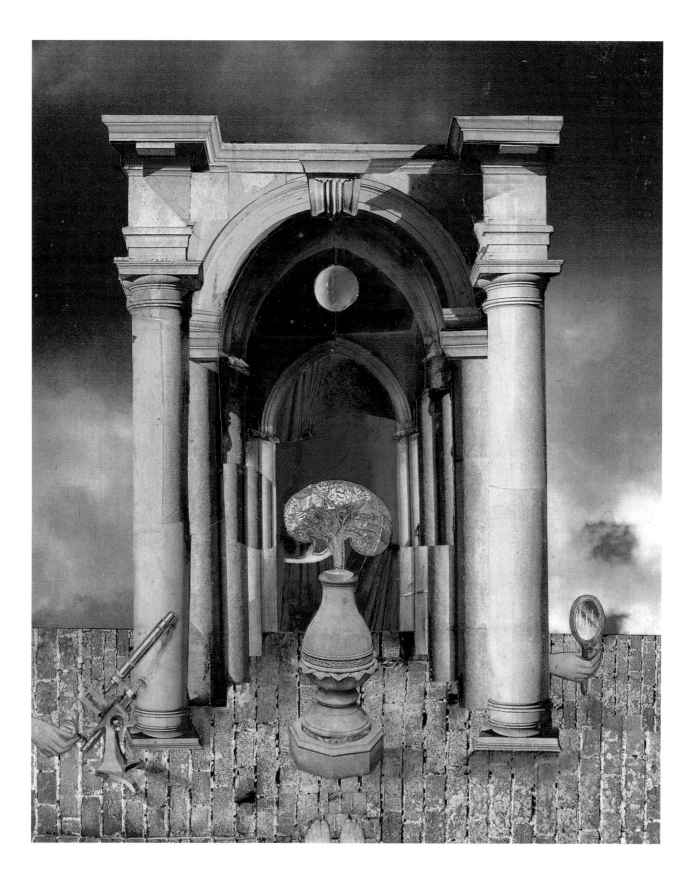

Introduction

The great 18th-century German poet and philosopher Goethe once quipped: "Know thyself! If I knew myself I'd run away." It is ironic, then, that the prestigious Goethe prize, awarded annually in the writer's honour, was won in 1929 by Sigmund Freud, the father of psychoanalysis. Freud's revolutionary belief that self-knowledge was essential in order to achieve the two main goals of life – to be able to love and to work – helped to change fundamentally the ways in which we think about ourselves. More than ever before, human beings are striving to know and understand themselves, and the 20th century has been marked by this relentless search for insight. But such insight is not easily won: in the 19th century, the American essayist Henry David Thoreau encapsulated the difficulties involved when he wrote: "It is as hard to see one's self as to look backwards without turning round."

The search for self-knowledge has been conducted through two fundamentally different approaches, distinguished by German psychologists as *Wissenschaft* (science) and *Verstehung* (understanding). The first is an objective search for medical insight, which in the case of psychological investigation relies on studies of groups of people. It will compare, for example, the measurable response or behaviour of one group of subjects who have been given a particular drug, with the response of a "control" group, who are similar in all ways except that they have not received the drug. The second approach is subjective and analyzes in detail the experiences of individual subjects given the drug as they report them, in order to reveal how these experiences have affected the whole person.

A central aim of the objective approach is to discover how the brain works. It is conducted in a scientific tradition that can be traced back to the early Greek doctors, such as Hippocrates in the 5th century BC and Galen in the 2nd century AD, who were the first to scorn the idea that diseases were punishments of the gods, maintaining instead that they were natural in origin. For example, on the subject of epilepsy (previously known as "the sacred disease") Hippocrates wrote: "It is not any more sacred than other diseases, but has a natural cause: that its origin is supposed to be divine is due to man's inexperience." Through experiment and dissection, the medical pioneers of the Greek and Roman eras were able to describe many diseases and disorders of the mind, often with surprising accuracy, and some of the medical procedures that they developed remain in use today.

Progress in understanding the mind, however, was interrupted after the fall of Rome. The experimental method came to be regarded with suspicion with the disappearance of the tradition of Greek science and philos-

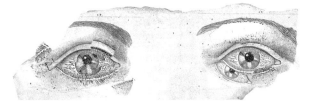

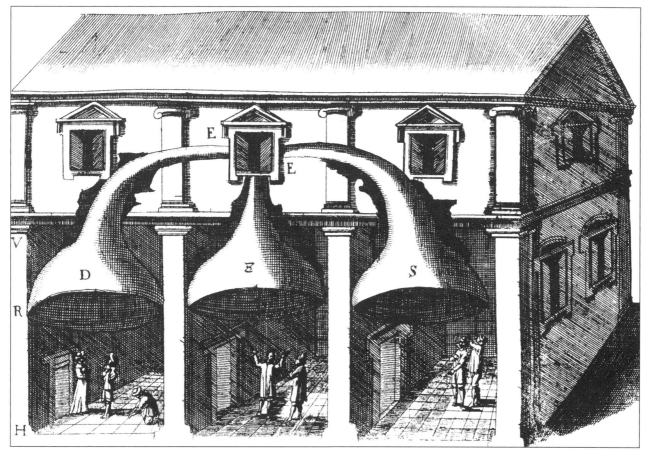

ophy, and dissection was forbidden by the Church, which interpreted it as a desecration of the dead. Doctors were purveyors of quack remedies, folklore and alchemical nonsense. Only in the 17th century, with William Harvey's discovery of the circulation of the blood, did medicine revive as a science. Even so, the revival was slow. The French playwright Molière's last play was *Le malade imaginaire* (1673) – *The Hypochondriac* – in which he satirized doctors as charlatans (Molière died on stage during a performance in which he himself was playing the part of the hypochondriac). And even in the 18th century, naive and wildly inaccurate theories of body and mind were still common cur-

rency. The Scottish lecturer and writer John Brown, for example, believed there to be only two types of disease (asthenic and sthenic) and, correspondingly, two cures (stimulant and sedative).

Molière's cynicism was relevant until the middle of the 19th century: although doctors learned how to handle some illnesses, their scientific knowledge lagged far behind other disciplines. For example, in 1825, at the time when the engineer George Stephenson built the first passenger railway, the dominant theory of brain function was phrenology. The practitioners of this science argued that they could divine the personality and abilities of an individual by studying the size and

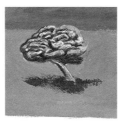

location of bumps on the skull. We now know that this is largely nonsense, because the brain, packaged for protection, "floats" slightly within the skull so there is no precise correlation between the shape of the brain and that of the cranium, but in its time this theory was considered unimpeachable. Even by 1905, when Einstein set out his theory of relativity, our knowledge of physiology was scanty, and drugs such as penicillin and aspirin that we now take for granted had not been dreamed of.

I have dwelt on history because it is important to realize how recently brain science has developed. Perhaps because of its short life, it has borrowed much of its underlying philosophy from other disciplines, particularly anatomy, physiology and biochemistry. This philosophy is predominantly reductionist, making the assumption that if one can plot every kind of cell, every kind of hormone, every kind of structure in the brain, and work out how they are related, one will arrive at a complete theory not just of how the brain works mechanically, but also of consciousness itself. Many distinguished brain scientists, including the biochemist Francis Crick, the co-discoverer of the structure of DNA, believe that this approach will one day bear fruit and allow us to isolate and define what at the moment we rather imprecisely call "the mind".

The reductionist approach has intriguing implications. Let us suppose that mind and consciousness are nothing more than the products of simpler brain processes, and let us assume that we have fully understood and mapped all of these processes. In principle, a highly sophisticated brain scanner – one not yet invented – would be able to reveal exactly what I, or any other subject, was thinking and feeling. This idea seems both sinister and improbable: sinister because it would pave the way for all kinds of mind control; improbable because the flow of thoughts, the mix of ideas, feelings and moods seems so quick and elusive that trying to pin them down long enough to observe them would be like trying to catch a mosquito with chopsticks.

In addition, the reductionist philosophy has been criticized on more concrete grounds, which can be expressed using an analogy from chemistry. It is possible to evaluate a cup of water, identifying its constituent molecules of H_2O, and we can isolate each molecule; but if we go further and separate H_2O into its constituent atoms (hydrogen and oxygen) we arrive at an explosion rather than a thirst-quenching drink. Reductionism, therefore, has its limits; and where to set those limits in the study of mind and consciousness is a thorny, and possibly insoluble, problem.

The intellectual antithesis to reductionist studies of the mind is the subjective method of Freud and his successors. This approach is innately pessimistic in that it offers no real hope of ever knowing what someone else really feels. Freud believed that the most complex neurosis was held in the brain as physical and chemical changes. He was not a soft anti-empiricist – in fact, he saw himself very much as a scientist. In 1895, he wrote his first essay, "Project for a Scientific Psychology", which was published only posthumously. In this, he began to develop a theory of memory and learning based on the concept of the brain as a mesh of interconnected nerve cells, organized in networks, which transmitted a form of energy. He later ignored this work to concentrate on what became the main thread of his research; he believed that the theories that he had proposed in the "Project" were premature, because the science of neurophysiology was still far too primitive to account for the experiences and phenomena revealed to him by patients in analysis.

Freud's caution was sensible. For today, while numerous psychological conditions – fears, phobias, fetishes, irrational and antisocial behaviours – have been well documented, in most cases we do not have the slightest clue where to start looking for the brain mechanisms that might be involved. For example, do disturbing childhood experiences, which Freud stressed in his theories of neurosis, lay down abnormal neural networks in the brain, or are their effects purely psycholog-

ical? Freud's example has spawned a huge therapy industry, the aims of which are to help people to describe and account for their subjective experiences, in order that they can achieve Freud's goals and live satisfying lives. The therapists' approach has been criticized by the reductionists as "fiction masquerading as science", and indeed, it does have its pitfalls – but without our personal insight into our states of mind, feelings and emotions, neuroscience would lack much of its reason to exist. The brain is interesting because it is the seat of our ability to express ourselves, of our complexity as human beings.

Although the title of this book is *The Secret Language of the Mind*, it is already apparent that the two different traditions of mind science have bequeathed us two very different languages – one is the language of objective science, which deals in the empirically tested facts of

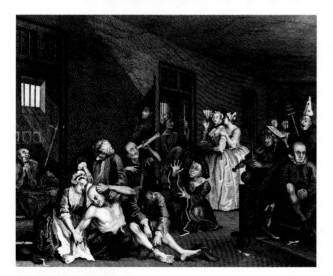

The way in which we treat people who display abnormal behaviour reflects prevailing attitudes to the mind. In the Middle Ages, the mind was believed to be a spiritual entity: insanity was caused by demons and treated by exorcism. The first hospital exclusively for psychiatric patients was opened in England in the 15th century: this was the hospital of St Mary of Bethlehem, commonly known as "Bedlam". Patients here received little treatment, and the hospital served more as a prison, isolating undesirable members of society. A somewhat sanitized view of Bedlam is shown here (left). Our fear of mental illness persists; and although studies of physiology and psychology have led to a partial understanding of the brain and the mind, mental patients are still treated cruelly in many countries.

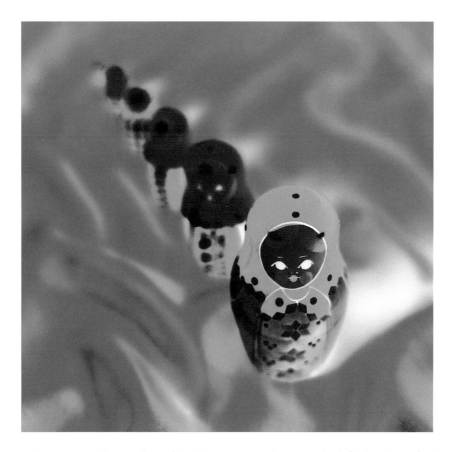

medicine and neuroscience; the other is the subjective language of personal insight and therapy (its critics call it "psychobabble"), which aims to give people ways of describing – and explaining – their feelings, hopes, intentions and disappointments.

One difficulty in combining the two approaches is the frank contempt each side can feel for the other. Hard-headed scientists dismiss those whom they call "romantics" as peddlers of obscure ideas. The late psychologist Donald Broadbent told me that, as an experimenter, it worried him that students took up psychology hoping it would give them insights into the way to live life. To the

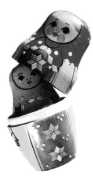

experimenter, insight is a trap: facts, not hunches, are needed to unravel the complex workings of the mind.

Others have become disillusioned with an over-emphasis on science and especially on artificial laboratory experiments. In his book, *Psychology Exposed* (1990), Paul Kline of the University of Exeter, England, laments that most results in experimental psychology are trivial, dressing up the obvious in scientific jargon.

While the tensions between the two approaches are somewhat less acute than they were 20 years ago, there is still a battle for the soul of psychology. It looks as if we will not arrive at a full understanding of the mind – one that is both intuitive and physiological – for a long while yet. But the search is exciting.

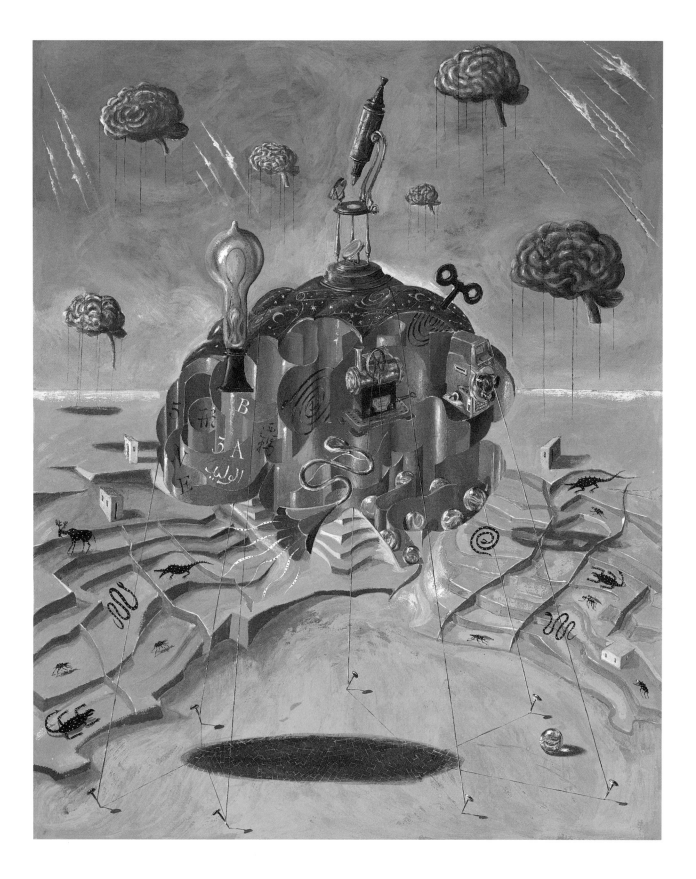

Mind and Matter

Many regard the linguist Noam Chomsky as one of the geniuses of the last 30 years for his pioneering work on the structure of language. Yet despite having successfully investigated one of the most complex processes of the mind, Chomsky is not optimistic about the future of brain research. In an interview with me in 1977, he said: "It may very well be that, among the theories we are unable to attain by our biological endowment, there is included the theory of mind ... it will appear that human beings have mystical, unintelligible properties because we, as biological organisms, will not have within our range the theory that would, in fact, explain it."

A full understanding of the mind is elusive. Imagine you are looking at a red triangle. You know that it is red and a triangle. Scientists may one day be able to plot every physical and chemical event that the triangle triggers in the retina and in the perceptual centres of the brain. But will detailed knowledge of which nerves fire and the patterns of nerve activity ever adequately describe the experience of seeing the triangle? Understanding the language of the mind means getting to know two different kinds of discourse: on the one hand, the physiological talk of neurons, networks and biochemical changes, the stuff of objective science; and on the other, the

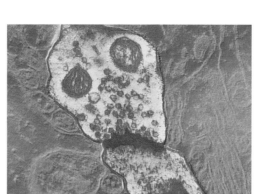

Neurologists have made enormous advances in understanding the biological process that might be equivalent to consciousness or "mind". They have revealed that the individual junctions, or synapses (above), between nerve cells in the brain are far more sophisticated than the "switches" in the most advanced computers. Each synapse is remarkably adaptable in its responses, and each nerve cell behaves like a miniature processor. Consciousness arises from the simultaneous functioning of billions of nerve cells communicating via trillions of synapses. The question is, how does that occur?

"psychological" talk about feelings, experiences and thoughts.

Not all experts agree with Chomsky's pessimism. Terry Sejnowski and Patricia Churchland of the University of California, recognized authorities on Artificial Intelligence (AI), attack the idea that solving the puzzle of the brain is beyond us. They condemn such views as "failures of imagination" and point out the remarkable advances in neuroscience over the last hundred years. Churchland and Sejnowski argue convincingly that biochemical expertise, the discovery of "brain waves", the revelations of DNA that have opened up genetic studies of the mind and improved techniques of psychological investigation and experimentation, now provide answers to questions once considered unanswerable.

Another difficulty is that many different professions, among them anatomy, physiology, biochemistry, genetics, neurology, psychiatry and psychology, are involved in brain research. Every discipline views the brain and mind from a very different perspective, each with its own fundamental concepts and preconceptions. Integrating these approaches will be a giant intellectual step that may help to solve some of the mysteries of the mind that have perplexed philosophers, psychologists and scientists for 2,000 years.

The Evolution of the Mind

When Charles Darwin published *On the Origin of Species* in 1859, he shocked scientists, clergymen and ordinary people with his scientific challenge to the Biblical account of creation. At the time, his notion that humankind had evolved from ape-like ancestors aroused anger and ridicule, but now his theory of evolution by natural selection is almost universally accepted as one of the cornerstones of modern science.

Few people today seriously doubt that the human brain is the product of billions of years of evolution by trial and error, but many find it difficult to grasp how such an "unthinking" process as natural selection could have generated the development from bacteria and single-celled organisms (protozoa) to human intelligence, creativity and self-consciousness.

Life is notoriously difficult to define; in the 19th century, the philosopher Friedrich Engels thought it to be "the mode of action of albuminous substances", by which standard a frying egg might be considered to be alive; the theologian Cardinal Newman perhaps came closer to the truth when he said, "Growth [is] the only evidence of life", because growth and self-replication are attributes of all recognized forms of life.

Living creatures, through their growth and reproduction, create an ever-increasing degree of order from the disorder around them. To achieve this, they must separate themselves from the less ordered environment with which they would otherwise merge. Accordingly, all organisms, from humans down to protozoa, have surrounded themselves with a physical boundary that separates the "entity" from the "nonentity". But the boundary does more than just prevent the organism from spilling out: it is also where organism meets environment, where useful substances are taken in and toxic ones expelled. And at this boundary, crucially, the organism responds to the outside world. Even a simple protozoan displays a basic responsiveness to external stimuli: it can retract part of its surface from a noxious chemical, or engulf a particle of food within its boundary membrane.

This sensitivity of cells is the starting point for the evolution of nervous systems. It is not difficult to see that cells with greater sensitivity to external stimuli would be favoured by natural selection – for example, a cell that retracts quickly from a predator would be more likely to survive (and therefore reproduce) than a slower cell. As organisms evolved from simple unicellular to more complex multicellular body plans, it is possible to envisage certain cells becoming specialized to carry information about external stimuli from one part of the body to another. This development allows the organism to respond to a stimulus not just locally, but over its entire body: so rather than just retracting part of its surface from a noxious substance, the whole organism can now contract, or even swim away to avoid the stimulus.

The most common simple nervous systems today are in sea anemones and hydras. A single neuron (or nerve cell; see page 26) receives a stimulus from one part of the body and conducts an impulse to another part, where it causes a muscle to contract. As this system becomes more elaborate in

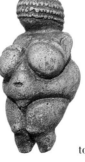

Human consciousness – as measured by our ability to devise and use symbolic representations of the world around us – probably evolved at some point during the Paleolithic Period (the Old Stone Age), which began 2.5 million years ago. The earliest human artifacts, which date from this period, express an awareness of the universe, of mortality and of the cycle of life. Among these artifacts are cave paintings, some of which are believed to be representations of the cosmos, and "Venus" sculptures (right), thought to symbolize fertility.

higher organisms, neurons differentiate into three types: some (which are known as sensory neurons) become specialized to detect stimuli; others (motor neurons) are specialized to activate muscles or groups of muscles; and others still (interneurons) to link together the two other types to produce a coordinated response. Animals with this basic nervous organization (for example, jellyfish) can display relatively sophisticated behavioural responses, such as capturing prey and swimming.

As animals became more complex and increasingly active, nervous systems continued to develop in sophistication. Sensory neurons collected in distinct organs, specialized for light, sound or smell. Over evolutionary history, these sense organs became concentrated at the front of the animal (the part that encounters the environment first) and connected to the motor neurons (which could activate muscles over the whole body) by interneurons, which became aggregated into a central nervous system that ran down the entire length of the animal's body. Over millions of years, the front end of the central

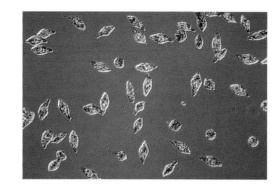

Even simple organisms possess fairly sophisticated mechanisms to respond to environmental stimuli. The protozoan Euglena *(left), for example, gains its food by photosynthesis and so needs light to survive. It swims by beating a long, thin projection called a flagellum. At the base of the flagellum is a light-sensitive area, near which is a pigment-filled spot called the "eyespot". When light shines on the* Euglena, *the eyespot casts a shadow on the light-sensitive area. The* Euglena *responds to the shadow by swimming toward the light, maximizing its chances of survival and reproduction.*

Archeologists have studied the cranial capacity of skulls to obtain a measure of how the human brain has grown (below). Australopithecus afarensis *(1), who lived around 3.5 million years ago, had a skull capacity of 500cc; by 2 million years ago, this had increased to 650cc in* Homo habilis, *the first of our ancestors to use tools (2); 1.5 million years ago* Homo erectus, *who could make fire, had a skull capacity of 1,000cc (3); and, surprisingly, Neanderthal* (Homo sapiens neanderthalis) *had a capacity of 1,400cc (4), slightly larger than modern man (5). Changes in skull size, however, cannot explain the evolution of consciousness.*

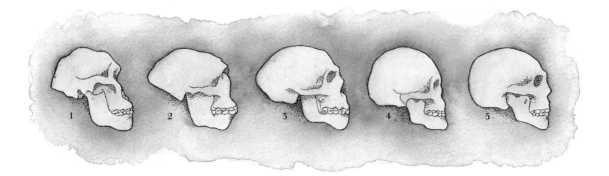

nervous system enlarged and grew in complexity, forming the brain, whose purpose was to integrate sensory information and coordinate the animal's motor responses.

All animals (except sponges and a number of highly-specialized parasites) possess a nervous system, built up from neurons. A neuron is a simple sub-unit – it can respond to a signal either by firing or by not firing, and the neurons of the human brain behave in more or less similar ways to those of other animals. The extraordinary level of consciousness of our own species arises not from any qualitative difference between our neurons and those of other species, but from differences in the scale, complexity and plasticity (see page 26) of the human brain, compared with animal brains. It is

possible to gain some insight into how and when these differences evolved by examining the fossilized skulls of our hominid ancestors (see page 17). One line of skull evidence, for example, suggests that the left hemisphere of the human brain became more developed and weighed more than the right hemisphere from around 300,000 BC. Neurologists now know that the left hemisphere controls speech and language in right-handed people, so one explanation for this asymmetry is that language, or at least some precursor of language, began to evolve around this time and thickened the left hemisphere. Such theories, however, are speculative, partly because the fossil record is patchy, and partly because the size of a skull tells us little about the number and complexity

The number and complexity of the interneurons in the central nervous system increased over evolutionary time. The organization of networks allowed sensory information to be processed before being sent to muscles. Three examples of simple networks are shown below: an incoming

impulse can diverge and pass to several motor neurons (left); impulses from several sources can converge on a single interneuron, which fires when it receives a number of inputs (top right); and an interneuron can feed an impulse back to itself, creating a loop (bottom right).

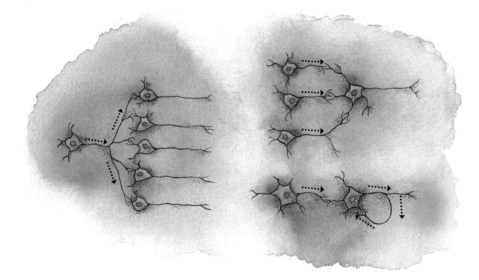

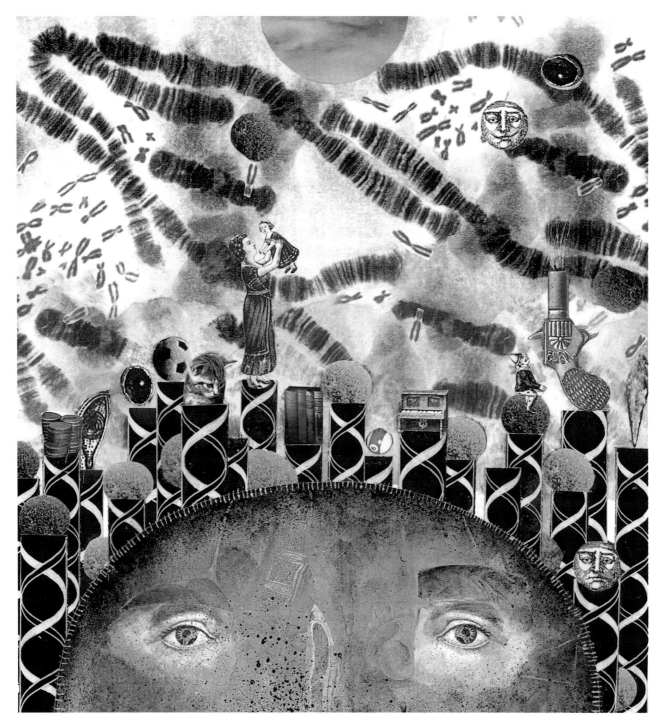

To what extent are higher human characteristics and behaviours – intelligence, creativity, altruism and so on – "wired" into the human brain? Some theorists suggest that these characteristics are determined by the genes we carry in the helical DNA molecules in each of our cells.

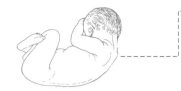

of interconnections between neurons in the brain, and it is these factors that account for much of the brain's potential.

If the fossil evidence is a little vague in places, we know in far greater detail how each individual brain develops from conception onwards. The brain starts as a slab of cells in the outer layers of the embryo. (It is interesting to note that, embryologically, the brain is derived from the same layer from which the skin develops – the crucial "boundary layer" that mediates between the self and the outside world.) After about three weeks, these cells become differentiated from the other cells in the embryo and then roll out to form a hollow cylinder, or neural tube. This forms the tube of the spinal cord. In a four-week-old embryo, it is possible to see three swellings on the front of the neural tube. These will develop into the three main regions of the brain, the forebrain, mid-brain and hindbrain (see page 22).

The brain grows more quickly than the spinal cord. Its dorsal lobes receive inputs from the sensory neurons of the developing eyes, ears, nose and mouth. Another structure to evolve rapidly in the embryo is the hypothalamus, which is responsible for controlling appetites and aversions,

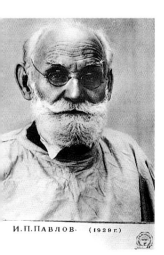

At the beginning of the 20th century, the Russian physiologist Ivan Pavlov (left) carried out a series of now classic experiments that showed that dogs could be taught or conditioned to salivate at an unnatural stimulus, in this case the sound of a bell. His speculation that such a conditioned reflex must be caused by physical changes in the connections between neurons in the brain has since been confirmed.

И.П.ПАВЛОВ. (1929 г.)

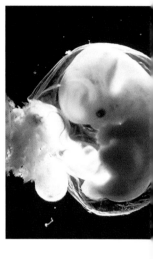

The human fetus (right) develops according to a timetable set by its internal genetic blueprint. For the 17th-century philosopher John Locke, the baby's mind at birth was a tabula rasa, *or blank slate, and the infant acquired its knowledge through experience. Today, most psychologists agree that nature and nurture interact to shape our mental development.*

hopes and fears. The hypothalamus helps to coordinate the development of the central nervous system and the endocrine system, the glands of which secrete the hormones that control growth, metabolic activity and sexual development. At birth, the newborn's brain is, anatomically, remarkably complete.

From this account, it appears that the brain has a fixed development program determined by the genes encoded in the DNA that we inherit from our parents. The wiring of some "pathways" in the brain is directed by our genes (the connections between the eye, the optic nerve, the optic chiasm and the visual cortex, for example, are genetically determined), but it is also true that other pathways in the brain are created through learning – even learning what one might call un-natural habits. The great Russian physiologist Ivan Pavlov proved that a dog could be trained to salivate to the sound of a bell; a response previously under inner physiological control could be triggered by a new and unnatural stimulus. Pavlov argued that this meant that a new neural pathway was created, connecting neurons that had previously had no links.

Most of the connections between neurons in the brain are forged in the first months after birth as the infant is bom-barded with sensory and motor experiences, and learns to

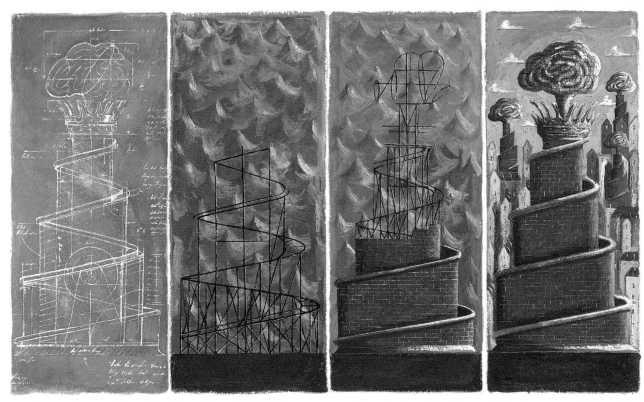

perceive, and to coordinate his or her actions. (The Swiss psychologist Jean Piaget argued that the first months of a baby's life should be called the "sensorimotor period"; see page 78.) But even while the child is in the mother's womb, the development of the brain is not just a matter of triggering a pre-arranged genetic code. A bad diet and too much alcohol or tobacco on the mother's part will harm the development of the fetal brain. More remarkably, Peter Hepple at Queen's University in Belfast has shown that if a fetus is exposed to specific types of music, it will respond to them after birth in a way that suggests it recognizes them from the womb. In other words, the brain does

not have to be out in the world for its neurons to form the kind of connections that were always supposed to have been formed only after birth.

Findings like Hepple's and other studies on the newborn cast new light on the long debate about the role of nature and nurture in human development – the influence of what is innate and what is learned. Such studies suggest that the terms of this debate may be out of date, because one of the key distinctions between the innate and the learned is that everything one is born with is innate. But if learning can start in the womb, it is much harder to make a clear distinction.

The Anatomy of the Brain

The long evolutionary history of the human brain suggests that it is a structure in which old and new elements exist side by side. Some anatomists have pointed out that certain areas of the brain – those involved with the regulation of automatic behaviour, such as breathing and emotions – show remarkable similarities to the brains of reptiles. So although we all possess the grey matter that makes possible a Shakespeare or an Einstein, we should not forget that we also have some of the brain of a crocodile.

The brain is an information-processing device. Receptors in the sense organs (the eyes, ears, skin and so on) and within the body (the heart, lungs, digestive tract and so on) receive information about the body's external and internal environment. This information is transmitted by the nerve fibres of what is known as the peripheral nervous system, which is made up of all the nerves that convey stimuli, in the form of electrical impulses, to the central nervous system, which comprises the brain and spinal cord. Here the information is processed, and a suitable response is made, usually by triggering effector neurons, which transmit a nervous impulse to a muscle, causing it to contract or relax.

Within the central nervous system, there is a hierarchy of control. Many simple stimuli are dealt with by reflexes: we quickly withdraw our hands if we touch a hot plate. The brain is not involved in reflex actions – they are "hard-wired" into

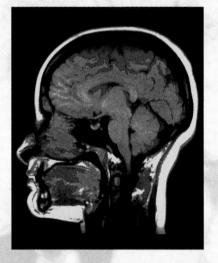

This image of a healthy human brain was made using the technique of MRI (see page 182), which allows neurologists to look inside the skull of a conscious subject. The colours (added by computer) identify areas of different density and so help to distinguish different structures in the brain.

the spinal cord – although it can override the reflex: we do not drop a hot plate loaded with food unless it is impossibly hot or we are under stress. It is the complex functions that are dealt with by the brain. Breathing, balance, swallowing and digestion – "automatic" functions of which we are not consciously aware but which nevertheless need delicate control and orchestration – are controlled by relatively ancient parts of the brain. Deciding, for example, whether to turn around when someone calls your name in the street is controlled by newer, "higher" centres.

This division is inevitably simplistic: the brain is an incredibly complex organ composed of tens of billions of cells, and its areas cooperate in a way that is far from fully understood. Even so, it is possible to break the brain down into a number of structural components, and, in a very general way, to assign functions to these structures.

Both the brain and the spinal cord are protected by bone (the skull and vertebrae respectively) and surrounded by cerebrospinal fluid, which acts as a shock absorber. Viewed from the side, the brain itself looks a little like a cauliflower, and it weighs an average of 1.2 kg (2lb 9oz) in males and 1 kg (2lb 3oz) in females. It can be divided into three major areas: forebrain, midbrain and hindbrain. Confusingly, these areas are not located where their names suggest they would be (the forebrain is not at the front, for example): this is because the

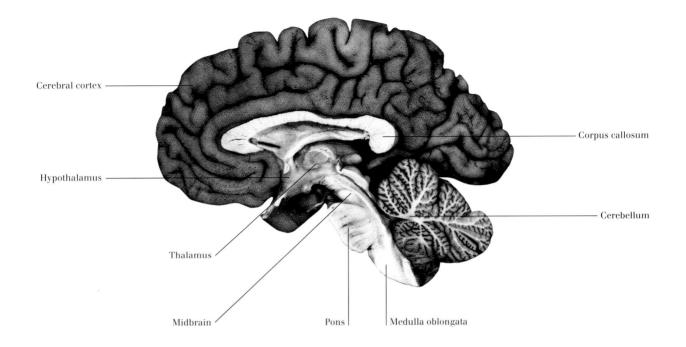

Cerebral cortex

Corpus callosum

Hypothalamus

Cerebellum

Thalamus

Midbrain   Pons   Medulla oblongata

(Above) This lengthwise section through an adult human brain exposes the main structures of the central nervous system. The forebrain consists of the cortex, the thalamus, the hypothalamus and the limbic system (not shown), and the hindbrain consists of the medulla, the pons, the cerebellum and the reticular formation (not shown). The midbrain is smaller in humans than it is in other mammals. (Below) The two hemispheres of the cerebral cortex in the forebrain (see page 24) are clearly visible when the brain is viewed from above.

names relate to the position of the different parts of the brain in the embryo, and these positions change during development of the fetus.

The hindbrain is situated at the base of the head. It comprises four functional areas: the medulla oblongata, the pons, the reticular formation and the cerebellum. The medulla is the point at which spinal nerves from the left side of the body cross over to the right side of the brain and vice versa. It controls automatic functions, such as heartbeat, blood circulation, breathing and digestion. The pons is a relay station passing information between the higher centres of the brain and, together with the reticular formation, it appears to be

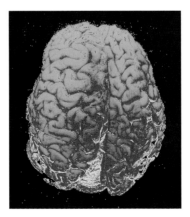

involved in determining whether we are awake or asleep. The reticular formation has a larger role in regulating arousal and attention – it seems to "activate" other parts of the brain.

To the side of these structures is the cerebellum, which, with its many convolutions, looks almost like a mini-brain tucked into our "real" brain. The cerebellum controls many functions that have become automatic but were originally learned and practised, including balance and coordination. When you walk without thinking about it, the cerebellum is in control of your movements.

The midbrain is a relatively small nerve centre. It contains a continuation of the reticular formation and it is responsible for some aspects of hearing and vision (such as eye movements). It seems to be more important in mammals other than humans: in our species, many of its functions have been taken over by the forebrain.

The forebrain is the largest area of the brain. Its most prominent feature is the cortex, which contains on average some 10 billion neurons. and lies on top of all the other brain structures. It is also the functional "summit" of the brain, responsible for the "higher" functions of thought, voluntary action and what we call consciousness.

Other key parts of the forebrain are the thalamus, the hypothalamus and the limbic system. The thalamus comprises a number of neural centres and acts as a "clearing house" for sensory and some motor signals, directing information from, for example, the eyes and ears to the approp-

riate part of the cortex. The hypothalamus appears to be involved in controlling the appetites for food and sex, and regulates other biological urges.

The hypothalamus, thalamus, midbrain and hindbrain (excluding the cerebellum) together make up what is called the brain stem. The brain stem is responsible for regulating all basic life processes, and it is lack of activity in this area that leads a physician to pronounce "brain death".

Between this central core of the brain and the cortex lies the limbic system ("limbic" comes from a Latin word that means "border"). Closely related to the hypothalamus in anatomical terms, this area of the brain allows us to control our instinctive drives (so that, for example, we do not immediately strike out at someone who accidentally treads on our feet). The limbic system contains three main structures: the

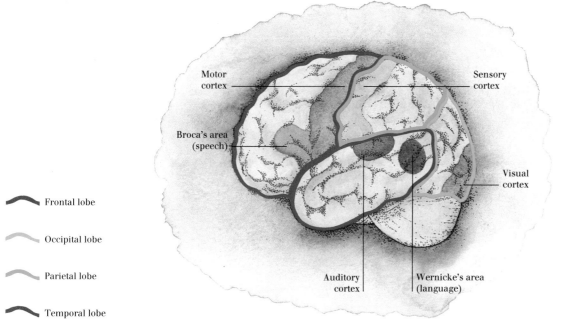

Motor cortex

Sensory cortex

Broca's area (speech)

Visual cortex

Auditory cortex

Wernicke's area (language)

Frontal lobe

Occipital lobe

Parietal lobe

Temporal lobe

amygdala and septum, which are involved in regulating anger, aggression and fear, and the hippocampus, which seems crucial to our ability to "record" new memories.

The cortex (or cerebral cortex) is a sheet of neurons, less than 5mm (0.2 in) deep but with an area of 155 sq cm (2 sq ft), that makes up 70 per cent of the brain. The folding of the cortex, necessary for it to fit into the human skull, gives the brain its characteristic wrinkled appearance. The neurons of the cortex process information; they are grey in colour (this is why the cortex has been termed "grey matter") and are extensively connected to each other and to other parts of the brain. The long connections that link widely separated parts of the brain are made by neurons covered in a fatty insulator – myelin – which gives them a whitish appearance (they are collectively known as "white matter").

The cortex itself is not uniform, but has a number of structural and functional divisions. The most obvious of these is the division between its left and right hemispheres. Some experts argue that each of these hemispheres is almost a brain in its own right (see page 32). The two hemispheres are connected by a large bundle of fibres called the corpus callosum, which helps to integrate the actions of the brain, telling the left what the right is doing and vice versa.

Another important division of the cortex is into four lobes – the temporal, frontal, occipital and parietal – named after the skull bone that lies closest to each. There have long been arguments about the extent to which functions are localized in different lobes or in smaller areas of the brain. The frontal lobe seems essential for attention and concentration, the temporal lobe for language and memory, the parietal lobe for sensory information and the occipital lobe for vision and perception. However, most cognitive processes appear to depend on the complex interaction of many parts of the brain.

LEARNING FROM THE BRAIN'S MISTAKES

It is no easy task to identify the function of any particular part of the brain. Much of our knowledge comes from investigations of people who have suffered localized brain damage. The assumption is that if damage to area X affects a person's ability to perform task Y, then X must be involved in controlling Y. But area X could be responsible for only one key aspect of achieving the task, such as controlling movements. The case of Phineas Gage, who was injured when blasting rock in 1848, highlights these problems. A crowbar transfixed his skull and left frontal lobe (right). Miraculously Gage did

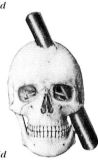

not die, but regained consciousness and seemed to make a remarkable recovery, although his personality changed dramatically. From being a steady workman, he became unreliable and prone to swearing and aggression. His case is

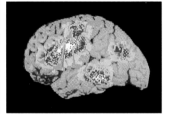

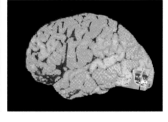

cited as proof that the frontal lobe governs personality. But did the crowbar affect Gage's perceptions or his ability to control his actions or brain chemistry? Today computer-aided techniques, such as PET scans (see page 183), allow neurologists to locate specific types of mental activity in a live brain (left).

The Basic Language of the Brain

Like any other organ of the human body, the brain is no more than an assembly of cells specialized to perform a particular function. Broadly speaking, the function of its cells, or neurons, is to pick up information (in the form of electrical impulses) from other neurons, synthesize the information received, and pass the (modified) information on to many other neurons. With a few exceptions, most physiologists believe that the "genius" of the human brain derives from the sheer size and complexity of this information-processing system. Best estimates suggest that there are around 200 billion neurons packed inside our skulls, each one of which is (on average) linked to around 5,000 others. This makes a total of one quadrillion neural connections – a figure greater than the number of phone calls made in the

United States in the last decade. Despite this volume, brain scientists have made spectacular progress in understanding the basic properties of individual neurons, and in decoding the language that they use to communicate with one another.

Although there are many different types of neurons in the brain and central nervous system, they seem to share a similar "body plan" and to work in the same way. Neurons have many features in common with other types of cell – for example, they possess a nucleus, which has overall control of the cell's housekeeping functions, and like other cells they are enclosed by fatty membranes – but it is obvious from their shape that they are highly specialized. While most human cells are roughly spherical, neurons are highly elongated – the perfect shape to transmit information efficiently from one place to another.

A human neuron has three relatively distinct parts: the cell body, the dendrites and the axon. The cell body contains the cell nucleus; radiating from this are short

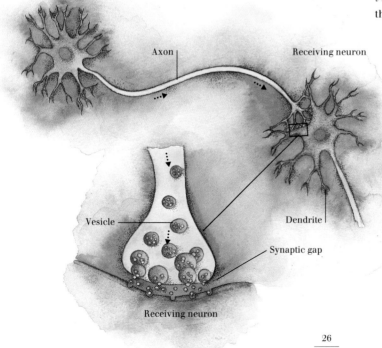

Sending neuron

Axon

Receiving neuron

Vesicle

Dendrite

Synaptic gap

Receiving neuron

A "typical" neuron in the human cortex has a diameter of less than one micrometre and is usually contacted by thousands of other neurons. Here, just one such contact is shown. An electrical impulse moves down the "sending" neuron's long axon toward the small swellings on its terminals. Here, the impulse triggers the release of tiny packets (or vesicles) of neurotransmitter chemicals into a small gap (the synaptic gap) between the sending cell and the branch-like projections (dendrites) of the receiving cell. These neurotransmitters diffuse across the gap and unlock chemical gates on the surface of the receiving cell, and this event causes the receiving cell to fire, sending an impulse down its own axon.

branches or dendrites (*dendron* is the Greek word for "tree"). Both the cell body and the dendrites receive inputs from other neurons. Projecting from the cell body is a long, slender, sometimes branched tube called the axon. In some cases, as in neurons that run the length of the spinal cord, the axon of a single cell may be several feet long. The axon is the neuron's "output cable": at its ends it forms junctions, or synapses, with the dendrites or cell bodies of other neurons, allowing impulses to be transmitted from cell to cell.

It is a feature of the nervous system that some neurons contact many other neurons; others contact few but are contacted by many. These differences in organization allow for differences in function: for example, Purkinje cells in the cerebellum (responsible for our learning to coordinate movements) are contacted by more than 200,000 cells each.

Physiologists often talk about a neuron "firing" as if it were a gun. But in fact, what happens when a neuron fires is that an electrical impulse moves down its axon, away from the cell body and toward the synapses. The impulse can only ever move in this one direction, is always of uniform intensity, and once moving down the axon, cannot be stopped or modified by the cell. In addition, the nervous impulse is not like a conventional electrical current that flows through a conducting wire; it is more like a "ripple" of electrical charge resulting

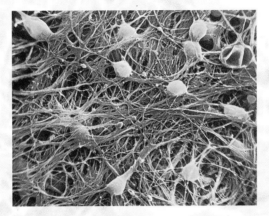

This micrograph clearly demonstrates the complex organization of neurons within the human brain. Neurons, however, are not the only type of cells in the central nervous system. They are, in fact, greatly outnumbered by glial cells, which perform the brain's housekeeping functions, notably nourishing the neurons and holding them in place.

from the movement of ions – charged atoms – in and out of the axon. It would be very tempting to think that this electrical transmission of information accounts for all brain activity, and that one neuron directly passes its electrical impulse to another in the same way that electrical signals race around the circuits of a computer. The story, however, is not as simple as that.

When an impulse reaches the end of the axon of one neuron (cell A), it cannot jump directly to the dendrites or cell body of another (cell B). This is because the two cells are separated by one or many synapses (a word derived from the Greek meaning "to clasp"), which are gaps just 200 nanometres wide. Instead, the impulse causes tiny vesicles (fluid-filled pouches) at the synaptic terminals of cell A to burst into the gap. These vesicles are full of neurotransmitter molecules, and when they burst, the neurotransmitter they contain is released into the synaptic gap. The molecules move the short distance to cell B and attach to specific receptors on its surface where they can affect the behaviour of the neuron, causing it to fire or not fire.

Not all neurotransmitters are the same: some will "excite" cell B, making it more likely to fire, while others are inhibitory and make firing less likely. We have already seen that a "typical" neuron in the human cortex (such as cell B) is likely to be connected to several thousand others. Of

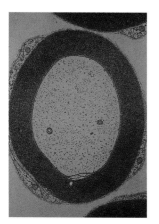

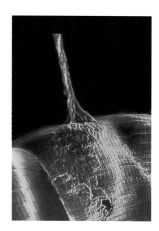

Neurons that cover long distances, carrying impulses from one region of the brain to another, or from the brain to the body, are usually coated with a white layer of fatty insulator called myelin, which helps to speed up transmission. In this image, left, the myelin "sheath" appears as a set of concentric rings around the central axon. The myelin is produced by other kinds of cells that wrap themselves around the axon, supporting it. If myelin is damaged or destroyed, nerve function is impaired. In sufferers of multiple sclerosis, for example, the myelin sheath is damaged at irregular intervals along axons in the central nervous system.

Neurons have specialized functions. Receptor neurons, such as the cells on the retina, respond to light and convert physical stimuli into electrical impulses. They are the points at which information enters the nervous system. At the other end are the motor neurons, which carry signals to the muscles and glands and produce outputs, such as movements. When a motor neuron fires, it produces a chemical change at the tip of the axon that makes a muscle fibre contract (above, right). Most neurons are neither receptors nor effectors, however, but interneurons that serve to relay impulses throughout the nervous system.

these, some will release excitatory neurotransmitters, others inhibitory. Each neuron has several vesicles, each containing a different neurotransmitter, as well as a number of specialized receptor sites, each primed for a specific neurotransmitter. Whether or not cell B fires depends on the complex sum of the activity of all the cells to which it is connected, and the types of connections that these neurons make.

In the human cortex the main excitatory neurotransmitter is the molecule glutamate, and the main inhibitory molecule is gamma-aminobutyric acid, commonly known by its acronym, GABA. But again the story is not that simple. Neuroscientists now know that there are at least 50 other neurotransmitters, which work alone or in combination to modulate the activity of the brain: some are excitatory, some inhibitory, and some can be either under different circumstances. Some generate a quick response, while others seem

to change the receptive state or overall activity of the brain; and some are present in one part of the brain and not another.

For many years, scientists believed that nerve impulses raced around the brain at immeasurably fast speeds. Today, however, we know that an impulse travels down a typical neuron in the cortex at a speed of around 1.5m (5 ft) per second – a little slower than a bicycle. However, in long axons coated with myelin, such as those that run the length of the spinal cord, the nerve impulse travels faster, up to as much as 100m (330 ft) per second.

The behaviour of certain types of synapses in some neurons can be modified by brain events: put simply, these synapses can be made to "remember" their previous pattern of firing. When such a synapse is stimulated in a particular way, it causes channels to open that admit calcium ions into the neuron. The presence of the ions within the neuron sets in

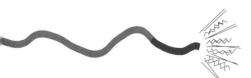

motion a complex, and as yet unknown, series of chemical reactions that potentiates, or makes stronger, the synaptic response to the stimulus that was received before. This process, known as long-term potentiation, provides a mechanism by which a neuron can fire more readily in response to a familiar stimulus – days, weeks or even years after the original stimulus. Some neurologists believe that this process underlies our ability to form and recall memories.

This inevitably brief description of the brain's basic "language" shows that our thoughts are the result of a complex, delicate interplay of electrical and chemical signals spread out over a network that takes in millions if not billions of individual cells. It is apparent that the neurologists who are trying to equate physical and chemical processes in the brain with mental events – thoughts, emotions and memories – face a formidable challenge.

It has become clear that imbalances in the production of neurotransmitters can lead to serious problems in brain functioning. An excess of the neurotransmitter dopamine is linked to schizophrenia: crudely, it is as if the neurons fire too easily, thus producing hallucinations and other disconnected thoughts. Conversely, a lack of dopamine is associated with the tremors and loss of coordination in Parkinson's disease. On the other hand, patients with Alzheimer's disease do not produce much acetylcholine, a neurotransmitter that is present notably in the hippocampus (part of the brain important in memory formation).

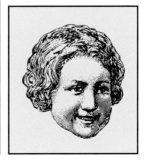

CHEMICAL CONSCIOUSNESS

Dramatic proof of the influence of neurotransmitters on human thought comes from the work of neurosurgeon R. G. Heath. During his operations on conscious psychotic patients, Heath dripped neurotransmitters onto the septal area, close to the amygdala, which is known to be responsible for some of our emotional behaviour. His patients responded with swift and profound changes in mood: one man, at first on the verge of tears upon remembering his father's near-fatal illness, suddenly started to grin very broadly and told Dr Heath that he was making plans for a hot date.

Today, specially designed molecules that mimic, inhibit or otherwise change the behaviour of neurotransmitters are used in the treatment of many mental disorders, from depression to schizophrenia. Some of these drugs, including the main types of antidepressants, increase the concentration of certain neurotransmitters; others – like Prozac (fluoxetine) – inhibit the response to selected neurotransmitters during transmission. Such substances are also the basis of many of the more potent "recreational" drugs: for example, the powerful hallucinogen LSD works by interfering with the action of the neurotransmitter serotonin, causing certain emotional parts of the brain to become overstimulated.

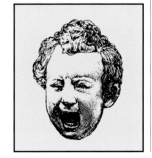

Models of the Mind

Scholars are always tempted to use analogies to clarify difficult concepts. Students of the mind are no exception, and the many, diverse models of mental function are proof that psychologists and others have rich imaginations. These models have always been influenced by the latest technology: some are historically interesting, others remarkably prescient. The ancient Greeks drew parallels with puppets controlled by strings (the word *neuron* is Greek for "string"). In the 17th century, the French philosopher René Descartes, heavily influenced by hydraulics and the beauty of fountains, saw nerves as fluid-filled tubes (although he was careful to leave some room for the soul in his hydraulic model in order to stay on the right side of the religious authorities). Concepts of the soul were abandoned altogether in the 18th century in models such as that proposed by the French physician Julien Offroy de la Mettrie in his book *L'homme machine* (1747). La Mettrie was the first to suggest that the mind was wholly material, simply a bundle of cells. Modern theories of the mind start from these types of mechanistic assumptions.

In the early 19th century, some anatomists argued that certain areas of the brain controlled specific characteristics such as memory, language, vanity, wit and wonder. They claimed that by feeling the bumps on the skull, one could tell how developed these qualities were. This science was known as phrenology, and its practitioners constructed "maps" of the head showing the location of human characteristics. By 1880, the phrenologists were ridiculed as charlatans but some of their ideas were not without merit.

In the early part of the 20th century, neurologists were seduced by models of the brain based on simple information networks. Like a telephone exchange, the brain could receive and send out signals, and although the signals were subject to interference or "noise" in the system, they were not radically altered as they passed through. The brain was, in effect, seen as a complex relay station.

These days, information-processing models dominate, and enormous effort goes into drawing parallels between the brain and computer architecture. You don't have to be a mystic, however, to see that the brain does much more than just process information. It appears to allow us to act out, and act on, our choices: we have, or at least seem to have, free will. The question of whether free will is an illusion remains one of the main problems that mechanistic models of the mind confront.

Until 1960, many students of the mind, especially in the United States, were only too willing to accept the view of humans as machines. They espoused a theory known as behaviourism. Psychologists such as John B. Watson (1878–1958) and B. F. Skinner (1904–1990) claimed that free will was an illusion. According to this theory, we may think that we buy toothpaste because we want to, but in fact we are doing so because of the influence of past experiences – every piece of behaviour is the product of past rewards and punishments. Another way of putting this is that we do not act, only react, according to what Skinner called our history of conditioning.

Skinner tried to show that one could "shape" (literally create) complicated behaviours that seem to be conscious and intentional by a subtle program of carrot and stick. In one spectacular experiment, he "shaped" the behaviour of pigeons so that they would play table tennis. If pigeons could be conditioned to do that, why couldn't humans be conditioned to perform all known human acts?

Skinner not only believed that people had no free will, but that the illusion of its presence was responsible for much human misery. In his Utopian novel *Walden Two* he described a peaceful, creative society that used rewards and the occasional punishment to bring up its young. Where the British writer Aldous Huxley saw a nightmarish "brave new world", Skinner offered a vision of a progressive, cooperative and controlled society.

Behaviourism influenced the whole discipline of psychology deeply from 1913 to the mid-1970s and was, in some ways, beneficial. It made psychologists focus on scientific method and design experiments that are easily repeated by other scientists in order to verify the results. Over the last 20 years, however, its limitations have been exposed and most psychologists now believe that consciousness has to be included in their theories. Apart from some die-hard reductionists, most accept that we will not obtain a proper account of how and why we do things until we can explain the basis of consciousness. The behaviourists argued that it was not possible to explore the mind objectively, so scientists would have to focus on the study of behaviour; however, cognitive psychology admits subjective evidence, including reports on one's own state of mind.

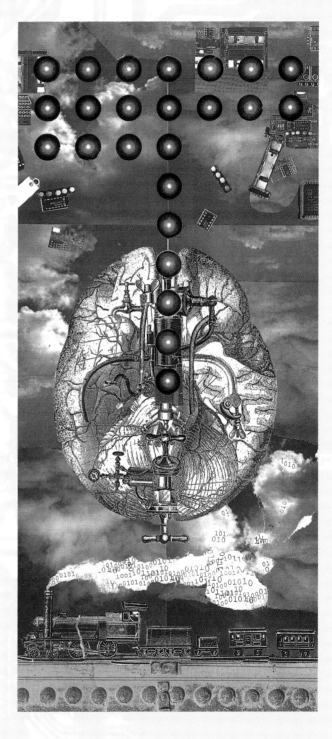

Left Brain, Right Brain

At first glance, the human brain appears to be perfectly symmetrical, its two cerebral hemispheres forming mirror images of each other. On closer inspection, however, it turns out to be rather lopsided, both in structure and function. The left hemisphere of the cortex is slightly larger than the right, and appears to be "wired" in a different way.

The left hemisphere of the cortex controls the right side of the body, while the right hemisphere controls the left side of the body. For example, a stroke to the left hemisphere is likely to lead to problems in controlling the right side of the face and the right hand. But it is not just a question of each hemisphere controlling one side of the body. Neurologists have also identified many functional asymmetries and speak of "cerebral dominance". In 90 per cent of people, and almost 100 per cent of right-handers, the left hemisphere is dominant, with individuals having stronger and more dextrous right hands.

Significantly, most infants usually point at objects with their right hands. It has been argued that this pointing is crucial to the development of language: first you point, then you name. If you point with the right hand, you engage the left hemisphere, and one might therefore expect language to be located in the left hemisphere (in right-handers at least). Long before psychologists studied how babies point, the French surgeon Pierre Broca showed in 1861 that damage to a specific part of the left cerebral hemisphere produced almost total loss of speech: this area of the brain was named Broca's area in his honour.

If language is localized in one part of the brain, to what extent are other brain activities similarly compartmentalized? This question has begun to be answered by neurologists in the last 40 years. In the 1950s, Los Angeles surgeon Joseph Bogen was treating epileptic patients by severing the corpus callosum – the broad neural highway that connects the two

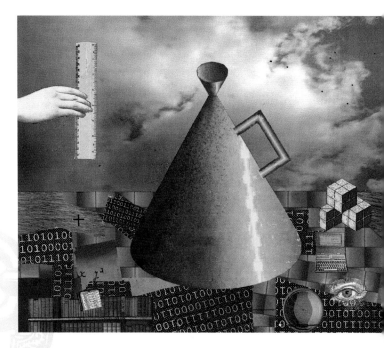

Direct evidence for the functional split between the left and right hemispheres of the brain comes from positron emission tomography (see page 183). The PET scan (below left) shows neural activity in the left and right hemispheres of a right-handed person asked to perform a linguistic task. The intense activity (yellow and orange) in the left hemisphere and the quiescence of the right indicate that language resides in the left hemisphere. In contrast, the brain of a left-handed person (below right)

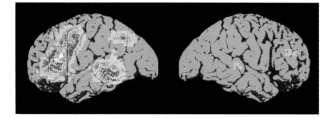

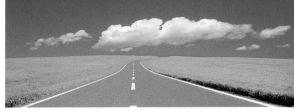

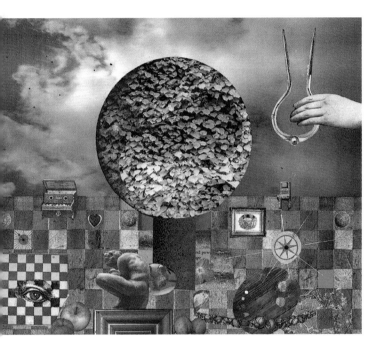

sides of the brain. He found that the uncontrolled firing of neurons that characterizes epilepsy could be checked by this radical operation, but he needed to know what the other consequences of this dramatic surgery could be. He took his problem to the psychobiologist Roger Sperry at the California Institute of Technology, who had been investigating the effect of severing the corpus callosum in cats and monkeys.

To assess the effects of the surgery on humans, Sperry presented information to one, but not the other, hemisphere of the "split-brain" patients. His first studies were on touch. The patients were blindfolded and given an object to hold in their left hand. This hand could reliably pick out the object again from a random selection but the right hand could do no better than chance. Similar experiments were performed on vision: if an image was briefly flashed on the left side of the visual field, it was "seen" only by the right side of the brain. The split-brain patient could not describe in words what he had seen but was able to pick out the image from a selection of pictures. These and other experiments gave rise to the notion that the left side of the brain deals with language, logic and "number crunching", while the right side is responsible for pattern and spatial awareness, creativity and musical talent.

Sperry's work also led to the intriguing possibility that we all have two different selves, one contained in each hemisphere. The most dramatic illustration of this was when one split-brain patient watched as her left hand made a particular response and insisted, "I didn't do that". Her sense of self, which in most of us involves language, seemed to have no connection with her left hand. Moreover, her left and right halves seemed to have different personalities. The former was a logical person and the latter wilder, more instinctive. This division appealed to some cultural commentators in the 1960s: the left brain conformed while the right was radical.

shows high activity in the right side and quiesence in the left. The split, however, does not apply to all individuals: ambidextrous people, and natural left-handers who have been forced to use their right hands, have language-processing areas in both hemispheres. In recent years, the strict localization of higher brain functions such as creativity, emotion and intelligence has been called into question by some neurologists, although others have built on Roger Sperry's theories (see page 34).

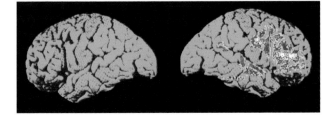

In Many Minds

Before Roger Sperry's ground-breaking experiments with split-brain patients in the 1950s (see page 33), few questioned the unity of the mind. One brain, one mind, one person, was the prevailing orthodoxy. Sperry's work changed the climate of research. Scientists such as Howard Gardner of Harvard University and Robert Ornstein of Stanford University built on Sperry's work and have devised complex theories that analyze the brain, breaking it into component parts that are far more subtle than the simple right/left split.

These theories posit the existence of discrete, semi-autonomous structural and functional "modules" within the brain. Sometimes these modules – termed "multiminds" by Ornstein and "multiple intelligences" by Gardner – cooperate; sometimes they compete. In any individual, some modules are likely to be more developed than others. The mind is not a whole, and one should not ask whether or not people are "intelligent" but how able they are at any of the particular skills governed by each of the modules.

Gardner's idea of multiple intelligences owes something to the work of the English psychologist Liam Hudson. In the 1960s, Hudson studied the problem-solving abilities of highly intelligent schoolboys, and found a sharp division between those who were verbally gifted and those who were scientifically gifted. In Hudson's view, the "artists" did not seem to have the same kind of intelligence, or mind, as the "scientists" had, and the true polymaths were few and far between.

Gardner identified not two, but seven, different intelligences: linguistic; logical-mathematical; spatial (used, for example, in map-reading or recognizing a pattern); musical; bodily-kinesthetic (which governs physical coordination); interpersonal (the ability to understand other individuals and to predict their behaviour based on that understanding); and intrapersonal (used in understanding ourselves). While the first three of these are more highly valued in the West, the other three have played key roles historically in Western culture and still do so in some non-Western cultures.

Gardner also claims that virtually all educational systems ignore the fact that some children may be gifted at one or more of these skills at the same time as they perform very poorly at others. His book *Multiple Intelligences* (1993) is a powerful plea for educators to recognize these different capacities and to acknowledge the awkward

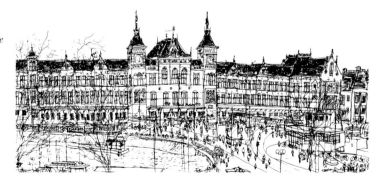

This drawing (right) is by British artist Stephen Wiltshire (b. 1975) who suffers from the problems of autism, but who has a visual memory so acute that he can view a building fleetingly and reproduce it years later with remarkable skill.

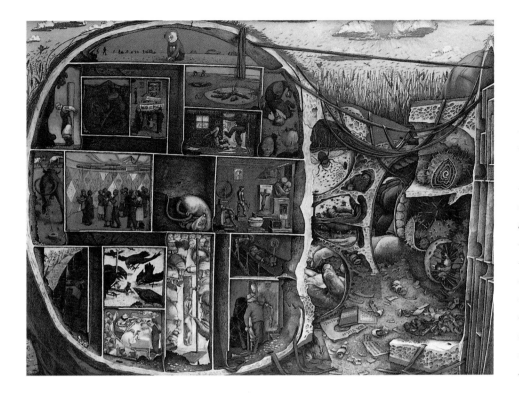

The concept that the mind is compartmentalized is illustrated vividly in The Maze, *by the Canadian-born artist William Kurelek (1927–1977), which he painted while he was a psychiatric patient in the Maudsley Hospital in London. He envisioned his brain as a maze of unhappy thoughts from which there was no escape for the exhausted and frustrated white rat curled up in a compartment in the centre, who, Kurelek supposed, represented his Spirit.*

fact that there may very well be little connection between these "intelligences".

Gardner's theory appeals to common sense. For example, there are many examples of academic "failures" who become influential leaders or captains of industry. The stereotype of the philosophy professor with his head in the clouds who is unable to fix a leaky tap may have more truth to it than we might like to think. But the theory is also supported by more concrete evidence, such as studies of the effects of localized brain damage on the distinct "intelligences" and long-term follow-ups of some exceptional individuals, sometimes called *idiots savants*. These people achieve low scores on conventional IQ tests, but they have one remarkable skill, or intelligence. For example, one case was a child called Nadia, who suffered from autism, a serious neurological dysfunction that left her very withdrawn, but who had a miraculous ability to draw horses.

Whereas Gardner suggests that we have seven separate intelligences or minds, Robert Ornstein is less definite about numbers. Maintaining that we should not view the brain as a unity, Ornstein sees a parallel between the structure of the brain, with its discontinuous layers (in which the cortex sits on top of the midbrain, and both sit on top of the cerebellum), and the operations of the mind, which are also discontinuous. He likens them to different and discrete programs that constantly compete for control of a "central executive".

No one has yet been able to locate the "intelligences" or "multiminds" within the physical brain (although Gardner has speculated as to their locale). But if this can be done, and if Ornstein's claim that "the logic of smelling is nothing like the logic of listening" is indeed correct, we may find that understanding the mind and brain demands an understanding not just of different languages, but also of different *kinds* of languages.

What Kind of Computer is the Brain?

The first digital computers – cumbersome, room-sized machines bristling with thermionic valves – were built in the 1940s. Although they possessed a fraction of the power of a modern laptop, their primitive abilities to perform tasks involving learning, processing and recalling information inspired the pioneers of computing to make ambitious predictions about the development of computer science. In the early 1950s, the British mathematician Alan Turing speculated that "thinking machines" would be a reality by the end of the century; moreover, he believed that these machines could be made to behave in a way virtually identical to a human by including a random element, like a roulette wheel. The quest for Artificial Intelligence (AI) has continued ever since, but opinion is still divided over whether machines will ever achieve intelligence, or even be able to mimic convincingly aspects of the human mind. Some experts in AI go so far as to say that it is only a matter of time before computers become as conscious as, or even more conscious than, human beings. While this extreme view tends to be held by computer scientists, there are few psychologists and neurologists today who believe that computers have nothing to contribute to an understanding of brain function. Many have been seduced by models of the mind that draw parallels between cortex and computer.

Among brain scientists it is important to distinguish between those adhering to the "hard" and "soft" AI positions. The soft position states that, in order to understand how the brain solves a problem, it is useful to examine how a computer solves a similar puzzle and look for helpful analogies. The hard AI position is not content to look at analogies: it claims that the brain is wired like a computer (albeit one not yet designed), and maintains that if a computer program can be written to perform a human task well, then the brain must be programmed in a similar way to perform that task.

The comparison between brain and computer certainly appears tempting: both computers and brains are composed of many simple sub-units – one has transistors and the other neurons. Computers work in a binary language – strings of "on" and "off" electrical pulses – as do neurons, which can either transmit electrical pulses or block their passage; and computer architecture claims to be inspired by new insights

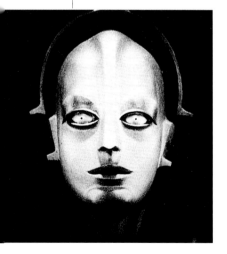

THE TURING TEST

In 1950, the British computer pioneer Alan Turing devised an "imitation game" designed to test whether a computer possessed human intelligence. Turing's test involved a number of written "conversations" between a man, a woman and an impartial "interrogator", who asked questions (none relating to physical appearance) of both. If the computer could take the place of one respondent and convince the interrogator that it was in fact human in 70 per cent of cases, then the computer would be deemed to be "intelligent". To date no computers have consistently been able to pass Turing's or other similar tests.

00111 01 001 11001 010110 110 10 00 0110 11001 010110 001

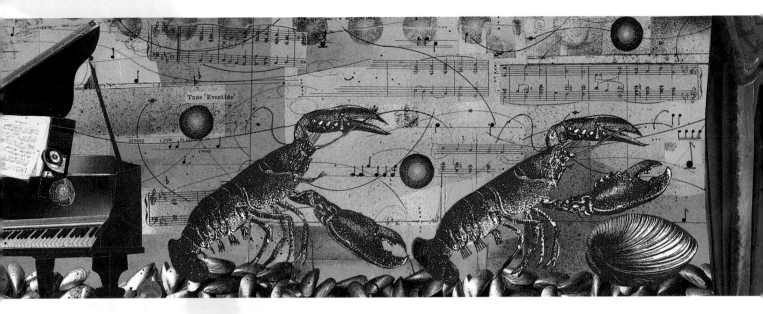

into the brain. At present, personal computers can process just 32 or 64 bits of information simultaneously, although they process these bits extremely rapidly. The brain, in contrast, can process millions of "bits" at a time, although it does so far more slowly. The trend in computer design is toward the "parallel processing" structure of the brain.

Many, however, are careful not to stretch the analogy too far. Philosopher Patricia Churchland and neurologist Terry Sejnowski argue that nervous systems are "naturally evolved computers ... whose modus operandi still eludes us". The brain has evolved without a "designer" to throw out older, obsolete models and replace them with new designs: it is almost certain to have wired-in ways of performing tasks that are no longer ideal but at one time represented the best evolutionary compromise – an observation contrary to the hard AI position. Churchland and Sejnowski also argue that the brain cannot be likened to a general-purpose digital computer because it cannot be programmed to run just any algorithm, or procedure. Instead, the brain seems to be a linked set of highly specialized systems that are very good at performing their tasks but limited in their flexibility. For example, the visual cortex cannot take on the functions of the cerebellum, because its cells have become specialized and are connected to certain anatomical structures. They also stress that theories of AI must integrate physiological facts, pointing to studies of the humble lobster and how it eats. Muscles that control the lobster's gastric mill, which grinds up food for digestion, are controlled by the stomatogastric ganglion, a structure composed of just 28 neurons. The basic electrophysiological and anatomical features of the 28 neurons have been catalogued, so in theory we should know how the structure works. But the lobster's stomach digests in a clear rhythm and, despite intensive study, no single neuron, or sub-set of the 28 neurons, has been found to be responsible for the digestive beat. If it is hard to compute just how the lobster digests, it is hardly surprising that many psychologists suspect that the computer models of the mind have more limitations than advocates admit.

00111 01 001 11001 010110 110 10 00 0110 11001 010110 001

The Non-Material Mind

A complete theory of mind needs to explain both the objective language of the brain and the subjective language of thought and experience. Computer models may be more limited than some enthusiasts suggest, because there are differences between organic and non-organic systems. Although these and other materialistic theories have become influential recently, there have always been scientists who have argued that such theories don't explain all the facts – and never will.

The late Sir Alistair Hardy made his name as a marine biologist, mapping the distribution of plankton in the oceans. But over 10 years from 1925, he also filed cuttings on all religious phenomena and spiritual experiences mentioned in the British press. He set up a Religious Experience Research Unit at Oxford University because he believed that psychology and physiology had to include the spiritual dimension.

Hardy was no neurologist, but his belief that brain activity cannot explain all mental behaviour is shared by physiologist Sir John Eccles, who won the Nobel Prize in 1963 for classically empirical work on the transmission of nerve impulses. In *The Evolution of the Brain* (1989), Eccles argues that while all mammals are conscious, human beings are special in being self-conscious. Although he accepts Darwin's theory of evolution through natural selection, Eccles believes there is a point at which the theory breaks down. This is the point at which our hominid ancestors started to show

MATHS PROBLEM

It is now possible to make sensible guesses about how higher brain processes arise from the biological system of the brain. But many mysteries remain. A study in the 1970s, for example, found that a number of mathematics students at Sheffield University, England, were missing large chunks of their brains. One had only 30 per cent of his cortex – the rest seemed to be water. But that did not prevent him from gaining a degree. No one is sure how that happened.

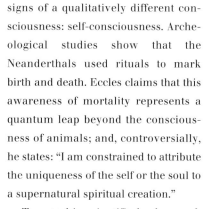

$$\sum \pi \% \notin \kappa = \Phi$$

signs of a qualitatively different consciousness: self-consciousness. Archeological studies show that the Neanderthals used rituals to mark birth and death. Eccles claims that this awareness of mortality represents a quantum leap beyond the consciousness of animals; and, controversially, he states: "I am constrained to attribute the uniqueness of the self or the soul to a supernatural spiritual creation."

True to his scientific background, Eccles has developed a model linking the material and non-material mind. He distinguishes the outer world (light, sound, smell, touch) from the inner world (thoughts, feelings, memories, dreams, imagining and intentions). Both, but especially the inner world, connect with the "liaison brain", which holds the ego, self and soul and is the seat of the will. The radical part of Eccles' theory is his contention that the liaison brain is not wholly material, and yet can influence the material brain.

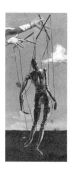

Eccles has tried to identify the areas of the brain that communicate with the liaison brain. He proposes that two areas of the parietal lobe in the right hemisphere of the brain make up what he calls the neo-neo-cortex. These areas are not well developed in apes and seem to develop late in the human fetus, so Eccles argues that they are late evolutionary additions to the human brain and are given over to creative and "gnostic" functions. They are, in other words, the link to the soul.

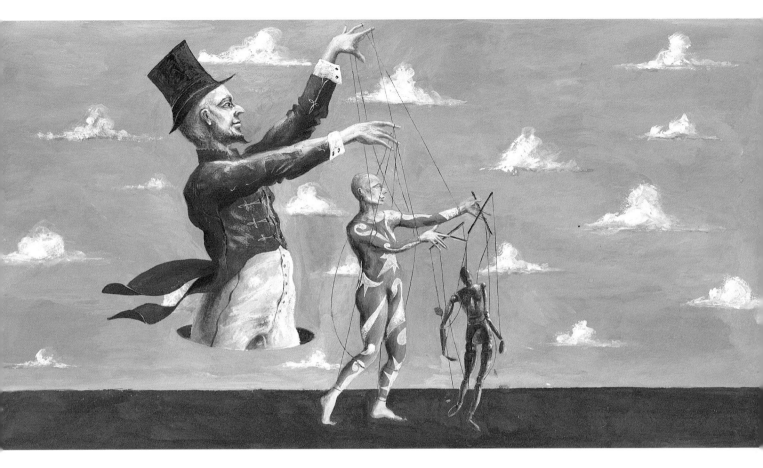

Eccles was tentative in putting forward physical theories to underwrite his model of the mind. However, his suggestions are at least feasible when viewed in the context of modern quantum physics. The uncertainty principle states that one can never simultaneously know the position and the energy possessed by a subatomic particle. If we measure the energy of the particle, we cannot locate it exactly, but can only describe its position in terms of probabilities. Since all matter is composed of such particles, it would seem that materialistic theories, which rely on patterns of direct cause and effect, are insufficient to describe the behaviour of a complex system such as the human brain, which could be said to behave as a "probability field". Moreover, one of the most astonishing recent findings of quantum physics is that the fate of a particular particle – whether it moves this way or that – depends on whether or not an observer is present. If we posit that the brain is always observing itself – the mind itself being the observer – we are at least part of the way to an explanation of free will, and closer to a scientific description of the soul.

Many scientists reject Eccles' theories (which certainly fly in the face of scientific orthodoxy), saying that his views represent a modern recapitulation of Descartes's belief that the soul resides in the pineal gland; but the precision and plausibility of his biological model has attracted some support, most notably from Karl Popper, one of the great philosophers of science over the last 50 years.

Psychodynamic Models of the Mind

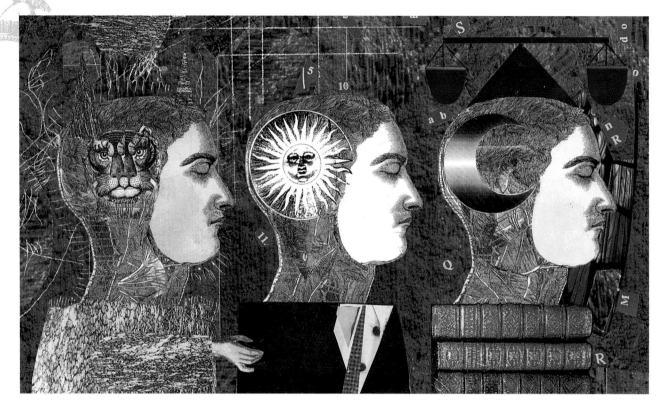

Understanding the mind requires the student to balance three very different kinds of theories: mechanistic, concerning the biology, physiology and biochemistry of the brain; phenomenological, dealing with how we perceive and interpret events in our environment; and psychodynamic, viewing the mind as an assembly of different sources of psychic energy. The analytic view is that behaviour is shaped by the dynamic interplay of these energies, which remain hidden from the conscious mind.

There have been many psychodynamic theorists – Carl Jung, Alfred Adler, Melanie Klein, Wilhelm Reich and D.W. Winnicott have all made important contributions to our understanding of the mind. However, most have drawn their inspiration from the work of Sigmund Freud who, in the 1890s, developed the principles of psychoanalysis – a way of revealing and examining our hidden psychic energies, of making the unconscious conscious.

Among Freud's central theories is the division of human thought into two fundamental levels – the conscious (that of which we are aware) and the unconscious (that of which we are unaware). Freud believed that unacceptable or taboo thoughts, wishes and memories (usually linked to childhood experiences concerning the basic biological urges) are repressed, or forced out of consciousness, but remain lodged

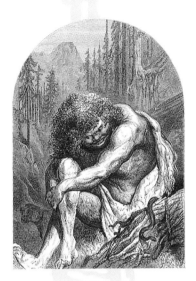

Sigmund Freud (1856–1939), who had a great love of Shakespeare, argued that Caliban (right), the half-man half-beast of The Tempest, *was an unmistakable representation of the id.*

in the unconscious. External events or associations can trigger this repressed material to rise back into consciousness, causing the subject to relive the anxiety and conflict that it originally elicited. Through that, the thoughts are pushed into the unconscious once more, resulting in constant unconscious conflict.

According to Freud, this unconscious conflict is played out between three distinct aspects of the personality – the id, ego and superego, which were famously described in his book *The Ego and the Id* (1923). The id (Latin for "it") is the individual's unconscious source of instinctual energy. It forms the great reservoir of the libido – a person's sexual passions and "life force". Ruled by the "pleasure principle", it seeks instant gratification regardless of cost. Out of this mass of urges develops the ego (Latin for "I"), which is the pragmatic, rational part of human personality: it tries to satisfy the id, but knows that it must do so within the constraints of the real world. The superego is the conscience that makes us either cowards or saints. It restrains the wild urges of the id and allows us to put libidinous energies to more "constructive" uses. The superego can also be seen as our unconscious blueprint of the rules and aspirations imposed by the society in which we live.

Human beings are in a constant state of largely unconscious conflict, with the ego trying to balance the competing demands of the id and the superego. The ego protects itself from this conflict through defence mechanisms that allow it to avoid dealing with frightening material. Freud's theory describes a number of defence mechanisms, a few of which are considered here. In "projection", we attribute our own unacceptable thoughts and desires to others. In "denial", we simply do not acknowledge that which is anxiety-provoking. In "repression", the unacceptable urge is driven back into the unconscious. And in "sublimation", the ugly impulse or thought is redirected into acceptable, even creative, behaviour.

Many commentators have criticized Freud's psychodynamic theories as unscientific and impossible to verify or disprove empirically. Hard-headed scientists such as Hans

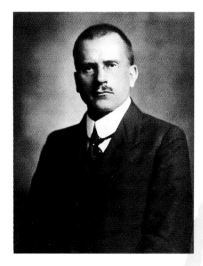

The Swiss psychologist Carl Jung (1875–1961) studied medicine at the University of Basel, and psychiatry at the Burghölzi clinic in Zurich. For many years he collaborated closely with Sigmund Freud, helping to develop psychoanalytic theory, but a rift occurred when Jung rejected Freud's emphasis on sex and began to explore spiritual aspects of the mind. With his theory of the duality of consciousness, meaning the distinction between the collective and personal unconscious, Jung attempted to place the human mind in a historical context, drawing inspiration from mythology, literature, spiritualism and alchemy.

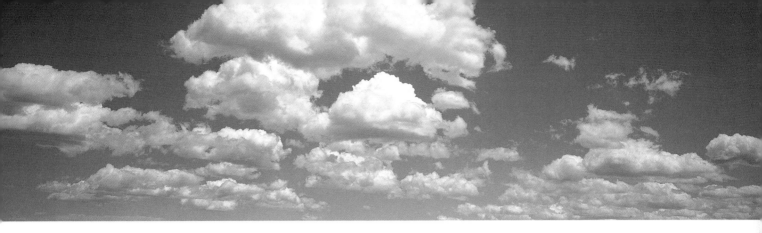

Eysenck observed that "what Freud said that was true was not new, and that what was new was not true"; the distinguished child psychologist Jean Piaget (see page 78) said that in 50 years of study he had found only one case in which Freud's ideas had been of any value; and even fashionable therapists argue that psychoanalysis is more of an art than a science. Freud, however, would have been appalled by this appraisal. The founder of analysis was a very competent neurologist and prided himself on his scientific credibility. Freud firmly believed that it would be possible one day to reveal the biochemistry of the dynamic processes in his patients, and his essay "Project for a Scientific Psychology" even outlined the kinds of cells and "engrams" that he was sure had to exist to "carry" such phenomena as repression.

Freud saw himself as a scientist, but other therapists have been more sceptical about the need to be scientific, viewing themselves more as latter-day shamans. Jung, for example, argued that a complete psychology had to include the spiritual dimension. While Freud saw religion as a neurosis, Jung considered it to be the true expression of an important aspect of human life and spirit.

Jung accepted much of Freud's basic theory, recognizing both conscious and unconscious elements in the human mind, but differed from Freud in the way in which he structured the unconscious. Jung believed that the unconscious has two distinct "tiers": the first, which he called the personal unconscious, is a reservoir of memories and repressed desires (grouped together in complexes) to which we can occasionally gain access through dreams or flashes of recollection; the second, lower tier, is the collective unconscious, the store of instinctive behaviours, patterns of thought, ancient fears and memories "inherited" from our ancestors.

Jung spent many years studying the myths, legends and religious practices of different cultures, and noted great similarities in their themes and modes of expression. He explained this finding by proposing that these stories and customs were all powerful expressions of archetypes – they were images rooted in the collective unconscious, the common inheritance of all humankind. Jung was also struck by the similarity

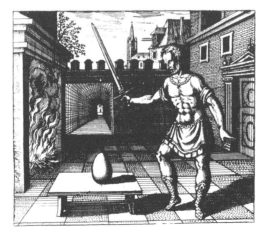

of the drawings produced by patients in analysis with the symbols of Western and Eastern religions and certain esoteric movements, especially alchemy (left), the medieval "science" of transmutation. Jung's belief that symbols represented higher forces caused the split with his friend and mentor Sigmund Freud, who believed that all symbols were concrete expressions of a known reality.

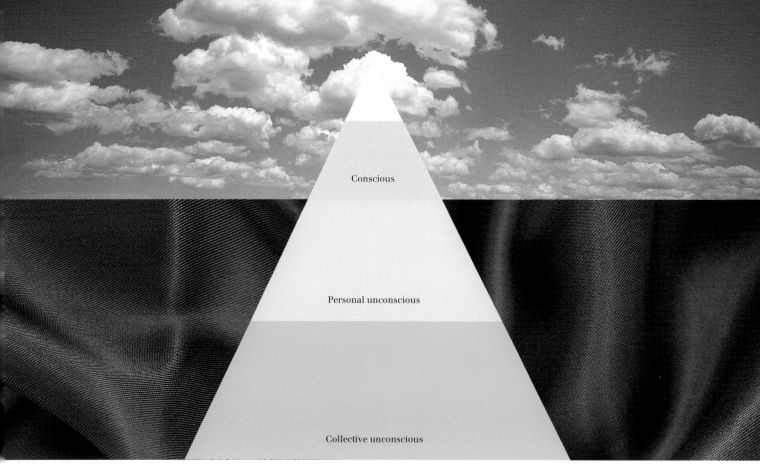

Conscious

Personal unconscious

Collective unconscious

For Jung, the conscious mind was underlaid by the personal unconscious – repressed memories and desires deriving from an individual's own experience. Deeper still was the collective unconscious, the memories and patterns of behaviour inherited from our common ancestors.

Because we all share the same distant ancestors, each of us is born with essentially the same material lodged in the collective unconscious. And just as the content of the personal unconscious is organized into complexes, so material in the collective unconscious is structured into archetypes – deep-seated tendencies to perceive and behave in particular ways. The collective unconscious cannot be accessed directly, and the archetypes emerge only as symbols, frequently taking on the male or female form. Jung recognized a number of archetypes that could be identified across cultures. These include the "shadow" (the part of ourselves that we fear or despise), the "animus" (the male side of a woman's personality), the "anima" (the female side of a man's personality) and the "per-sona" (the part of ourselves that we display to the world). By analyzing the archetypal symbols that appeared in his patients' dreams (see page 117), Jung believed that he could gain vital clues about their psychological problems. And by unlocking the meaning of the symbols, the patients themselves could gain insights into their own minds that would help to resolve the inner problems and conflicts that affected their relationships with others.

Jung's ideas are even more impossible to test scientifically than most psychodynamic ones. But even if all analytic ideas are one day proved to be entirely false, it will be impossible to ignore their significance, because they have undoubtedly changed the way in which we think about ourselves.

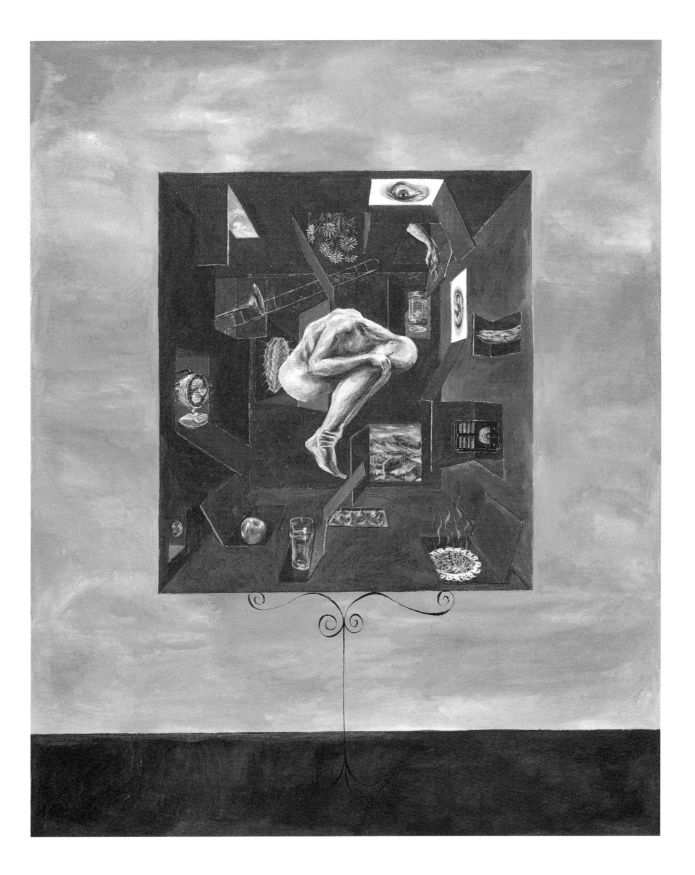

Sensation and Perception

The body of the nematode worm, *Caenorhabditis elegans*, is composed in its entirety of just 811 cells. Yet this simple organism has a sensory system that allows it to detect changes in light intensity, temperature, touch and chemicals on its body surface; and it is able to respond to these sensations by moving toward a "good" stimulus, such as food, or retreating from a "bad" one, such as excessive heat. Senses make the nematode, or for that matter any other organism, a more efficient survival and reproduction "machine", and their progressive refinement over time is a prominent feature of evolutionary history.

Our bodies are intricate machines made up of billions of cells. But our senses differ from those of the nematode in more than just sophistication and complexity. The nematode can experience only "raw" sensations, which tell it what is happening at its body surface and on which it acts reflexively. It does not and cannot actually "know" anything about its environment. So, for example, while it may feel heat on its body, it has no conception that this heat comes from the sun. We also feel raw sensations – green light, fierce heat and so on – but, unlike the nematode, we deduce that the colour comes from grass and that the heat comes from a log fire. This ability to know what is "out there", rather than just "what is happening to me", is the process of perception. It

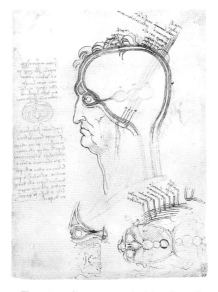

The extraordinary anatomical drawings of Leonardo da Vinci reflect 15th-century beliefs about the organization of the sensory system. The eye was considered to be a geometrically designed organ, superior to the other senses: it communicated directly with the imprensiva *(the receptor of senses), the intellect, the memory and with the other senses at the* sensus communis *(confluence of the senses).*

involves building up a symbolic internal representation of the environment that we can interpret and even call to mind long after the original stimulus (with its sensory information) has disappeared.

Perception allows us to interpret a visual pattern of lines and curves on the retina of our eye as a rose, or the particular mode of vibration of the sensory hairs in our inner ear as the sound of a cello. This makes perception fundamental to all higher brain functions, because while sensations are entirely subjective (for example, I can never know that your direct experience of "red" is the same as mine), perceptions are more objective – we can both agree that we are looking at a red rose. Without this basic level of common understanding, we would never be able to think, let alone communicate effectively with one another.

Natural philosophers have always been interested in the relationship between sensation, perception and the external world. Is what we perceive real or merely a representation that may have only a passing relationship with what is "out there"? Philosophers fall broadly into two camps. Realists such as John Locke (1632–1704) believe in "the certainty of things existing *in rerum natura* [in nature] when we have the testimony of our senses, for it is not only as great as our frame can attain but as our condition needs": our senses do not lie.

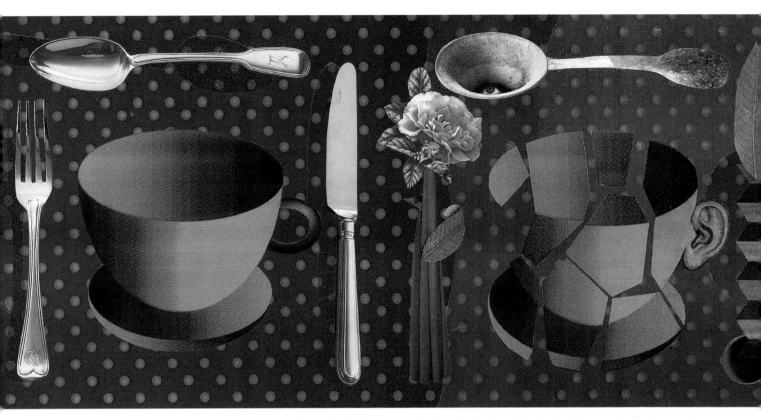

Opposing the realists are the idealists, such as the Irish bishop George Berkeley (1685–1753), who argued that "*esse est percipi*", to be is to be perceived, which, taken to extremes, suggests that a tree only exists when I or you or God see it. Berkeley was concerned with the idea that illusions can make it hard to be sure of the "real" existence of things. For example, if I look at a stick half immersed in a glass of water, it appears bent because light is refracted (bent) as it passes out of the liquid into the air. But if I feel the stick, it seems straight: my perceptions of the object are contradictory. Such paradoxes lead philosophers to argue that we can never be sure of the truth of our perceptions: all we can be sure of perceiving are sense data – information that our sensations give us. I may be able to doubt that I see a table because I

may be the victim of an illusion, but I cannot doubt that on the retina of my eye is a visual pattern that looks like a table, or at least the sense-data of a table. To realists, this seems fanciful.

Since 1900, huge advances have been made in our knowledge of the physiology and biochemistry of our senses. We know how the eye converts an image into a stream of nerve impulses, and how the ear can distinguish between differences in pitch. However, we still know comparatively little about the process of perception, and it has become clear that the relationship between sensation and perception is not simple. Perception is not a one-directional process in which stimuli received via our sense organs cause "brain events" that in turn get converted into an internal experience of an outside occurrence. Stimuli cause "brain events", but the

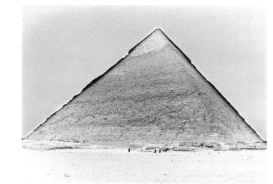

way in which those events are coded depends partly on what the brain expects and remembers. The old proverb "Seeing is believing" would read more accurately as "Believing is seeing" – we tend to see what we expect to see. This phenomenon was investigated experimentally by psychologists of the Gestalt (the German word for "form") school early in the 20th century, which maintained that the whole was greater than the sum of its parts. We tend to look for familiar patterns in what we see, filling in the blanks in such a way as to make sense of them, and we discriminate between those elements that are essential and those that are dispensable for our understanding of the whole.

A remarkable property of perception is that, in some rather exceptional cases, it can be divorced from sensation. We can know what is "out there" without perceiving it through the senses. Many people have had direct experience of this phenomenon, known as subliminal perception. This mental process makes us nervous because it suggests that we can be aware of things that we do not sense. In fact, what occurs is that we see an image so fleetingly that it does not "register" as a sensation, only as a perception – and we do not trust that perception as being true because it is removed from its usual sensory accompaniment. We become confused and doubt the truth of the perception. The existence of subliminal perception has been verified by laboratory studies. In one, subjects

Donald Broadbent (1926–1993), one of the most distinguished British psychologists of the post-war era, argued that it was impossible for a human being to perceive the same thing twice. Let us assume that you viewed the Great Pyramid at Giza 15 times from the same spot, when the sun was at precisely the same angle in the sky. Your 15th perception of the Pyramid would be subtly different from the others because it would activate the neural networks that "held" perceptions 1 to 14.

were flashed a word for ten milliseconds, after which they were shown a second word for a longer period of time; they were quicker to recognize the second word if it was related to the first than if it was not. In the 1960s this phenomenon was used by unscrupulous advertisers, who tried to influence television viewers subliminally by momentarily flashing an image that reinforced the desirability of a product.

Modern physiology makes it possible to be very precise about how the brain breaks down the signals that arrive at the body's sense organs: the ears, the eyes, the skin, the tongue and the nose, and we have even been able to describe some of the essential characteristics of perception. But there is a major puzzle remaining to be solved: how do we, in our brains, reconstruct these signals into what we experience as an image, a sound or a sensation of being touched?

In the 17th century, Isaac Newton used a prism to split white light into its component colours. He was aware of the distinction between sensation and perception when he wrote: "Rays, to speak properly, are not coloured. In them there is nothing else than a certain power ... to stir up a sensation of this or that colour."

Vision

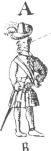

The human eye has often been compared to a video camera. To an extent, this is not a bad analogy. With a camera, light passes through the lens and falls onto a plate divided into hundreds of thousands of individual, minute, light-sensitive areas, or pixels, which convert the patterns of light and shade into a stream of electrical pulses. Depending on the available light, the camera operator can change the size of the aperture, letting more or less light pass into the camera. And by moving the lens elements, near or distant objects can be brought into sharp focus. Similarly, the amount of light entering the eye is controlled by the automatic opening and closing of the pupil; and a lens within the eye can be made to change shape to bring objects into focus on the light-sensitive part of the eye – the retina. Here, millions of individual light-sensitive elements – rods and cones – convert patterns of light and shade into a stream of nervous impulses.

But there the analogy ends, because when we open our eyes, we do not see the world as a collection of sensory bits and pieces – the pixels of the video camera – but as distinct

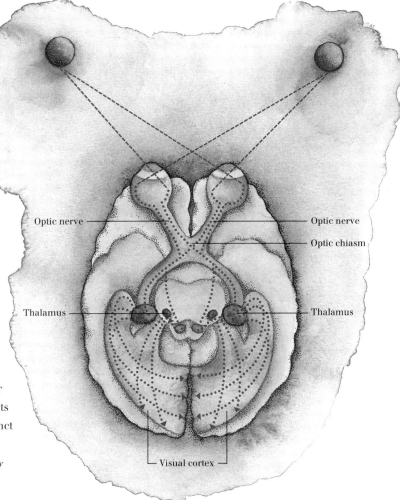

Densely-packed rods and cones in the retina of the eye are clearly visible in this electron micrograph (below). The rods, rendered pink by computer colouring, are more numerous than the cones (mauve) except in the fovea – a small area of the retina where daylight vision is most acute. Different types of cones contain pigments sensitive to red, green or blue light. The combined nerve impulses from the three types of cone are interpreted by the brain as different sensations of colour.

The optic nerves meet to form the optic chiasm (above). From here, signals from the right side of the retina (which carry information about the left side of the visual field) are routed, via the thalamus, to the left side of the brain. Signals from the left side of each retina follow a corresponding path. This means that information from the left side of the visual field is processed by the same side of the brain that controls the right hand.

VISION

objects, shapes and colours. The ability to achieve this alone makes the human visual system remarkable, far outstripping the most sophisticated attempts at computer perception. How do we "know", for example, where one object stops and another begins? How do we recognize a human face seen from a variety of angles as belonging to the same person? And how can these perceptions occur in "real time" – quickly enough for them to be able to guide our responses and movements?

We still do not fully understand the process of visual perception despite the extensive wealth of knowledge that scientists have accumulated about the physics and chemistry of vision and the organization of the human visual system. As far back as the 17th century, doctors assumed that cells in the retina reacted to light. It was only in the 19th century, when physiologists and physicists such as Gustav Fechner began to experiment on how the eye adapts to the dark, that it became clear that the retina contains two types of sensory cells: rods and cones, named after their appearance under the microscope. We now know there to be around seven million cones in the retina of the human eye: these cells respond to bright light, and can detect the fine detail and colour of an object. They are specialized: some cones contain pigment sensitive to red light, some to green and some to blue. Rods are more numerous (approximately 100 million) and respond to dim light and motion,

THE POWER OF VISION

Sight is considered to be the most important sense, providing crucial perceptions of the world. Because of this, it has always been a powerful symbol in the mythologies of many cultures, where the all-seeing eyes of the gods hold us in judgment. For example, Horus, the falcon-headed sky god of ancient Egypt who watched over the application of law, is symbolized by the eye (below).

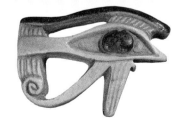

but are unable to distinguish colour. They are responsible for our monochrome "night vision". Every rod and cone is filled with a small amount of photoreceptor pigment. When hit by light, the shape of the pigment molecules temporarily changes, triggering a chain of chemical events that results in the firing of a nervous impulse. The impulses from the rods and cones first pass to bipolar cells and then to large ganglion cells, the long axons of which extend out of the eye as the optic nerve.

The nerve fibres from the both eyes are directed, via the thalamus (a structure in the forebrain that acts as a relay station for incoming sensory information), to the visual area of the cortex, located at the back of the brain. The critical importance of this area in vision was discovered by neurologists during the First World War. They noticed that a significant number of soldiers who had been blinded without any apparent injury to the eye had sustained injuries to the rear part of the cortex. Ever since then, the working assumption has been that it is in the visual cortex that the messages coming from the retina are analyzed and constructed into our experience of vision.

Vision consists of events on the retina being processed in the brain. For example, we all have a blind spot because there are no photoreceptors in the place where the optic nerve leaves each eye. However, the blind spot of the left eye is not the same as that of the right eye, and the brain uses the infor-

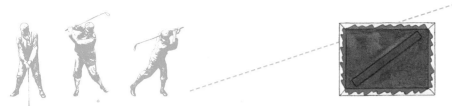

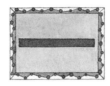

mation from one eye to compensate for a lack of information from the other. Similarly, our brains receive slightly different images from each eye, because of the physical distance between them – the closer an object is to the eyes, the greater the discrepancy. However, the brain fuses these two pictures to the extent that we are not aware of any discrepancy between them: "double vision" occurs when, for some reason, the brain does not effectively fuse the two images – for example, after a concussion or excessive consumption of alcohol.

To most of us, seeing is second nature: it does not have to be consciously "learned". Rather, the visual system is programmed to mature as babies are exposed to light and especially to moving faces and objects. By the age of three months, babies are thought to see in the same way as adults. As their eyes begin to see more "normally", neural connections are laid down and refined within the cortex, establishing the networks needed to process visual information. Only if something radical occurs does vision fail to develop. Studies have shown that kittens placed in an abnormal environment, such as one in which they only see curved lines, do not develop normal vision: if they are shown straight lines, there is no firing from the relevant cells in their visual cortex.

Patients who recover from life-long blindness experience problems that come from never having "learned" to see. One of the earliest such cases was reported in 1728 by William Cheselden, who removed opaque cataracts from the eyes of a blind fourteen-year-old boy, thus restoring his sight. He reported that the boy had no sense of shape and could make no judg-

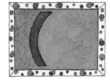

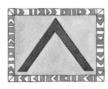

ments of distance but thought that everything was very close to his eyes. He would use touch to confirm what he was seeing – for example, he found it hard to tell the difference between a cat and a dog, until one day he picked up a cat and petted it; it was only by combining touch and vision that he was able to distinguish between the two animals. The boy was also amazed by pictures, especially a locket that held a likeness of his mother: he could not understand how his mother's face could be compressed into a tiny locket. Oliver Sacks in *An Anthropologist on Mars* (1995) reviewed the trauma that often results when such patients get their vision back.

Some of the most sophisticated research on the visual language of the brain was carried out by David Hubel and Torsten Wiesel, who shared the Nobel prize in 1981. They painstakingly traced the paths of neurons in a cat's brain all the way from the rods and cones of the retina through the thalamus to the visual cortex, and found that each neuron in the visual cortex could be "mapped" onto a corresponding small region of the retina. They then exposed a "mapped" part of the retina to a variety of visual stimuli and used electrodes to measure the response of the corresponding neuron in the cortex. The results were astonishing. Rather than responding simply to the presence or absence of a point of light on the retinal field, the cortical neurons fired only when they "saw" highly specific features. Some neurons fired in response to circles, others straight lines, still others particular angles or curves. Some were stimulated by particular contrasts of dark against light or light against dark, or thickness of line or figure. Some fired when presented with

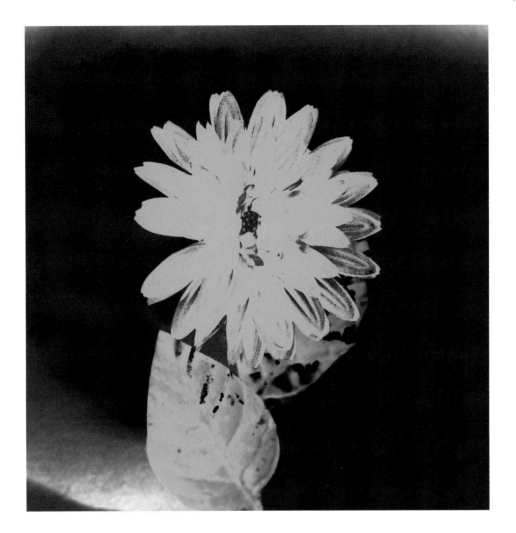

a moving object, and others only in response to stationary objects. Each specialized group of neurons is known as a "feature detector". The suggestion is that when we look at an object, a network of cortical cells, specialized in seeing that type of object, fires, registering a cascade of line segments – fundamental graphics – which, at a higher level of operation, the brain somehow synthesizes and converts into an internal symbolic representation of what we are observing. Hubel and Wiesel's research was on cats, but it has generally been assumed that a similar system operates in the human brain.

If the lights in a room are extinguished, we temporarily see nothing, but it takes only about 10 minutes for our eyes to adapt to the low light conditions. Our pupils dilate, allowing in as much light as possible, and our rods, which function in the dark, take over from our cones, which work in bright light. The eye's extraordinary ability to adapt to new light conditions does, however, have some physiological quirks. In 1825, the Czech biologist Johannes Purkinje noticed that, at dusk, the red flowers in his garden darkened much more quickly than his blue and violet flowers. This is because, at low light intensities, our eyes are more sensitive to the shorter wavelengths of blue light.

This model can be more clearly explained by example. Imagine you are looking at a golf ball about to be propelled from the tee. The ball forms an image on a small part of the retina, onto which are mapped thousands of neurons of the visual cortex. At first, the ball is stationary, so neurons sensitive to still, circular lines fire. When the ball moves off at 45 degrees, a second set of cells sensitive to movement at this angle fire; each time the angle at which the ball is travelling changes by 10 or 15 per cent, a different set of neurons fires. In our mind, this switching is experienced as the image of a ball in continuous flight.

Following on from Hubel and Wiesel's work, others have proposed that the groups of cells in the visual cortex are at the bottom of a hierarchy of feature detectors. Suppose a number of these cells feed into a single higher-level detector, or complex cell; and many complex cells feed into a hypercomplex cell. It is possible to imagine that these high-level cells fire only in response to a very specific feature or stimulus, such as a face, a car or a pair of shoes.

Hubel and Wiesel's theory presents a credible mechanism by which we can detect patterns. But this in itself does not constitute perception, which involves knowing what the pat-

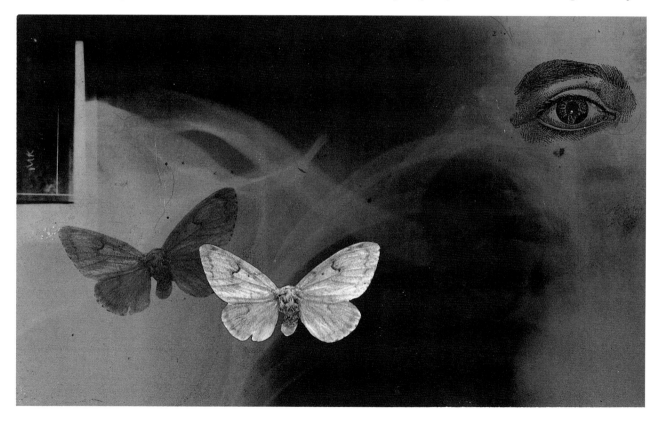

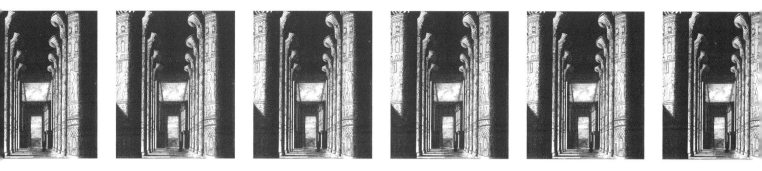

tern represents – recognizing what is "out there" (see page 45). A number of theories have been put forward to explain how we recognize patterns, but perhaps the most plausible are the feature-matching theories.

These propose that an object is recognized when certain of its features (which could correspond to the line segments or higher-level features of Hubel and Wiesel's theory) are matched up against a library of features held in our memories. In each case, cognitive parts of the brain decide which is the "best fit" and place this information into consciousness, allowing us to "know" that a particular collection of lines and curves projected onto our retina is in fact a dog.

This explanation is undoubtedly simplistic – intuitively, it seems unlikely that analysis of lines and curves can account for the richness of our perceptions. However, other established phenomena reinforce this hypothesis. The "word superiority effect", first noted in the 19th century, is a case in point: this notes the fact that letters are more readily recognized when they appear in the context of a word. For example, if the letter "a" is briefly flashed before your eyes, you are more likely to perceive it if it is enclosed in the word "cat" than if it stands alone. This phenomenon is not consistent with a simple line-matching perceptual mechanism, which predicts that the letter should be perceived just as readily whether or not it is part of a word. Thus, it is likely that context and expectations are extremely important parts of perception – a theory borne out by the existence of the numerous artificial and natural visual illusions (see page 98).

Visual perception is one of the most complex processing tasks that the brain is called upon to perform. It is not surprising, then, that when it goes wrong, the results can be dramatic. One of the most peculiar disorders of perception is visual agnosia, made famous by neurologist Oliver Sacks who described the case of the man who mistook his wife for a hat in a book of the same title: this patient tried to lift his wife's head off and place it on his own head, as if it were his hat. Sufferers appear to have a fully operational visual system – there is nothing wrong with their eyes or the visual pathways to the cortex – but they make errors when interpreting the information presented to their brains. For example, some sufferers can perceive separate details of an object but are unable to identify the object as a whole. Others may be unable to recognize faces or even inanimate objects – they may be able to identify a chicken but not a bus.

It is significant that unlike disorders of the visual system, which may cause degradation of the image, blurring, loss of colour vision and so on, visual agnosia causes only gross errors in perception. This suggests that perception works through a high-level "language" that can be compared with the written word in its level of specificity. For example, if we see a misspelling of the word "boot" as "boat" in a specific context, we do not arrive at an image of a misshapen shoe, but of an entirely different object, because each word is a discrete unit. Our visual perception seems to work in the same way, by "seeing" or perceiving objects as complete forms, not as sums of their constituent parts.

Hearing

When Vincent van Gogh cut off his ear, he did not damage his hearing. While other animals can use their facial muscles to move the external ear toward the source of sound, in humans beings the ear flaps, or auricles, play a negligible role in concentrating and focusing sound. The real process of hearing begins deeper within the skull, in the middle and inner ear.

Anything that produces sound – the string of a violin, the surface of a loudspeaker or the human vocal cords – vibrates, alternately compressing and rarefying the air around it, producing a series of sound waves that move through the air away from the source at a speed of more than 300m (1,000 ft) per second. The distance between successive compressions gives the frequency of the sound, and the degree of compression gives its intensity. Physically, then, sound is nothing but a series of vibrations, which carry no inherent sensory qualities. The brain perceives frequency as pitch and intensity as loudness; timbre is established by the multiplicity of frequencies. As with other senses, these perceptions are private to each of us. But before it can be passed to the brain for decoding, the information carried by waves of sound must first be converted into the language of electrical pulses that can be understood and manipulated by neurons. This process is performed by sophisticated mechanical, chemical and electrical subsystems within the ear. As sound waves enter the ear, they pass down a tunnel, known as the external auditory canal, at the end of which is a taut membrane called the eardrum. The drum vibrates in sympathy with the incoming sound waves and passes its movement on to an assembly of three bones in the middle ear: the malleus, incus

and stapes (hammer, anvil and stirrup). These bones behave like a tiny mechanical amplifier, increasing the intensity of the vibration before transmitting it to the spiral-shaped cochlea in the inner ear (the word "cochlea" comes from the Latin for "snail"), where the sound vibrations are transduced into nervous impulses.

The cochlea is a long, tapering, bony cavity, coiled up on itself to save space. It is divided by membranes into three long, parallel channels each of which is filled with fluid. When vibrations are passed to the cochlea from the bones of the middle ear, the fluid is disturbed. The vibrations, or sound waves, move down the length of the cochlea in the form of "bulges" – areas of high and low pressure – within the fluid.

One of the membranes inside the cochlea (the basilar membrane) carries thousands of specialized sensory cells (see page 28), called hair cells because they possess hair-like projections that extend into the fluid. When the bulges of pressure pass by this membrane, they push the hairs up into contact with another membrane (the tectorial membrane). As a hair is pushed against this membrane, the hair bends, causing its "parent" hair cell to generate an electrical impulse. This impulse is picked up by an auditory neuron, which conveys it to the brain. The auditory neurons are bundled together to form the acoustic nerve, which reaches the auditory cortex of the brain via the thalamus – the brain's sensory "sorting office" (see page 24). It is interesting to note that the auditory nerve comprises some 30,000 individual neurons as compared to the million or so neurons of the optic nerve: seeing, it might be concluded, is a considerably more complex job than hearing.

Anyone who has blown across the top of a partly-filled bottle knows that the pitch (or frequency) of the sound produced depends on the level of the liquid within. Blowing across it causes the air inside the bottle to resonate (vibrate intensely) at a particular frequency, which is determined by the height of the column of air in the bottle. This piece of elementary physics helps us to understand how the ingenious design of the cochlea allows us to distinguish between different frequencies of sound. The cochlea, as we have seen, is tapered. Each point along its length can be thought of as a bottle filled with a slightly different amount of liquid,

Sound is produced by any physical vibration and is transmitted as a succession of sound waves: trains of compressions and rarefactions of air molecules. In the human ear, sound waves are picked up by the eardrum and amplified by the three bones of the middle ear before they pass down one fluid-filled channel in the cochlea (red) and back up another (green); as they do so, fluid in a third channel (yellow) is compressed. These compressions are detected by hairs (inset photograph) attached to sensory cells in the third channel. The sensory cells convert differences of pressure into neural impulses, which travel to the brain via the auditory nerve.

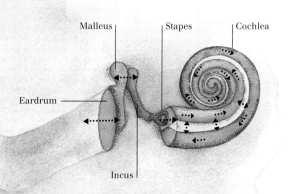

Malleus   Stapes   Cochlea

Eardrum

Incus

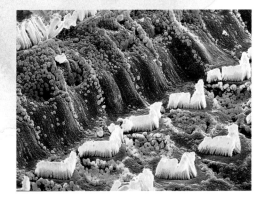

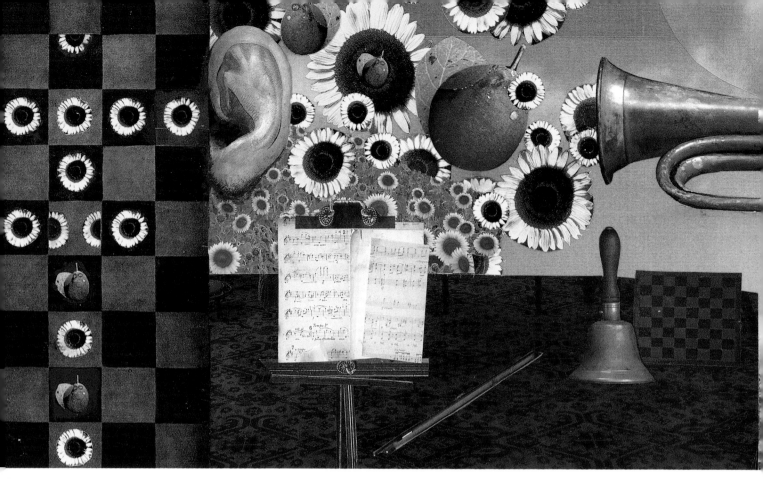

and so each point has its own natural and preferred frequency of vibration. When sound coming into the ear matches this frequency, this particular point of the cochlea will vibrate more than any other point, and its connected auditory neurons will fire more than any other auditory neurons. The brain "hears" this as a particular pitch of sound.

While there are similarities in the ways in which the brain processes sound and visual images, there are also many differences. One of the key differences relates to attention. We have much greater control over what we choose to look at than what we choose to listen to – when we want to look at a particular object, we can turn our heads and focus our vision. To perceive sound, we can also turn our heads to direct one ear toward the source of that sound, but in many situations there are conflicting sounds. However, there is a more effec-

tive method: we can mentally choose to focus on certain sounds, blocking out other conflicting stimuli – the phenomenon known as selective listening. For example, if a different text is read into each ear of an experimental subject, he or she will usually report "hearing" just one story. However, there is also some evidence that we do hear something of the "unheard" information, even though we do not perceive this information consciously (see page 47).

Many species have more sensitive hearing than humans, and can detect a far wider range of frequencies. Human hearing, however, must contend with one major challenge not faced by other animals – language. Our capacity to speak, and our need to listen, have affected the way in which the human brain processes sound, with the result that our auditory systems expect to hear not disconnected sounds, but coherent

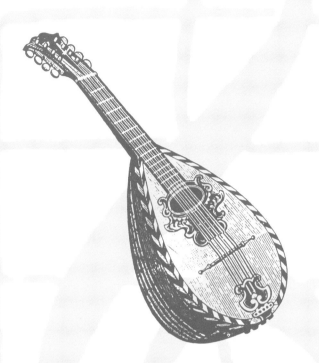

handicap to contend with: often they are dis-criminated against because they are seen as being of below average intelligence. Many deaf children have problems with the syntax of written language, but this is because sign language has a distinctive grammar and syntax of its own, which differs substantially from spoken and written language. Another problem is that the normal process of linguistic development may be disrupted in deaf children who are encouraged to speak "normally" before they learn to sign: they then spend their formative years struggling with, rather than learning, what comes naturally to others – language.

The brain's bias toward detecting regularities in sound, and constructing narratives from noise, is also evident in our ability to produce and appreciate music. In general, music that is said to be "easy on the ear" is relatively predictable in rhythm and melodic progression. Even someone who is completely untutored in music theory can detect a "bad" or jarring note in a musical phrase in the same way that he or she can identify an inappropriate word in a sentence. This has led some theorists to speculate that music, like language (see page 70), has an inbuilt grammar with which we are endowed at birth. We enjoy a piece of music when its grammar matches the unconscious rules held in our minds. This theory is hard to prove or disprove, but the use of dissonance in some modern music (particularly jazz), as well as cultural differences in musical styles, suggests that the brain cannot be wired from birth to appreciate only conventional harmonies.

stories that make sense. Just as with vision, our expectations affect our perceptions. Surrounded by a babble of voices in a crowded room, for example, we can pick out the sound of our own name in a distant conversation. A number of experiments support the idea that our brains try to impose patterns on what we hear. Human hearing has become remarkably attuned to the nuances of conversation, such as the almost imperceptible pauses that act as cues to speak or to listen, and the minute differences in intonation.

The importance of sound in language and communication makes deafness a particularly isolating condition – perhaps more so than the loss of any other sense. Deafness is more common than is often imagined: one child in every thousand is either born deaf or develops severe hearing difficulties early in life. But deaf children do not just have their physical

Touch, Pain and Pleasure

In many ways, touch stands apart from the other senses. It is not localized in specialized sense organs, but rather it covers our entire body surface, and it provides three distinctive types of sensory information – pressure, temperature and pain. Even the language we use to describe touch is different. While we say that we *perceive* visual objects, sounds, tastes and smells, we talk instead about *feeling* texture, heat and pain. We also use our sense of touch less than the other senses. As adults, we rarely test the texture of an object to determine its identity. Furthermore, what we see and hear changes constantly, so our eyes and ears are always active; but what we touch often remains the same for minutes or hours at a time and is excluded from consciousness – we are only aware of the feel of our clothes, for example, when we first put them on.

Unlike the other senses, touch often carries an intense emotional charge – a mother cuddles her baby, lovers caress each other – and many studies have demonstrated the positive psychological effects of touch. Premature babies gain weight more quickly when they are picked up and hugged; stroking a pet allegedly reduces stress and can actually lower heart rate; and experiments on monkeys have shown that touch seems to reinforce the development of normal social interactions. One of the most extraordinary examples of the emotional power of touch comes from

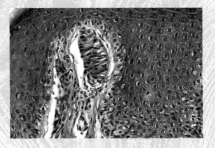

Buried in the dermis of the human skin are touch receptors called Meissner's corpuscles (above). They are particularly numerous on the fingertips, soles of the feet and erogenous zones.

Temple Grandin, a designer of agricultural equipment who has been autistic since birth. Like many autistic people, Grandin could not bear the sensations or the intimacy of being touched. In her book *Thinking in Pictures* (1995), she writes that she always hated being hugged, but describes one kind of touch that she has found re-assuring. As a teenager staying on her aunt's ranch, she noticed that some cattle seemed to feel reassured when held in a cattle squeeze. Grandin developed a similar machine for autistic people, because she found that its dispassionate pressure was extremely comforting and helped to ward off anxiety.

The biology of touch does not shed much light on these psychological complexities. In 1895, the physiologist Max von Frey argued that there were five basic kinds of sensation – touch, displacement of hairs, pressure, temperature and pain – which are detected by five different kinds of receptor cells in the skin. However, it now appears that there are only two types of receptor, one type dealing with touch and the other with temperature and pain. Physically, the touch receptors are nerve cells that have globular swellings on the terminals of their dendrites: they are buried at different depths within the skin and respond to different types of touch, from the light brush of a feather to deep pressure. Pain and temperature receptors are free nerve endings lacking the globular swellings on their terminals. Not surprisingly,

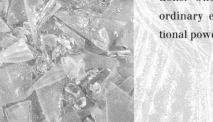

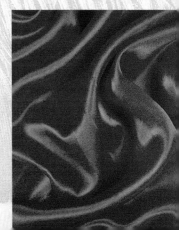

sensitive parts of the body, including the hands, lips, face and tongue, are more richly endowed with receptors than areas such as the knees and back, where sensory discrimination is not at a premium. The amount of cortex devoted to different body parts is sometimes represented graphically in the form of a "homunculus", or small human, the size of whose limbs is proportional to their sensitivity (see illustration, right).

The sensory neurons then connect with nerves in the spinal cord: here, some pain receptors make direct links to motor neurons, forming the pathways responsible for involuntary reflex actions. Other spinal cord nerves carry signals up to the brain: they pass via the thalamus (the sensory sorting office) and sometimes the limbic system (an area of the brain associated with memory and emotion) before arriving at the somato-sensory cortex – that part of the cortex in which touch, pain and temperature are perceived. Each part of the body "maps" onto a specific area of the somatosensory cortex, and those parts of the body with a high density of receptor neurons have correspondingly large areas of the cortex dedicated to them. Some parts of our bodies have highly refined sensitivities to different stimuli: for example, on the cheek or the belly, we can perceive a weight as small as 5mg (0.00018oz), and with our fingers we can distinguish between two points separated by less than 2mm (0.085in). It is harder to measure sensitivity to temperature because we can adapt quite easily to cold or warmth, and what we define as warm or cold is generally relative to our body temperature at the time. However, on more sensitive areas of skin we can detect minuscule temperature drops.

While pressure and temperature are external phenomena that can be measured objectively, pain originates within the body. Whenever tissue is damaged, neurotransmitters are

Our skin is highly sensitive to external stimuli, acting as a barrier against the outside world at the same time as it is collecting a wide range of essential information. It can sense minute changes in pressure, temperature and movement – as particular as the movement of a single hair – bringing us pleasure or, if the stimulus is too strong, pain. However, different areas of the body have different degrees of sensitivity. A "homunculus" (left) maps these differences graphically, representing the size of each part of the body in proportion to its sensitivity. Around half the somatosensory cortex concentrates on receiving information from our hands and face, the most sensitive parts of our body.

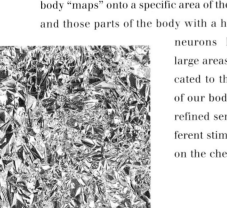

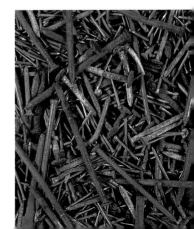

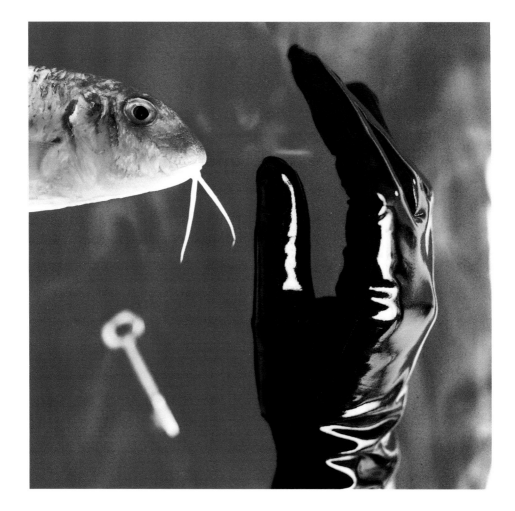

released that cause "high threshold" receptor neurons to fire, and it is the arrival of these impulses at the cortex that gives us our perception of pain. As with the other senses, pain perception is highly subjective: it is as much a matter of mind as of physiology, and can be strongly influenced by attitude, personality and cultural factors. For example, studies have shown that extroverts routinely report more pain than introverts (see page 88).

Psychological techniques are used, with some success, to help the chronic pain in cases of serious illness or if conventional drug therapy is inap-

propriate: patients may be asked to imagine that they are soldiers, with the pain as an army to be defeated, or simply encouraged to visualize scenes in which pain is alleviated.

That pain can be controlled or enhanced by thought alone has led to a new theory of pain perception called the gate control theory. This proposes that in order for pain to be felt, it is not enough to receive "pain" signals at receptor neurons: these signals must also be sufficiently intense to force their way through a pain "gate" that protects us from feeling trivial pains that need not

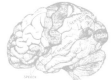

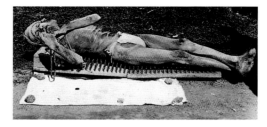

concern us. Supporters of this theory claim that the gate is not just a concept but corresponds to a real anatomical structure in the spinal cord. As well as receiving sensory fibres from the skin, the gate is also fed by nerve fibres from the cortex, which secrete endorphins (see page 129): these neurotransmitters have strong biochemical similarities to morphine and heroin, and are the brain's natural painkillers. Their release can effectively close the pain gate, decreasing the level of pain experienced.

The gate theory may go some way to explaining the ancient healing technique of acupuncture. This was developed in China around 2500 BC, from the belief that illness and pain

Whether or not we feel pain is clearly determined by more than just the nature and intensity of the external "pain-inducing" stimulus. The degree of pain experienced is influenced by expectations and habituation, as well as cultural factors: to many Westerners, for example, some of the feats performed by Indian fakirs (above) would be beyond tolerance.

were caused by an imbalance between the opposing dark (Yin) and light (Yang) forces in the human body. By inserting needles into specific points around the body, a skilled practitioner can restore the balance between the Yin and the Yang, thereby effecting a cure. An alternative explanation holds that the needles, placed on trigger points also familiar to Western medicine, stimulate the neurons of the pain gate, producing a strong analgesic effect.

The highly individual nature of the perception of pain and pleasure is nowhere more apparent than in people's sexual preferences. In 1886, the pioneer sexologist Richard von Krafft-Ebing published his *Psychopathia sexualis* (The Psychopathology of Sex) which introduced the terms "sadism" and "masochism". Krafft-Ebing found that some people could be aroused to orgasm by pain that, for most, would be excruciating, and others could be aroused by fetish objects, including shoes, feet and gloves. At the time, his discoveries were felt to be so shocking that they almost led the Vienna Medico-Psychological Association to cancel his membership, and his book, considered too lurid for the masses, appeared only in Latin. Krafft-Ebing's study of fetishes raises an unanswered question: do masochists feel pain in the same way as the rest of us, but accompanied by associations that "overwrite" these sensations with pleasurable ones? Or is their sensation of pain qualitatively different, so that when they are being whipped, for example, they feel simply pleasure?

PHANTOM LIMBS

That pain is psychogenic (generated by the mind) is supported by the testimony of people who have damaged nerves in a limb or who have lost limbs. Around 40 per cent of these people report feeling tingling, burning, cramping or crushing pains in the "phantom" limb. This arises because the neural circuits in the somatosensory cortex that are associated with the limb are still "in play" even though the limb itself has been lost. Many amputees often become angry and frustrated when they feel sensation or pain in their missing limbs, and part of their rehabilitation is to learn to accept and cope with the pain, which can in some cases may last for years before eventually subsiding.

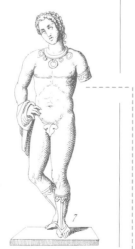

Taste and Smell

Historically, philosophers and psychologists have been more interested in vision and perception than in the characteristics of smell and taste, which were thought to be "gross" animal senses. It is indeed true that these senses have a less prominent role in humans than in other animals, and there is much to suggest that they are more ancient and primitive than vision. Smell receptors, for example, appear to have an older connection to the brain than the other senses: they are wired directly into the cortex, while the other senses are routed to the cortex via the thalamus.

It appears that smell is the only human sense to have been blunted over evolutionary history: our primate relatives have much larger areas of the brain devoted to smell, and compared with dogs we are virtually "scent blind". A German Shepherd dog has 30 per cent of its cortex devoted to smell: in humans the figure is less than five per cent.

Another characteristic of the human sense of smell that points to its evolutionary age is the uncanny ability of odour to trigger intense emotional memories – an ability explored by the 19th-century French novelist Marcel Proust in his

Different areas of the tongue are preferentially sensitive to each of the four basic tastes – bitter (purple), salty (blue), sour (yellow) and sweet (red).

largely autobiographical *Remembrance of Things Past.* Proust wrote that the smell of a *petite madeleine,* a cake he had eaten as a boy, evoked chains of childhood memories. Smell receptors are wired into the limbic system, a relatively early development in the brain that also controls some aspects of memory and emotion.

The human olfactory system (which governs smell) is simple. Air drawn through the nostrils passes into the nasal cavity and over a layer of tissue called the olfactory epithelium, situated just behind and below the eyes. Within this layer, about 1 sq cm (0.15 sq in) in area, are many receptor cells from which project tiny hair-like cilia. Specific chemicals on the cilia react to smells carried in the air, producing a nervous impulse. The impulse moves along nerve fibres, eventually reaching the olfactory region of the cortex on the temporal lobe of the brain. Here, different smells are processed and possibly "perceived".

A professional perfumer or whisky blender can distinguish more than 100,000 different odours; and even a normal nose can recognize more than 20,000 smells. But not all substances can be smelled. Glass, for example, has no smell because all its molecules are locked up in a solid structure and cannot be released into the air. Likewise, substances

Smells are detected by receptor cells in a layer of tissue called the olfactory epithelium, which is situated at the top of the nasal cavity. Hair-like cilia (right) on the receptor cells increase the surface area, over which an astonishingly wide range of scents can be registered.

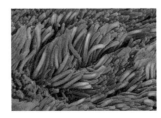

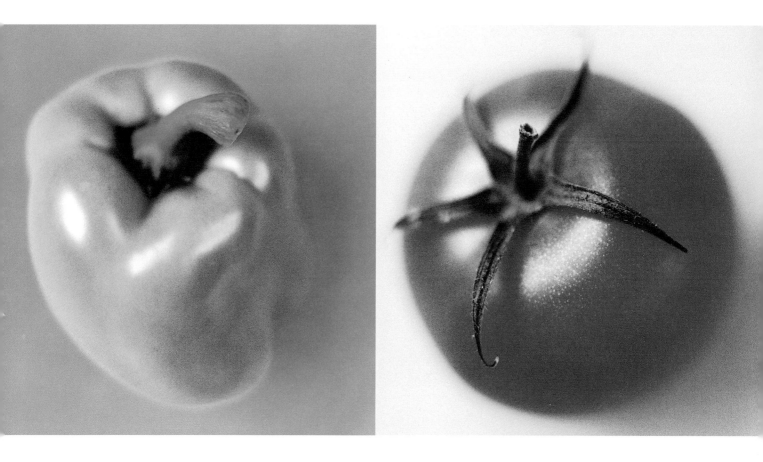

that are not soluble in fat cannot pass through the fatty cover-
ing of the smell receptors and so are not detected. Several
experts have proposed classifications of smells, but there is
no satisfactory classification that is consistent with everyone's
experience, partly because smells cannot be resolved into
basic components (such as colours) but must be described by
likening them to past olfactory experiences.

We use our tongues much more than our noses. The
tongue is used for speech, taste and touch, and is involved in
swallowing and breathing. This is why so much space in the
somatosensory cortex (see page 59) is devoted to the tongue:
one would not want to confuse the actions the tongue
requires for eating with those needed for talking. The tongue
is a rough patch of muscle covered in small bumps – the taste

Our sense of taste resides only partly in the tongue: the smell, texture and
appearance of food all have an important role to play in producing the
overall perception of taste.

buds – on which are clusters of taste receptor cells. Like the
olfactory receptors, these cells are covered with short hairs
that make contact with solutions in the mouth and respond by
producing nerve impulses that pass via the thalamus to the
somatosensory cortex. Compared with our sense of smell,
however, our sense of taste is crude, allowing us to distinguish just four basic flavours – salty, sweet, bitter and sour.
Much of the sensory information credited to taste comes from
smell, as anyone trying to enjoy a gourmet meal with a
blocked nose can testify.

Sensory Deprivation

The brain is a sensation addict, demanding a continuous stream of information from the sense organs. Faced with a sensory vacuum, even a partial one such as blindness in a portion of the visual field, the brain may turn to invention, with hallucinations and delusions substituting for real experience. And under extreme conditions of sensory deprivation, it may interpret the lack of stimulation as painful, even as a crisis.

Sensory deprivation has long been used in forms of punishment or torture. In his account of life in a penal colony in the 1920s, the French safe-breaker Papillon reported that he was haunted by endless paranoid fantasies after six months' solitary confinement in a dark cell. The technique is still used as a form of punishment in some "enlightened" penal systems, even though its dangerous psychological effects are recognized.

The scientific study of sensory deprivation can tell us much about brain function, but it also has real applications in understanding the stresses imposed on prisoners and people living and working alone. The first studies, however, were driven by more sinister motives. Between 1945 and 1950, the CIA became convinced that Communist psychiatrists had perfected brainwashing techniques in which a crucial part of "softening up" the subject was a long period of isolation.

Because of concerns that American scientists were falling behind in their knowledge of brainwashing, resources were poured into sensory deprivation experiments, and their perceived importance to the freedom of the West helped to remove many of the ethical objections to such work. In one Canadian study, subjects were placed in a dark, sound-proofed room in which there were no objects to touch. Within 36 hours, 25 of the 29 subjects began to hallucinate. Some saw dots and flickering lights, but others reported seeing quite complex scenes, and many felt a loss of self-identity – experiences not totally dissimilar to the symptoms of schizophrenia. The experience was so unsettling that after 48 hours, most subjects refused to undergo another period of deprivation. Perhaps the most startling finding was that although they had spent only a limited time under these conditions, many subjects found returning to the outside highly traumatic.

Sensory deprivation studies took a new turn in 1976 when J. C. Lilly, famous for his work with dolphins, argued that lack of stimulation did not have to be stressful. He immersed subjects in a dimly-lit water tank, telling them that they would find the experience interesting, rather than warning them of possible traumas. In the event, the subjects reported reductions in stress. Similar studies carried out later found that voluntary sensory deprivation for short periods could promote increases in creativity and relaxation, providing an opportunity for "greater insight, habit modification and beneficial self-directed behaviour change".

The difference between Lilly's and the Canadian experiments was one of motive. The Canadian subjects saw sensory deprivation as something that was being done to them rather than something they could control for themselves. In Lilly's experiments, the tone was positive. Subjects were collaborators in the experiment and were encouraged to make use of the opportunity. This will not surprise social psychologists who have often shown that the setting of an experiment, and even the experimenter's expectations, can have an enormous effect on the results.

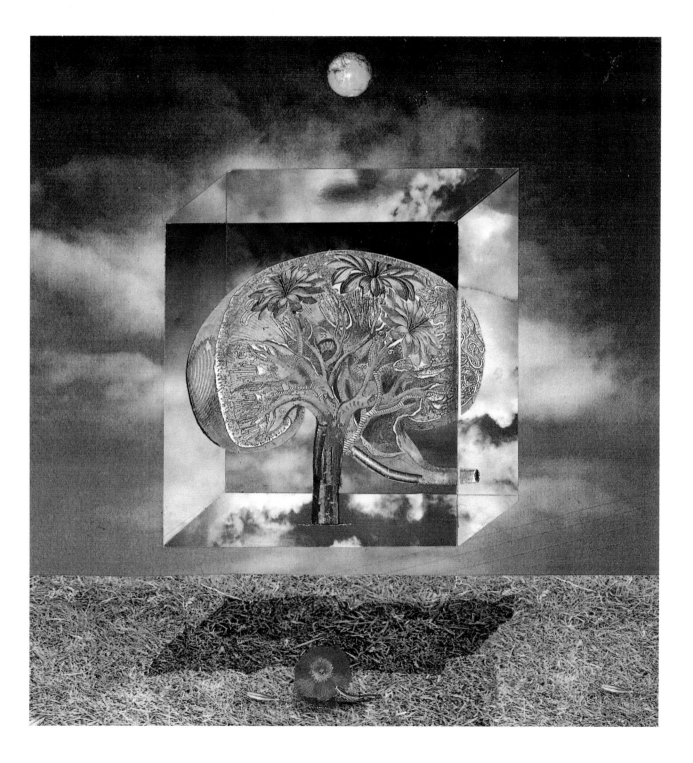

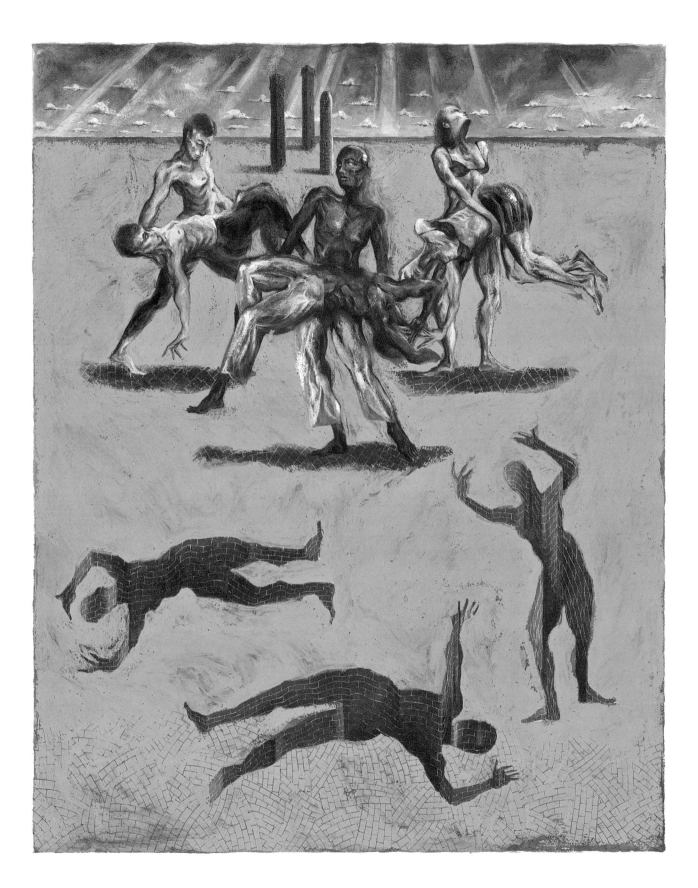

Consciousness

The philosopher Ludwig Wittgenstein warned that language was a trap that could lure us into trying to define the indefinable. Consciousness may well be one such indefinable concept, but this has not prevented a procession of the world's greatest thinkers from engaging willingly in what Wittgenstein termed "puzzles that do not really exist".

At the end of the 19th century, William James (see page 74) saw consciousness as the state of mind in which we weigh up the various possibilities of what we might be perceiving, and then select the most likely. The neurologist Antonio Damasio now argues that consciousness is "a concept of your own self, something that you construct moment by moment on the basis of the image of your own body, your own autobiography and a sense of your intended future". Although no broad consensus exists as to the precise meaning of consciousness, it can be described as the state of mind that allows us to "know" our own mind, to entertain thoughts about thoughts, to monitor our selves and our environments, and to use this information to make plans and formulate hopes and fears.

In some respects, consciousness can be equated with the traditional philosophical concepts of mind and soul. These concepts have a long history, which has inevitably influenced the development of theories about the nature, origin and location of consciousness.

For the ancient Greeks, the soul (or *psyche*) was the self: it

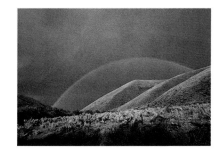

While theologians once saw consciousness, or the soul, as God-given, some modern neurologists maintain that it is no more than a by-product of the physical and chemical processes that take place in the brain. Consciousness emerges from interactions between these processes in the same way that a rainbow, although beautiful and seemingly purposeful, is merely the result of the interplay between light and water droplets.

was the principle of life that animated the body. Aristotle, in *On the Soul*, argued that the *psyche* was "the first actuality of a natural organic body" – meaning that to possess a *psyche*, or soul, is to possess a body – and he even located the soul in the heart. Despite this error of anatomy, Aristotle's view was remarkably prescient, because he tried to explain behaviour and emotion in terms of physiology: he suggested, for example, that the boiling of blood around the heart causes anger.

With the rise of Christianity, Western theologians were greatly influenced by the idea of the immortal, non-physical soul. The soul gave us free will, the risk of Hell and the promise of Heaven, and separated us from animals. Human beings were not biological machines. The Christian belief in an all-powerful God undoubtedly shaped the philosophy of René Descartes, whose dualistic theory of mind and body dominated thinking about the mind from 1650 to the early 20th century. Descartes' ideas still give pause for thought. He claimed that the world contains two qualitatively different types of substance – physical matter, of which the body and brain are made, and the indivisible "substance" of thought, which comprises the mind. Brain and mind somehow run in parallel, although the mind is pre-eminent, steering the brain in the same way that a pilot controls an aircraft.

Despite its flaws, dualism was influential for many years (some scientists and philosophers still believe that it holds true in a modified form), and passed into everyday thought: when we say, "The flesh is weak, but the spirit is willing," we are acknowledging the divide between mind and body.

In recent years, dualism has fallen from favour as neurologists have begun to demonstrate the ways in which states of mind are dependent on functions of the brain, and have put forward models of the mind in which the notion of "self" has an entirely neural basis. In these models (which are highly speculative), a particular state of consciousness is not just associated with a particular pattern of neural activity, it *is* that pattern of activity. For example, Francis Crick (the co-discoverer of DNA) believed that consciousness emerges from the simultaneous rapid firing of neurons in different parts of the brain, while neurologist Antonio Damasio proposes that it is mediated by particular neural centres, or convergence zones, in the brain. According to Damasio, thought is not pure logic – the brain does not work by manipulating logical formulae, but by handling representative images. At the convergence zones, disparate images are merged together: thought, memory, experience and emotion collide, setting the agenda for our immediate attention, and it is this that corresponds to consciousness. Damasio locates his convergence zones in the prefrontal cortex, which has for many years been identified as the seat of the soul, ego or personality (for example, consider the case of Phineas Gage on page 25 of this book), and backs up his model with neurological studies of people who have suffered damage to the frontal regions. These

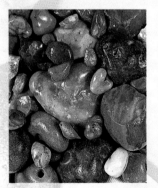

René Descartes (1596–1650), considered to be the earliest philosopher of modern times, made significant contributions to the study of science and mathematics. Descartes developed his own method of rational enquiry – the "method of doubt" – in which he resolved to doubt anything that was not entirely certain. Everything Descartes saw or heard might be an illusion or dream, but the one thing he could not doubt was that he was doubting. At the centre of this mental process there was a consciousness, an "I", even if all the "I" did was to doubt. This was expressed in one of the most famous soundbites of philosophy: cogito ergo sum, *I think therefore I am.*

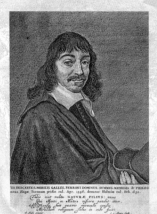

people appear to be unable to link thought with affect (or emotion); but rather than being cool-headed and rational, their lack of emotion makes them incapable of making decisions or coping with the demands of life. However, Damasio does have his critics, such as Daniel Dennett of Tufts University in the United States, who argue that consciousness is not located in only one identifiable area of the cortex but emerges out of all the brain's activities.

Homo sapiens means "humankind the knowing". Built into the name of our species, therefore, is the idea of consciousness, an ability to "know" that is central to our identity and distinguishes us from other forms of life. But how secure are we in our belief that we share consciousness only with our fellow humans – and not with other animals, plants and inanimate objects? Curiously, perhaps, there is no convincing answer to this question. The best that we can do is draw con-

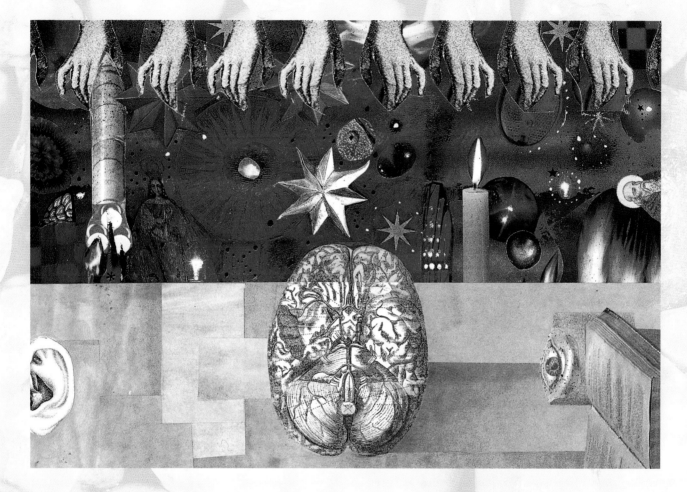

clusions from analogies. So, because my mind and consciousness derive from my brain, and you have a brain, I suppose that you too have a consciousness; a pebble, with no brain, does not. Similarly, because you behave rationally (respond to stimuli in the same way that I do), communicate information as I do and display emotional responses similar to my own, I suppose that you also have consciousness. This dependence on mere similarity of behaviour in attributing consciousness is reflected in the way in which we treat animals: some of us might say that a warm-blooded mammal, such as mouse, is "more conscious" than a lizard, because of the mouse's physiological similarity to humans.

Some neurologists believe consciousness to be located in the frontal lobes of the brain: others argue that it is a property of the entire organ.

Similarity tests are used by students of Artificial Intelligence (AI): if a computer can convincingly display human responses, it is judged to be intelligent. But does the computer "feel" conscious? Should we treat the computer with the respect that we accord to other humans simply because of its intelligence? These questions point us back to the controversies about the nature of consciousness and the long, often bitter, battles that philosophers and scientists have waged. We should keep Wittgenstein's caution firmly in mind.

Language

According to many experts, language sets human beings apart from other animals. Our faith in our superiority, however, has been challenged over the last 30 years as various enthusiasts have tried to show that some primates (and also dolphins) either have language or can acquire it. Their studies have made celebrities of "talking" chimpanzees like Washoe and Nim Chimpsky (named playfully after the linguist Noam Chomsky), but despite the attention lavished on individual animal subjects to try to get them to speak or to use sign language, the results have been disappointing. Nim Chimpsky, for example, could understand and produce two- or three-word phrases in American Sign Language; but his use of language was based on repetition and imitation, and he showed little evidence of grasping the rules of grammar – not the simple rules of punctuation and noun–verb agreement that we all learn in school, but the structural framework of language that is needed to construct new sentences and ideas.

Language, it would seem, is an extraordinary and almost wholly human attribute, and one that emerges very early in

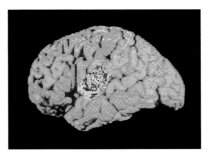

Although the idea of an innate grammar may seem at first strange, it is entirely consistent with what we know about the brain. Since the 19th century, neurologists have been aware of language centres in the brain, such as Broca's and Wernicke's areas, and modern technology allows us to visualize the areas of the brain involved in language. This positron emission tomography (PET) scan reveals the activity of language centres in the brain of a subject asked to perform a verbal task.

life. At the age of 12 months, bright toddlers can utter a few words. And by the age of four years, most can put together quite complicated sentences that express nuances of intent, understanding and emotion. The early development of linguistic skills has raised questions about how they are acquired. Is language learned, just as we learn any other unnatural action, such as how to ride a bicycle, or is it somehow wired into our brains, in the same way that the ability to fly is programmed into the brain and body of a newly-hatched chick?

Some psychologists have proposed that children pick up language by imitating their parents and other people around them, who obligingly speak in simply, clearly inflected sentences: certainly, imitation is important in some aspects of communication, such as gaining a grasp of the syntax of speech (see page 80) – the almost imperceptible cues that set the rhythm of conversation. But imitation is too simple a theory to account for many observations: why is it, for example, that infants begin to speak with one- and two-word phrases, rather than speaking in sentences?

Another theory, proposed by the influential behaviourist B. F. Skinner, is that language (which Skinner insisted on calling "verbal behaviour") is learned through conditioning. Children hear the speech of others and associate sounds with particular objects: when they subsequently make those sounds in response to the correct objects, they are rewarded. Gradually, through repeated rewards, their utterances come to approximate to the words and sentences of adult speech. In effect, parents teach their children how to speak. But one familiar fact contradicts the learning (and imitation) theories as the sole explanations of language acquisition: children often produce new and original phrases that they have never heard before and that they have never been rewarded for using – this means that they could not have "learned" these phrases, in Skinner's sense of the word.

Around the age of seven or eight months, most infants begin vocalizing nonsense syllables. These are the same no matter what language their parents speak – they are the sounds that are the most common across languages. How do we account for this?

The American linguist Noam Chomsky provided an answer. In his important book *Syntactic Structures* (1957), Chomsky showed that there were certain constant elements in all human languages. For example, they all seemed to have a distinction between subject

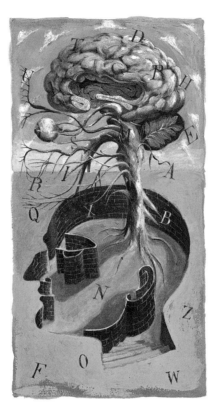

and object, and between nouns and qualifiers. For Chomsky the existence of these common elements suggested that the fundamental structure of all languages was the same.

It follows from Chomsky's theory that an infant's brain is wired so that it will respond in precise, set ways to these fundamental structures. The brain has an innate ability to extract first words and then rules of underlying syntax from the language that it hears. Conversely, as a mental construct, language is also built around these fundamental structures.

Chomsky's theory is supported by many observations: children from a variety of backgrounds, and with widely different abilities, seem to acquire language at more or less the same rate, as would be expected if language were partly innate and not exclusively learned. In addition, deaf children learn sign language in stages very similar to those followed by children with normal hearing as they learn to speak. And all children show a remarkable ability to apply unlearned rules of language structure to new objects and events in order to construct new and meaningful sentences.

Human consciousness depends greatly on our ability to form and interpret symbolic representations of the outside world. It seems that this ability – like seeing, hearing and remembering – is only partly a matter of learning.

States of Knowing

The different meanings we attribute to the term "consciousness" suggest that it is a cloudy concept. We can say, for example, "John is not conscious," meaning that John is asleep or in a coma; "John isn't conscious of anything in particular" suggests that he is daydreaming rather than paying attention; and "John is not conscious of his wife's hostility" means that he is not sensitive to her emotional state. It seems that consciousness is less a state of being, more a state of knowing.

Even the distinction between conscious and unconscious states is far from clear-cut. When I am asleep, most people would agree that I am unconscious; but I may well be dreaming that I am walking down the street, seeing my reflection in shop windows. In my unconscious state, I am conscious of myself, of the I. Then I wake up. Now I am conscious of what I was thinking when I was unconscious. These ambiguities have led some psychologists to talk in terms of a continuum of consciousness.

Within this continuum, however, it is useful to recognize three types of behaviour. At one extreme is fully conscious behaviour, when we use the reflective capacity of the mind to

Scientific research into sleep, which began in the 1930s, has revealed that different states of consciousness and unconsciousness are characterized by marked changes in the electrical activity of the brain. This activity can be measured by attaching a number of sensitive electrodes to the scalp of a subject: these detect the feeble electrical potentials generated by the firing of neurons in the brain and feed the output to a pen recorder. The resulting jagged trace is called an electro-encephalogram, or EEG. When the subject is fully awake (1), the EEG records "brain waves" that oscillate between 8 and 12 times per second. In the earliest stage of sleep, which is an intermediate stage between wakefulness and sleep (2), the waves become more rapid and irregular. As the subject progresses into deeper, non-dreaming sleep (3, 4 and 5) the oscillations become progressively larger and slower. During the deepest sleep, the subject is hard to wake up (4 and 5). During dreaming sleep (or REM sleep; see page 114), the brain waves more closely resemble those of the conscious state (6). As we sleep, we move quickly from one stage of sleep to another, and we repeat the various stages throughout the night.

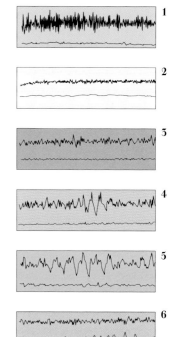

During deepest, non-dreaming sleep, the body is relaxed and the mind is quiet. During dreaming sleep, however, the brain, heart and eyes are very active while the rest of the body is virtually paralyzed.

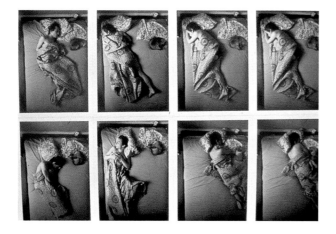

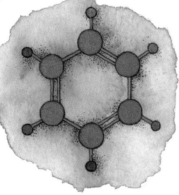

its utmost, when we struggle to find the appropriate word in writing a letter, or when we pay full attention to a practical or mathematical problem.

In automatic behaviour, we are still conscious, although not conscious of carrying out the actions and thoughts in question. This is sometimes known as the preconscious level. Walking is one example of automatic behaviour. I walk from point A to point B. If you ask me whether I had meant to walk from A to B, I will say that I had, although I did not have to will each step, or indeed pay attention to the action at all. Only if an unexpected event had interrupted my walk would I have become more conscious and fully aware of my actions: for example, if I had tripped on my shoelace, I would have consciously looked around for an object to grab in order to break my fall.

The thoughts and actions involved in automatic behaviour are somehow separate from the rest of consciousness. These thoughts are not "unconscious" in the Freudian sense of being repressed and accessible only through psychoanalysis and dream work (see page 114), because they can be brought into awareness at a moment's notice. For example, you are not conscious of knowing the meaning of each word you speak or read, but you are able to bring each meaning to consciousness if you need to. Similarly, when you drive a car, you do not talk yourself through each stage of the action, but if you had to describe the action of driving in detail, you would be able to. Automatic behaviour can also coexist with con-

The 19th-century German chemist August Kekulé reputedly solved the puzzle of the chemical structure of benzene while asleep. In a dream, Kekulé saw the image of a snake biting its own tail while in whirling motion: this led him to the idea that the benzene molecule was a ring-shaped arrangement of carbon atoms, rather than a straight chain as had previously been supposed.

scious thought: we can drive quite safely while carrying on a conversation or planning our day. Indeed some psychologists suggest that we actually focus better on creative tasks when engaged in automatic behaviour. The crime writer Agatha Christie claimed that she made up most of her plots while washing the dishes. She could make Poirot and Miss Marple live while her hands were deep in soapy water.

The third type of behaviour is unconscious. Freud argued that there is constant seepage between the conscious and unconscious minds, and that occasionally material from the unconscious can surface and guide our behaviour. I may do something I cannot later recall, make an inexplicable mistake, or find myself unable to explain why I did or said something. The unconscious also intrudes upon the conscious in the form of remembered dreams. Unconscious processes are sometimes constructive. For example, the French mathematician Jules Henri Poincaré (1854–1912) once awoke to find in his mind the solution to a set of complex mathematical problems known as the Fourier functions: it may be that the answer came to him unconsciously.

The Stream of Consciousness

Over the centuries, many philosophers and psychologists have struggled to characterize the nature of consciousness. Few, however, have been as influential as William James (1842–1910), whose observations and analyses of conscious experience set out in his *Principles of Psychology* (1890) continue to inspire students of the mind a century later.

James argued that consciousness has four key attributes. First, it is personal. Every thought is owned by someone. Second, consciousness is always changing. We can never be in exactly the same state of consciousness twice, or in James' words: "No state once gone can recur and be identical with what was before." This assertion can best be clarified by an example. Let's suppose I think of Anna in a pink frock on Sunday. If then on Monday I find myself thinking of Anna in pink again, my second state of consciousness of "Anna-in-the-pink" must somehow include the first state of consciousness of "Anna-in-the-pink", so the two cannot be quite the same. Third, James argued that consciousness is continuous, and it is this continuity that gives us our sense of self.

He summarized these ideas in the apt metaphor of the stream of consciousness. Just as a stream is always a stream in spite of the fact that the water that defines it is constantly changing, so identity is maintained by the flow of thought, or consciousness. And just as the stream flows continuously in one direction, so consciousness is never stationary, but is a dynamic state that is never exactly the same from one moment to the next.

Finally, James argued that consciousness was selective, capable of filtering out the irrelevant material from the hundreds of impressions bombarding our brains at any one time. On this point, it appears that James was largely mistaken:

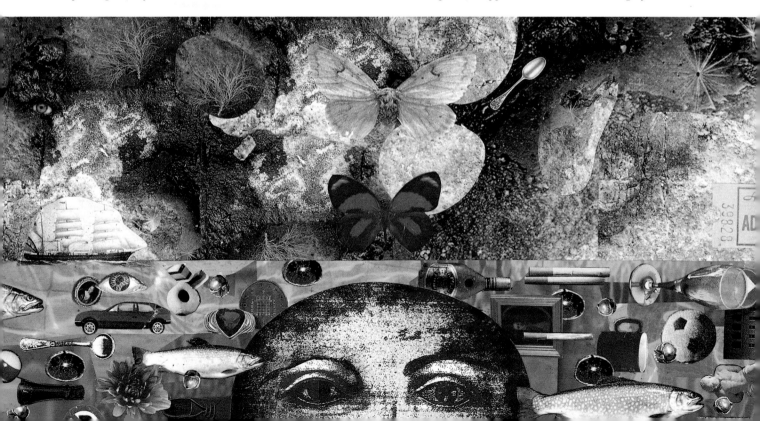

these filters in fact work on an unconscious and preconscious level (see page 38).

Given his conviction that the stream of consciousness glued the self together, it is not surprising that James was fascinated by exceptional cases of multiple personality in which the "glue" appeared to fail. In 1889, James had the chance to study one such case in great detail – the surprising story of Ansel Bourne.

Bourne was a preacher in Greene, Rhode Island. In July 1887, he left his home and withdrew $551 from the bank. His family expected him home that night, but Bourne did not return. When they started looking for him, they were told that he had been seen taking a train to Pawtucket. Despite placing notices in the local papers, they could find no trace of Bourne and began to fear that he had been murdered.

Seventeen days later, residents of nearby Norristown saw that an unassuming man, Mr Brown, had taken over the lease of a small stationery store. Brown attended the local church and surprised the congregation by speaking eloquently. On 19 September of the same year, Brown woke up in a panic. He had no idea what he was doing in Norristown running a store. He told customers that his real name was Ansel Bourne and that he was from Greene. They were utterly baffled, but on wiring Greene, they discovered his story to be true.

William James went to interview Ansel Bourne. Having hypnotized the preacher, James quickly made contact with

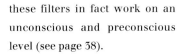
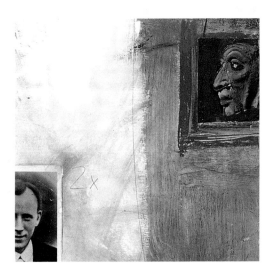

Robert Louis Stevenson's classic The Strange Case of Dr Jekyll and Mr Hyde *was published in 1886, just as reports of multiple personality cases were emerging from the asylums. His fiction was deeply influenced by, and undoubtedly exercised an influence on, how we see cases of multiple personality.*

Brown, who remembered everything that had happened after his arrival in Norristown. Brown said that he knew of Bourne but had nothing to do with him, and was indeed rather dismissive of the preacher. Bourne, however, said that the name Brown was familiar, but had no idea who he could be. James was convinced that Bourne was not "acting": his one mind really did contain two separate consciousnesses.

Interest in multiple personality has burgeoned over the last 40 years, and many dramatic cases have been documented. These include that of Chris Sizemore, whose three "other" personalities – Eve White, Eve Black and Jane – were the subjects of a Hollywood film, *The Three Faces of Eve*. In some of these cases, the alternative personalities differ not just in "character", but also in physical attributes, such as body posture, voice and handwriting, and there may even be shifts in brain activity, heart rate and blood pressure. The theories put forward to account for these extraordinary changes include that of Frank Putnam of the National Institute for Mental Health in the United States. Putnam believes that multiple personality disorder is a response to childhood trauma. The child who is being abused cannot bear what is happening to him or her and creates out of his or her unconscious another character. The new character becomes the person who suffers, who is beaten or sexually abused, and in this way, the child's normal self does not have to cope with the pain and anxiety.

Introspection

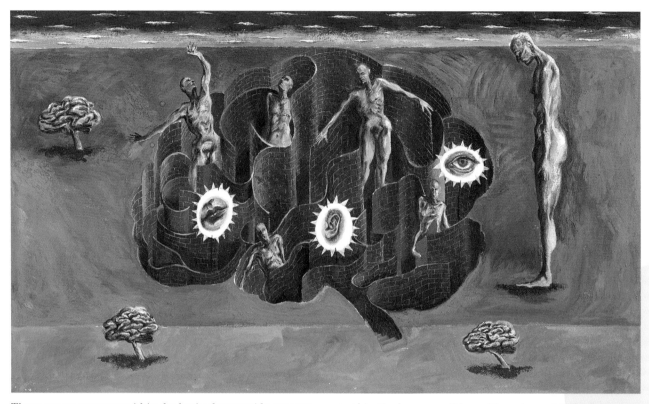

There are no neurons within the brain that provide sensory information about brain activity: this means that, literally, we cannot physically sense what we are thinking. We know very well that we are conscious. However, there is no way that we can prove that fact conclusively to anyone else. For years philosophers and psychologists have struggled with this issue, searching for ways to study the thoughts and thought processes of other people – in fact, to study consciousness – in an objective fashion.

Scientists have long been frustrated by the lack of direct access into the brains of their human subjects. They have had to rely on asking subjects to report on their thought processes as objectively as possible – although most have been concerned that such a process must be unavoidably subjective.

Sir Francis Galton (see page 169) was one of the first to attempt a scientific, experimental approach to the investigation of consciousness. He presented subjects with a variety of stimuli and asked them to keep in mind the images that they associated with them. He then asked them how vivid and clear these images were, and how long they lasted. (This marked the first use of standard questionnaires in psychology.) A group of German psychologists took a similar approach in the 1890s. They believed that immediate sensation was the fundamental building block of consciousness.

They therefore tried to describe the sensations that subjects (often their own carefully trained students) experienced when they were exposed to a stimulus for a very short period. In a typical experiment, a subject would be shown a flashed image of a yellow circle and would then be asked to describe and define the experience. These early experimenters could not draw generalized conclusions because they found to their dismay that no two people had exactly the same response to any stimulus. For example, if somebody's mother always wore a yellow hat, he or she would have a different response to the flashed yellow circle than would somebody who always used a golden circle as a focus for meditation.

Introspection fell out of favour among mainstream academic psychologists with the rise of behaviourism in the early 1900s, because it was all too clear that the data that introspection offered, based on private events, were not objectively measurable and verifiable. Behaviourists excluded the study of consciousness from psychology and concentrated on studying behaviour as they tried to achieve what they defined as a "real" science.

Other psychologists continued to use introspective methods. Indeed, introspection is the basis for psychoanalysis. Freud's methods consisted almost wholly of listening to patients. Although he knew that the analyst could easily become less than objective, he believed that there was no other way of studying consciousness. He also resisted coding

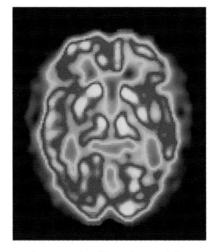

Images produced by positron emission tomography (PET) are able to show which areas of the brain are most active at a given time by measuring the expenditure of energy – more active areas are tinted yellow.

objectively the content of analytic sessions. Carl Rogers, the founder of client-centred therapy, recorded therapeutic sessions and analyzed them to understand the process of therapy. The transcripts that he published, especially in his book *Counselling and Psychotherapy* (1942), offer a wealth of data on what seems to be going on in patients' minds. The Rorschach test (see page 165) is similar to the 19th-century studies. Patients are presented with a stimulus – the inkblot – that is more or less free of personal associations, and their commentary on the thoughts that are evoked are the basis for assessments of personality and state of mind.

Since the 1960s, there has been new interest in investigating consciousness, as psychologists realized that their science had to account for the subtleties of being human. At the same time, technology has been catching up with psychology's desire for quantitative investigations of consciousness. First developed in the 1920s and since refined, EEGs sensitively measure electrical activity (see page 72) in the brain, although many time-consuming baseline studies must be made before any interpretation is possible. Functional MRIs and PET scans (see pages 182–3) can illustrate graphically levels of activity in the brain. These techniques can elicit the sort of objective information that even the most skilled introspection could never hope to achieve – but without some very human, subjective thought, the meaning of the scans remains obscure.

How Babies Become Conscious

A newborn baby is barely able to see. He or she knows nothing, cannot speak a word and has no idea what an idea might be. He or she has no sense of identity. Within 36 months, this creature has changed into a toddler who can speak, feel feelings, make plans and follow (and, irritatingly, disobey) rules. The baby knows what it wants now, and knows what it wants to happen in a few minutes time: by most people's definition, the toddler is conscious.

There have been many attempts to describe and account for this transition. Sigmund Freud stressed the idea of psychosexual development (see pages 41 and 91), in which a child progresses sequentially through a number of distinct stages, each with its own dominant "theme". The idea of staged development was also central to the work of the great Swiss psychiatrist Jean Piaget (1896–1980), whose theories have shaped how we think about the emergence of intelligence and "mind".

Piaget claimed that motor movements are the first steps to consciousness. In the first two years of life, babies touch, grasp, sit up and crawl. Through these movements they learn to coordinate eyes, hands and other limbs, and begin to develop intelligence. And coordination makes it possible for babies to have intentions: a nine-month-old can crawl with great determination toward that interesting red balloon. Piaget called this phase of development the sensori-motor stage. But clearly, coordination on its own does not equate with consciousness. In Piaget's next stage (which begins around the age of 18 months) infants start to be able to make symbolic mental representations of their actions: they acquire schemas or internal "theories" of how the world around them works. If a child encounters a new object or event, it tries to make the new experience fit into a pre-existing schema – a process Piaget called assimila-tion. If the object cannot be assimilated, the schema is modified to take in the new information – a process called accommodation. Children do not see, touch and hear passively: as the environment acts on the child, the child responds, constantly reorganizing itself as the result of the incoming information.

Human thought would be impossible without our capacity to represent and symbolize objects and events (especially by using words and language). This ability allows us to think beyond mere perceptions, beyond the here and now. Piaget stressed the difference between symbols and signs. Whereas a sign is fixed (three red flags, for example, always means "enemy ships on the horizon"), a symbol is not so rigid. When a baby learns (or devises) a sound that symbolizes a bottle, it may make the sound whether or not the bottle is there – for example, if it wants to express pleasure or need. And a child at play can equally use a brick to symbolize a car or a soldier (not all symbols are words).

So according to Piaget, a baby's intelligence and consciousness result from assimilation, accommodation and an increasing ability to symbolize. The baby is seen as a miniature scientist, testing internal hypotheses by manipulating the world around it, and then using the results of its experiments to construct "ideas" (schemas). Piaget developed these theories after years of observing children, including his own, and he saw young children as egocentric, not really concious of others. Many critics, however, claim that this model of development is rather one-sided because it ignores the fact that babies are social creatures.

Studies have shown that, from a very early age, babies can make real social contacts with their parents and other children and that they are are much more sensitive to others and

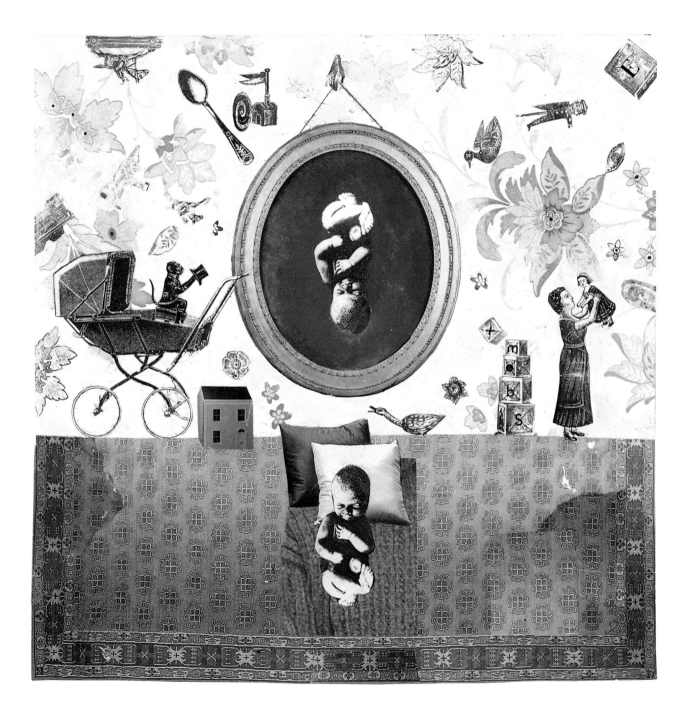

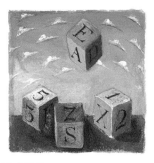

The evolution of consciousness in a human infant has a number of prominent landmarks:

1. The infant learns to coordinate and control its movements by manipulating and dropping objects.

2. The infant learns that there is a boundary between self and others.

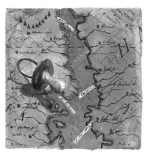

less egocentric than Piaget believed. A baby's sense of self and its consciousness develop not just out of "experimentation" and schema-forming, but also out of interactions with its mother, father, siblings and other human beings.

Only in the 1970s did psychologists really begin to expand on theories that acknowledged the role of social interaction in development. To many, this approach is more true to life. After all, in general human beings do not live in isolation. We exist in groups, we are brought up in families, we join "gangs" of friends when we are children. As we are so social, it is not surprising that our sense of self grows through the way in which we relate to other human beings.

There are good reasons to believe that some key steps in developing consciousness depend on social interactions. The ability to perceive objects, to recognize the boundary between

self and others, to communicate, to reason and to have intentions are all, to some extent, mediated by the presence of others. For example, most parents notice (with some delight) that their newborn baby can imitate their facial expressions, and by its third month the baby can respond to a parent's strange or inconsistent behaviour with an "appropriate" expression of fear or sadness. This observation suggests that the baby becomes sensitive to, and able to express, subtle differences in mood at an extremely early age.

An infant will also gain from its parents the hidden rules of communication – the knowledge of when to speak and when to listen, the rhythm of conversation – which is as important as the individual words it also gradually learns. This rhythm is set by many subtle cues – eye contact and little nods of the head – which the infant learns as it engages in "baby talk"

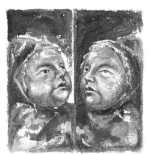

5. The infant develops a body image and starts to recognize its own image in a mirror.

6. The infant begins to point: this seems to be crucial in learning language, because we first point at something and then name it.

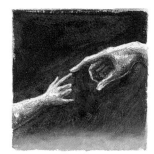

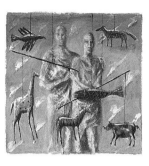

3. *The infant learns to recognize father, mother and other significant people.*

4. *The infant learns to recognize its own name.*

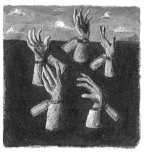

with its mother and father. Analyses of such dialogues have shown that, even at the age of two months, the baby shows some grasp of the patterns of adult conversation.

Studies of the game of "peekaboo" have made it possible to see how babies start to have wishes, intentions and plans through playful interactions with their parents. Jerome Bruner (1983) mapped the progress of Jonathan's play between five and nine months. At five months, Jonathan responded if his mother started to play peekaboo, but he showed no signs of initiating the game himself. By nine months, Jonathan could signal to his mother that he wanted to play: he was becoming conscious both of his wish to play and of his ability to cajole his mother into starting to play.

The role of imitation and play is crucial to the development of consciousness (see page 82). In the words of psycho-analyst D. W. Winnicott: " It is largely through play ... that a child begins to allow these other [people] to have an independent existence." Play helps infants to establish that there is a boundary between themselves, their parents and the rest of the world. They are then ready to take the next crucial step – becoming aware that other people are conscious just as they are, and have minds, thoughts, wishes of their own. American psychologist Henry Wellman found that this capacity is present in three-year-olds, who are able to see situations from the perspective of others if they are clearly explained.

These lines of evidence support the idea that children are less egocentric than Piaget believed, and that they may achieve adult consciousness earlier than was previously thought, although there is no clear point at which we can say that this transition has occurred.

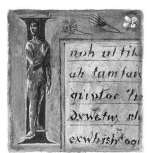

7. *The infant starts to use sentences that begin with "I".*

8. *The infant recognizes that other people have thoughts and intentions different from its own.*

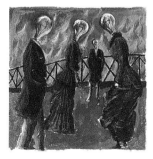

Lying and Pretending

When Shakespeare's Richard III mused, "Why, I can smile and murder whilst I smile," he affirmed the extreme nature of our ability to lie. Lying is one of the great triumphs of human self-consciousness because it requires holding at least three contradictory elements in mind simultaneously. When I tell an untruth, I must know that I am saying A; I must know that I don't believe A; and I must know that I really believe B.

Most children begin to lie when aged between two and three years. Their earliest untruths are simple denials: a child is asked if he hit his brother and replies "No". Often the child betrays him- or herself by laughing nervously at the same time as uttering the lie, and body language continues to identify a child's lies even as he or she gets older. Three- and four-year-olds typically place a hand in front of the mouth when fibbing – the mouth has to be hidden because it is not speaking the truth. Five-year-olds are sophisticated enough to know that anything so obvious will make it clear that they are lying, but many still cannot help betraying themselves through body language signals – they often look down at their feet, avoiding eye contact as they lie, almost as if they are not quite ready to hold two different thoughts in mind at the same time. Children become confident liars only when they are eight or older.

Even in adults, the body offers clues as to whether or not a person is lying. Like children, adults tend to look away when they are telling a lie: often they look down and a little either to the left or the right of their feet. In addition, studies have shown that facial expression can give liars away. Whereas genuine facial expressions are symmetrical, false ones are

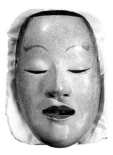

asymmetrical – but even the most practised observers cannot gauge this every time.

For all that it is difficult to read, facial expression may be a better indication of honesty than polygraphs (lie detectors). These machines measure a number of physical indicators of stress, including heart rate, respiration and the electrical conductivity of the skin. Polygraph tests measure the stress levels generated by different questions, some ostensibly harmless (When were you born?) and some more challenging (Did you rob the bank?), and the results are read by skilled interpreters. However, feelings of stress do not guarantee that someone is lying, and even the most experienced reader cannot identify skilful liars who do not feel stress when they lie.

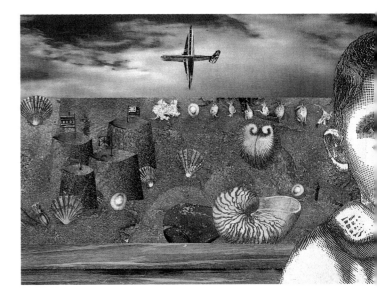

Closely linked with our ability to lie is our ability to pretend, although there is an important difference between the two. Whereas lying is concealment, pretending is an open conspiracy, and it plays an important role in our development. Children learn to pretend, and to recognize the pretence of others, well before they can lie – at the age of about 15 months. One often sees that at the start of "pretend games", the child puts on an exaggerated play face, a non-verbal signal that says, "This is not for real." Adults also have their own "pretend games", which they share in order to cement close emotional relationships. Often these are childlike, perhaps because adults strive to achieve in close relationships the intimacy that they had with their parents as infants.

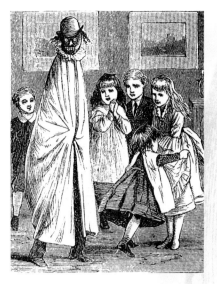

From the age of about 15 months, most children are able to pretend and react appropriately to the pretence of others.

Psychologists used to think that pretending was an interesting but relatively insignificant behaviour, but it is now becoming clear that it is central to learning a variety of social and cognitive skills. In their pretending games, children test out their own identity – so that if a child pretends to be Superman, but knows that he is pretending, he learns something about who he really is.

This idea is supported by recent work on the condition of autism (literally "self-concern"), which affects 0.04 per cent of children. Autistic children usually develop normally up until the age of around two years, at which point they become extremely withdrawn (avoiding eye contact, hugging themselves and recoiling at being touched), and cease to develop normal social and language skills.

Early theories of autism, which suggested that the condition was triggered by emotionally cold mothers who never hugged their babies, have been disproved, but there is still debate over whether autism is psychological or physiological in origin. One theory holds that autistic children are frightened of some of the stimuli that are typical of play – especially loud noise. And while they play with toys fairly normally, they find it impossible to play pretending games. Researchers such as Uta Firth and Simon Baron Cohen of the Cognitive Development Unit in London argue that this is at the heart of autism, because one way in which we learn how to behave socially is through pretending: lack of this ability impedes our social and emotional development.

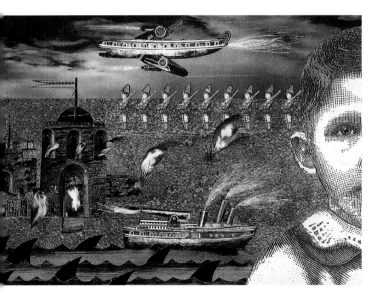

Memory and Forgetting

How can I know who I am if I have forgotten what I have done? This question reveals the central role of memory in maintaining a sense of identity. It glues together fragments of consciousness, allowing us to construct narratives of our lives. Not surprisingly, memory has attracted the attention of psychologists and neurologists, who have tried to describe its characteristics and to probe its biological basis.

Among the earliest scientific studies of memory were those conducted by the German psychologist Hermann Ebbinghaus toward the end of the 19th century. Ebbinghaus, experimenting on himself, examined the way in which he recalled and forgot "neutral" information, such as nonsense syllables – groups of letters such as VRA and GOJ, which he believed carried no meaning. By separating memories from meaning, he believed that he could formulate a set of "fundamental laws" that would describe and quantify the processes of remembering and forgetting.

Ebbinghaus' approach has been criticized on the grounds that memory is clearly influenced by our intellectual and emotional responses to stimuli, which build up associations in our minds – we are far more likely to remember the name of someone to whom we are briefly introduced at a party if her name is the same as our mother's. It is not possible to remove all such associations from verbal constructs, even apparently neutral ones like nonsense syllables. However, most studies still rely on this method; only a few follow a different approach. For example, Marigold Linton of the University of Arizona has used her own life as a memory experiment, critically examining her own recall of everyday events – With whom did she play tennis? Did she go to the dentist or to the bank? (see opposite).

Although theorists now doubt the existence of "neutral" stimuli, Ebbinghaus did much to ensure that the study of memory would follow a scientific path, and this has yielded some important results.

Perhaps the best known of these is the division of memory into long-term and short-term stores. Short-term memory (STM) is where immediate information is held temporarily. If you tell me your phone number because I need to call you back immediately, the number will be held in STM. If I am distracted for a matter of seconds before making the call, the number may well vanish from my consciousness, but this does not happen if I "rehearse" the number, silently repeating it to myself over and over again.

Psychologists such as Ebbinghaus have revealed some of the curious characteristics of STM. First, it seems to be able to hold only between five and nine (most commonly seven) items of information. It is almost as though STM were a letter rack with seven available slots: once these slots are filled, a new incoming item will displace one of the earlier items in the rack, which will be permanently deleted from STM. The overall amount of information stored in STM can be increased by chunking – grouping items together. So while we may have difficulty storing and recalling the following

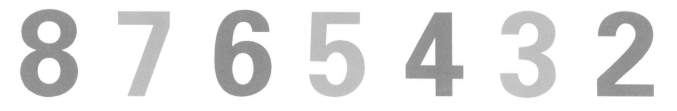

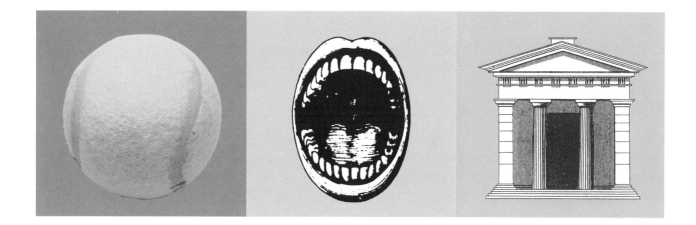

dry sequence of nine letters ELTOTSIRA, it becomes easier when we realize that it spells ARISTOTLE in reverse, because we then need to store and recall only one item. Information can also be lost from STM as it fades away through disuse – unless of course it is rehearsed by repetition, a process that seems to restore the information to "full strength".

Second, much of the information in STM is held in an acoustic form. If we try to remember a phone number, we tend not to remember the constituent numbers by their shape (the angularity of a 4), or by the associations we make with them (3 blind mice), but by the sound made when the number is spoken. This differentiates short- from long-term memory, where, as we shall see, information is remembered through its meaning.

Non-verbal stimuli, such as pictures and symbols, clearly cannot be recorded in short-term memory as sounds, so they

Marigold Linton studied memory by applying objective methods to herself. Every day, she would write down three important events that had occurred, and months later would see if she could recall them. Linton found that only six per cent of the events dropped out of memory in the course of a year, but most others slowly became jumbled. It would seem that we tend to confuse information in our long-term memory rather than forget it completely.

Research on memory has revealed a curious phenomenon known as state-dependent learning. We are slightly more likely to recall information learned in a particular environment or context when we are back in the context in which it was learned in the first place. It has been experimentally demonstrated that deep-sea divers find it easier to remember facts learned underwater when they are underwater again – and one is slightly more likely to remember information acquired while drunk when drunk again.

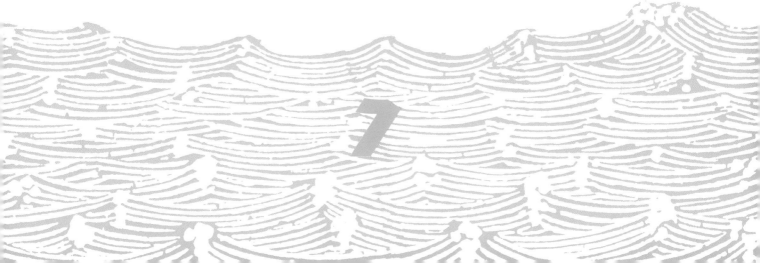

7

are processed in a different form. If we briefly look at a photograph, we can, for a few seconds afterwards, recall certain of its details by examining a "mental sketch" of the image. The apparent existence of separate visual and acoustic memory centres has led memory experts such as Alan Baddeley to develop working models of STM. Baddeley claims that short-term memory has three components. One is an articulatory loop in which words and sounds are stored for up to two seconds. When you give me your phone number, it is first stored here. By saying the number to myself, I feed it back into the system, increasing the strength of the memory trace. Another component is a visuospatial sketchpad, storing visual information for up to five seconds. The third component is a central executive that coordinates the total activity of the STM.

Long-term memory (LTM) is where we store information acquired minutes, hours or even years ago. It differs from STM in that long-term memories are usually remembered semantically, by their meaning, rather than by their sound. A student reading a textbook remembers the meaning of the material it contains, rather than the sound or the appearance of the text. And it is common knowledge that information can be remembered more readily if it is imbued with meaning: in trying to commit facts to memory, many people use mnemonic techniques that weave together disparate bits of information into a meaningful sentence or into a story (see box, right).

MNEMONIC DEVICES

Many people use mnemonic (memory-aiding) devices to help them remember lists, speeches or other important information. All these devices rely on making meaningful connections between otherwise unconnected information. Schoolchildren, for example, use the acronym HOMES to help remember the North American Great Lakes (Huron, Ontario, Michigan, Erie, Superior), and some musicians remember telephone numbers as tunes (each number corresponding to a position on the musical stave). Perhaps the most famous of these techniques, however, is the method of loci. This ancient method (used by the Roman orator and lawyer Cicero to remember his speeches) depends on imagining a familiar setting (the rooms of your home) or journey (the road to work or school). Each of the items to be remembered – a shopping list, for example – is mentally placed in a particular location (apples in the kitchen, eggs in the hall, and so on). In the supermarket, one simply takes an imaginary stroll through one's house and recalls each of the items in turn.

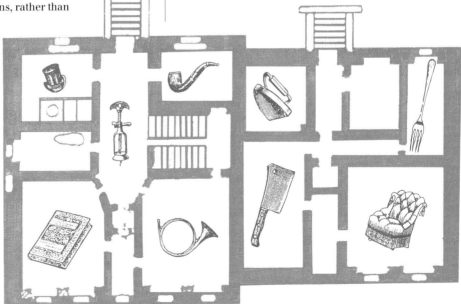

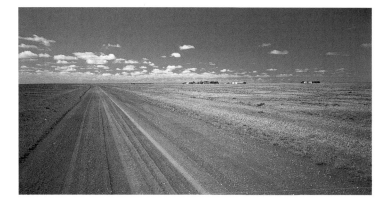

This is not to say that all long-term memories are semantically based (we can, for example, learn poems by rote without taking in their meaning), only that this is the preferred way of storing such memories.

Few people forget their first kiss. It seems that long-term memories are remarkably robust, particularly when they carry an intense emotional charge. The physiologist and Nobel Prize winner Sir John Eccles told me about a vivid memory of a day 88 years ago, when he was not quite three years old and living in the Australian outback. He remembers clearly having to leave home quickly with his father, and meeting the local doctor riding toward their house. It turned out to be the day that his sister was born. Perhaps such memories persist because we rehearse them over and over, but some psychologists suggest that emotional memories are recorded in a different way from neutral memories.

Our long- and short-term stores do not operate in isolation: clearly they must be linked in some way for us to be able to remember new information. Some experts maintain that rehearsal is the key to transferring items from STM to LTM. When we rehearse (repeat) an item in the short-term store, it persists for longer, and so has more chance of being transferred to the long-term store. Others stress the importance of making meaningful connections between the material in STM and what we already know: this helps us to integrate the new fact or facts into pre-existing hierarchies of information stored in LTM.

Although the exact mechanism of transfer from STM to LTM is still not clear, we know something of its neurology. Studies on rats by Richard Morris at the University of Edinburgh in Scotland indicate that the hippocampus, a structure beneath the cortex in the brain, plays a vital role in the retention of memories. Rats were placed in a large tank of water in which there was a hidden platform. Because rats do not like swimming, finding the stable platform on which they could stand was a great relief. The first time they were placed in the water and found the platform, normal rats formed a cognitive "map" of the tank, so that the next time they were put into the tank they found the platform much more easily. But if the hippocampus was surgically removed, the rats took the same amount of time to find the platform each time they were put in – clearly they were unable to retain a memory of the layout of the tank that would have made the task quicker.

Although long-term and short-term memory are clearly different phenomena, it does not follow that they "reside" in different parts of the brain. Indeed, the question of whether memory is localized in specific parts of the brain, or spread over the entire organ, has not been conclusively resolved. Broadly, there are two rival theories. The "field" theory was developed by Karl Lashley, a student of John B. Watson (the founder of behaviourism), who trained rats to negotiate a maze. After small areas of a rat's cortex had been removed, the animal did not completely forget how to get around the maze, but its overall ability to do so became degraded in proportion to the amount of cortex lost, suggesting that the maze memory was not stored in one specific group of neurons but spread out over the whole cortex. Lashley's model has been likened to the way in which a holographic plate stores a

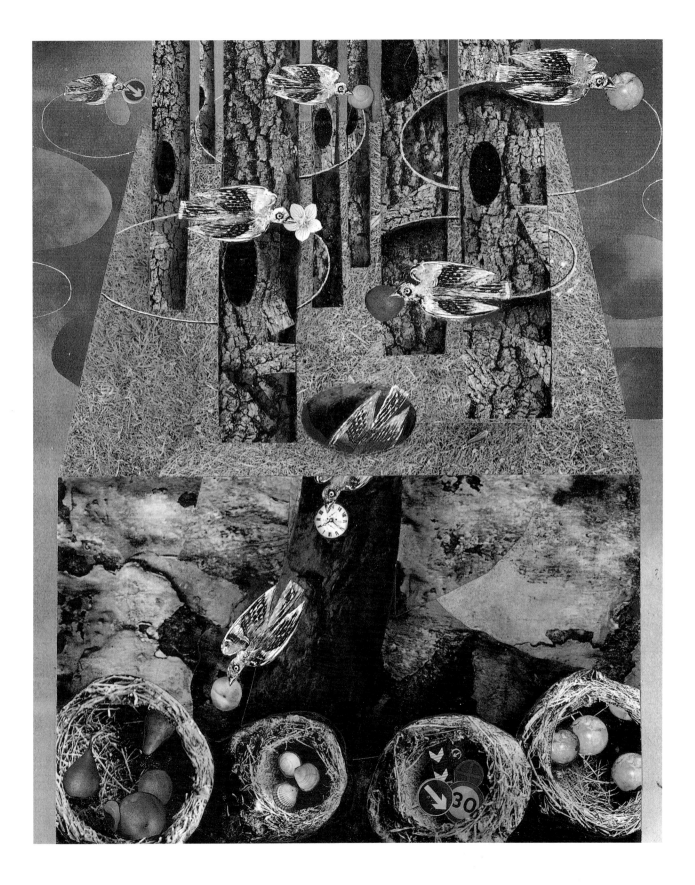

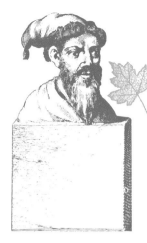

three-dimensional picture (information about every part of the picture is stored in all parts of the plate, so that damage to a small part of the holographic plate does not cause loss of a small chunk of the image: instead the entire image becomes poorer). This theory is favoured by information scientists rather than neurologists, most of whom subscribe to the assembly theory developed by Donald Hebb and Wilder Penfield in the 1940s.

Hebb argued that memories were held in sets of neurons interconnected by synapses (see page 27), and that this combination could be modified by experience. A particular memory (such as the name of your dog) would be held in a particular assembly, which he called cell assemblies but which we would now call neural networks. The work of the neurosurgeon Wilder Penfield supported the assembly theory: during surgery to alleviate epilepsy, Penfield electrically stimulated parts of the temporal lobe and noted that this evoked strings of specific memories in the conscious patients (who were under local anesthetic).

If it is true that specific memories are associated with particular cell assemblies, one might expect to observe biological changes in these assemblies when a new memory is recorded. One study of learning in chicks found just such a change. From the moment they hatch, chicks explore their environment. By pecking at objects on the ground, they learn to distinguish between what tastes good and bad. A group of neurologists found that this learning was accompanied by a noticeable increase in the number of synaptic vesicles – the bodies that contain neurotransmitters at the synapse – in parts of the chicks' forebrains. If these areas are surgically

Scientists once believed that memories were encoded by specific molecules, and that by transferring these substances from one brain to another we could literally transplant memories. Memory does have at least a partly biochemical basis, but fortunately it is more difficult to understand and manipulate.

removed, the chick is unable to learn to discriminate between food and non-food. This is consistent with the hypothesis that learning discrimination forms new cell assemblies in the chick's forebrain.

As well as increasing the number of vesicles present in a particular synapse, learning has been shown to cause biochemical changes that make it easier for one neuron to trigger another: it is as if the neuron "remembers" a familiar pattern of firing and is more likely to fire in this pattern once again. According to some neurologists, this represents a memory trace. The precise biochemical mechanism involved (known as long-term potentiation) has already been described on page 29. Suffice it to say here that it depends on the presence of specific receptor molecules (NMDA receptors) at the synapses involved. These receptors are present in neurons in the cortex and are particularly abundant in the hippocampus, the brain structure that we know to be intimately involved in memory formation.

Memory is one of the higher brain functions, and is crucial to the normal functioning of the mind and to the phenomenon of consciousness. It is a major breakthrough, therefore, that scientists have begun to understand how biological and biochemical changes can account for the way in which we record events as memories, and how these memories are associated with one another.

Personality

Personality theory is an area of psychology that has been enthusiastically assimilated into popular culture. We often hear people describe their acquaintances as extroverts or introverts (terms popularized by Carl Jung) or as being anally or orally fixated (terms from Freudian theory), and many popular magazines run questionnaires inviting us to "assess our personality".

Our interest in personality – the term that we use to describe an individual's particular "style" of thought and behaviour – goes back to the ancient Greeks. Around 400 BC the physician Hippocrates proposed that personality was determined by the nature of a person's bodily humours (fluids), and he identified four different character types: choleric (angry), because of excessive yellow bile;

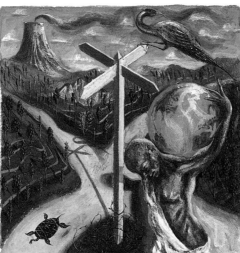

In Hans Eysenck's theory of personality traits, extroverts are sociable, impulsive, sensation-seeking and optimistic and tend to make careless mistakes, while introverts are more meticulous, reserved and passive. Stable personalities are calm, good leaders, and can shoulder responsibility, while unstable personalities are restless, prone to mood swings and have a short fuse.

melancholic (sad), because of an excess of black bile; phlegmatic (lethargic), because of an excess of phlegm; and sanguine (what modern thinkers would call "well-adjusted"), because of strong blood. Greek and medieval philosophy saw these four types as exclusive. You were, or were not, choleric; there was no scope for being partly choleric and partly melancholic according to the situation.

PERSONALITY TESTS

Objective personality tests use hundreds of simple questions with yes/no or true/false answers. The subject's answers are compared with a standardized sample to provide a separate score for each personality trait. A combined analysis of all traits can be plotted on a graph to give a visual sketch of a subject's personality. The questions used are similar to the following: Do you like going to parties? Do you enjoy talking to strangers? Do you see yourself as shy? Do you get bored easily?

Some psychologists criticize the use of such questionnaires because they are too remote from real life, and the choice of

answers is too limited. For example, I may not feel like going to parties because I am too lazy, but if someone turns up to see me unexpectedly, I will be very sociable indeed. In addition, subjects may not answer truthfully, choosing instead to give the answers that they believe are "correct" or that would lead to a more favourable impression. Cultural differences may also be reflected in a subject's answers.

Other tests are less rigid. The subject may be asked to read meaning into a neutral or ambiguous visual stimulus, such as an inkblot (see page 165). It is up to the tester to deduce information about the subject's personality from his or her response.

Although the Greek classification, with its bizarre physiology, is no longer held to be true, the Greeks, as is so often the case, had something significant to convey: there do seem to be personality "types".

Sigmund Freud's theory of personality stresses the importance of events in the first five years of life in determining character. According to Freud, we pass through a sequence of phases of psychosexual development in our early years – the oral, anal and phallic stages. During each stage, our pleasure-seeking impulses (see page 41) seek gratification through different parts of the body and their associated functions. Any trauma or problem at a particular stage can arrest our development and affect our adult personality. For example, someone taken away from his or her mother's breast at an early age may become an oral personality, overly dependent on others and seeking gratification through oral pleasures, including excessive eating, drinking and smoking.

To many, the classification of personality into a few "types" does not do justice to human diversity. Wilhelm Wundt (1832–1920), one of the founders of experimental psychology, argued that people previously classified as melancholic or choleric, sanguine or phlegmatic, shared reactions to many stimuli: they were not as different from each other as once was believed. Wundt's ideas influenced modern personality theories that emphasize the notion of personality traits – the supposed fundamental units of psychological organization – varying along a continuum, rather than being discrete categories. British psychologist Hans Eysenck recognizes two traits – introversion–extroversion and stability–instability –

and seeks to identify where on the continuum personalities lie. Other psychologists identify as many as 16 traits, including such factors as intelligence, boldness, sensitivity, warmth and emotion. The trait approach forms the basis of "objective" personality tests, which plot an individual's position on the variable scale for each trait (see box opposite).

Eysenck argues that an individual's personality is determined biologically – that the brain of an introvert is different from that of an extrovert. The difference, he suggests, lies in levels of cortical arousal: extroversion is caused by low levels of cortical arousal and introversion by high arousal. At first glance, this appears incorrect (an active extrovert might be expected to have high levels of cortical arousal), but Eysenck explains that one function of the cortex is to control and inhibit lower, more emotional centres of the brain, such as the limbic system. Cortical arousal, therefore, produces a high degree of control over the spontaneous side of our natures.

For other theorists, personality is shaped by the environment: we learn our responses through our lives from our own experiences, receiving rewards or punishments for our behaviour, or by watching others do the same.

In the 1940s, the American physician William Sheldon claimed that personality was related to body shape, or somatotype. Ectomorphs (tall and thin) were introverted and artistic; mesomorphs (well-built) were bold and energetic; and endomorphs (soft and round) were easygoing and sociable. However, there was little evidence to support his claims.

Gender

Nothing seems more basic than gender. Children become aware of their gender identity – of being either male or female – around the age of two; and differences in gender roles – sex-related behaviour patterns – are enshrined in the formal and informal rules and expectations of every society. Neurologists and sociobiologists often claim that gender differences are wired into the brain, making male and female brains qualitatively different. However, many psychologists and anthropologists support social learning theories that propose that we develop sex-related behaviour by imitating role models of our own sex and being rewarded for doing so.

In the early stages of pregnancy, the embryo shows no signs of gender, even though its sex is already determined by its genes. At eight weeks its embryonic gonads – testes or ovaries – begin to secrete sex hormones. Although both "male" and "female" hormones are present, it is the "male" hormone, androgen, that is critical to the development of sexual characteristics. If sufficient quantities are produced, the embryo develops male genitals; if there is little androgen, female genitals develop. This is the most obvious effect of sex hormones, but scientists have found that the brain too is awash with sex hormones, and it may be that its development is affected by them.

Structurally there are slight variations between the brains of men and women. Taking into consideration differences in overall body weight, there is no significant disparity in the average weights of their brains. Of potentially more interest is the difference in weight distribution: the two cerebral hemispheres in women are more equal in weight than in men. Psychologists have tried to correlate this asymmetry with the functional division of the brain (see page 32). For example, one might expect women to be equally good at verbal and spatial skills (controlled by the left and right hemispheres

respectively): this is not borne out by school tests in which girls seem to perform better in verbal tasks than spatial ones. There are possible physiological explanations for this. Functional MRI scans (see page 182) show that when presented with a spatial problem, women use both hemispheres of the brain, while men are more focused in their brain activity, using only the right hemisphere. Similarly, in women, linguistic activity is less focused than it is for men and is located in both hemispheres of the brain; this may mean that they find it easier to combine the language function with the cognitive activities that are required to produce coherent speech.

The social learning theory offers an alternative explanation for why boys are better on average at spatial skills. It sug-

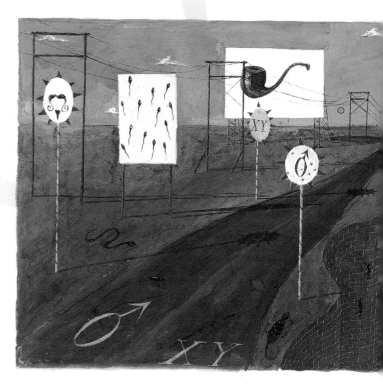

gests that boys excel in those areas in which they were more encouraged by parents, teachers and peers. Because traditionally society has assumed the possession of these skills is a male characteristic, boys will be encouraged to develop them, while girls will be more encouraged to develop their verbal skills. The same can hold true with other kinds of behaviour: expression of emotion is another example. Studies have shown that men report feeling complex emotion and that they demonstrate the same physiological responses as women do (see page 94), and developmental psychologists suggest that the emotional differences between boys and girls should not be exaggerated. However, boys may be influenced to internalize their feelings

Practitioners of alchemy, an occult system of belief that is thought to have originated in ancient Egypt, held that enlightenment could be attained by the union of opposites. This idea is embodied in the alchemical symbol of the androgyne or hermaphrodite (left).

and thus may not develop the same expressive style as girls, and this difference increasingly comes into play with age.

The range of influences to which children are exposed is vast. At first, their parents are their primary role models, but as young children become more social, they may confront different definitions of gender roles to those of their parents. Peer pressure can be a key influence, and in fact, children may be more concerned with gender roles than their parents and teachers are. However, studies have found that children who are taught that gender is a fixed, biological attribute are less concerned with gender stereotypes than others: perhaps they feel more secure in their gender identity and do not fear that it will be taken away from them if they act in ways that do not conform to popular conceptions.

There is an alternative view of gender identity, which does not see male and female characteristics as mutually exclusive. Sandra Bem, an American psychologist and author of *The Lenses of Gender* (1993), argues that there is evidence to show that individuals who are not restricted by gender stereotypes tend to be psychologically healthier. By advocating "gender depolarization" – a form of psychological androgyny in which gender-stereotyped behaviour is revealed to be no longer relevant – Bem echoes the philosophy of the ancient Greeks and the alchemists, and the psychology of Carl Jung, all of whom acknowledged that we possess both male and female principles, which must be reconciled in a complete human being.

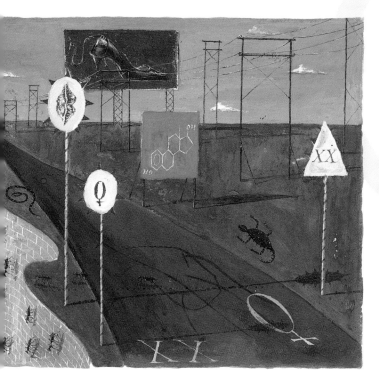

Emotions and Feelings

When we are asked to smile for a photograph, we usually summon up an expression that has little of the honesty of a natural smile. The reason for this was discovered in the 19th century by Guillaume Duchenne, a French neurologist. He found that one of the muscles involved in "natural" smiling – the *orbicularis oculi* – could be activated only involuntarily, or in his own words, by "the sweet emotions of the soul".

Facial expression is the most obvious external manifestation of emotional experience. The expression – a frown, a smile, a fierce look – communicates that emotion to other people and evokes a response: they offer their sympathy, they share in your joy or they avoid confrontation. Charles Darwin noted in his book *The Expression of Emotions in Man and Animals* (1872) that many of these expressions are shared not only across cultures but also across species. This finding has inspired many psychologists to define a group of core emotions; although the lists vary, they all include happiness, fear, sadness, disgust and anger. These emotions have obvious evolutionary value: for example, we feel anger when we are blocked in obtaining a goal, but this can lead to behaviour that will allow us to overcome the obstacle.

Although many psychologists agree in their identification of emotions, they still have not conclusively defined the nature of emotional experience. William James, in the 19th century, developed the first psychological theory of emotion. He believed that emotion was the result of physiological arousal. In James' view, "We feel sorry because we cry, angry because we strike, afraid because we tremble, and not that we cry, strike or tremble because we are sorry, angry or fearful."

The body certainly is involved in emotional experience. The sympathetic nervous system becomes very active. Heart rate increases, as does the volume of blood pumped by the heart; breathing becomes quicker; blood vessels to the skeletal muscles dilate (making us flushed); parts of the gut contract; and there are even changes in the responsiveness of the immune system.

But everyday experience tells us that James's explanation is inadequate. We do not feel truly angry simply because we are clenching our fists. Furthermore, many of the stimuli for emotions are internal – thinking about a particular situation can make us happy or sad. And many of our emotions are complex, such as feelings of pity or regret, which cannot be reduced simply to physiological responses.

One of the chief critics of James's theory was his son-in-law, the physiologist Walter Cannon. According to Cannon, the brain rather than the body registers emotion, and only after the emotion has been felt does the brain instruct the body to become physiologically prepared for action.

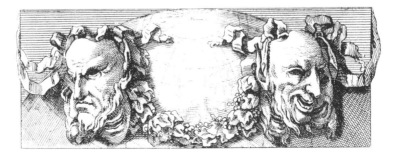

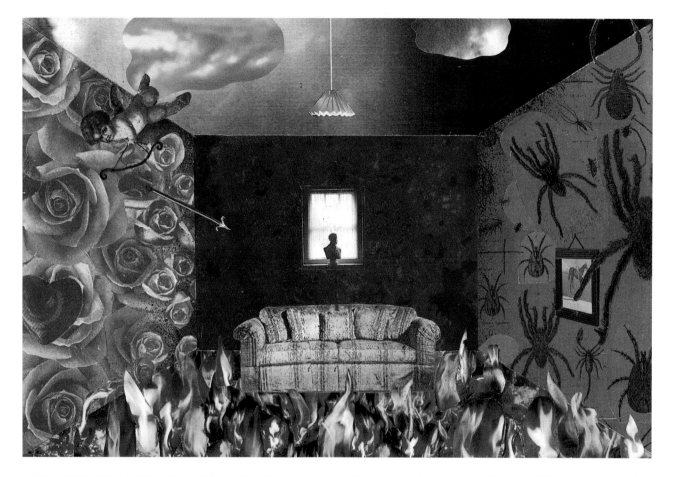

If Cannon's idea is correct, it would be reasonable to search for an emotional "control centre" within the brain. Various anatomical studies have identified the limbic system as crucial to emotional response. One component of the limbic system, the septum, is associated with anger and fear, while another, the amygdala, is involved in aggression: recent research in the United States has found that many violent criminals have damage to the amygdala.

It is possible that James and Cannon could both be right. As in the James model, a stimulus puts our bodies into a state of physiological arousal, but the emotion we feel depends on cognition – the ways in which the brain labels this arousal. This two-component theory of emotion was first proposed by Stanley Schachter and Joel Singer in 1962, and has served as the basis for further research into emotions.

The cognitive model is useful in the understanding of complex emotions. Imagine, for example, that you are standing on the street for some time, trying to hail a taxi-cab; another person flags down the first taxi to come and is driven away. You feel anger, including its physiological effects, because you have not achieved your goal. If the other person had been waiting as long as you had, you would perhaps be less angry with him: you would be more angry with your fate. But if he had just arrived and jumped in, then you *would* be angry at him. In this incident, our emotional response is not so instinctive – it is defined through a cognitive process.

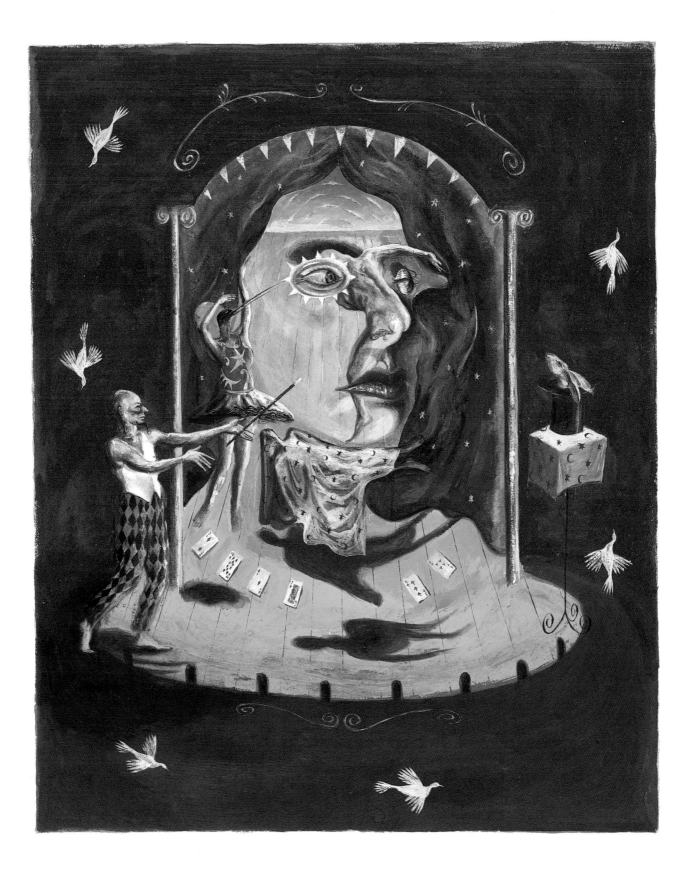

Illusions, Delusions and Deceptions

Imagine it is a clear night over the Mediterranean. The full moon hangs near the horizon, appearing so large that it seems close enough to touch; after two hours, it will have risen high in the sky, resembling nothing more than a small luminous disk. For some ancient cultures, this phenomenon was taken at face value – people believed that the moon grew and shrank every day – but today we know that we are experiencing a visual illusion. All our perceptions, not just the visual, can fall prey to error. We call these errors illusions when what we perceive is at odds with what we know to be true or think to be likely.

There are many different types of illusion, which cannot all be accounted for by a single theory. Some are due to quirks in physiology. We see an after-image when we stare for too long at a bright light. To someone who has been standing in the snow for an hour, a cold bath feels tepid or warm; but to someone who has been in a tropical jungle, the same bath feels ice-cold. More interesting and illuminating are illusions with a cognitive basis – ones that arise from errors of interpretation when perceptions are processed in the brain.

The moon illusion described above falls into this category, but there are many more examples. Some illusions are expe-

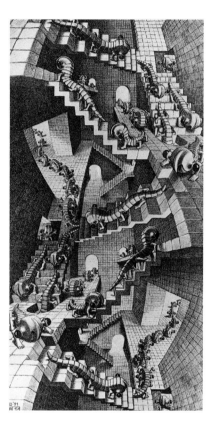

What we perceive is, in part, shaped by what we expect. However, our expectations can be subverted and the impossible can be made to seem possible, as in the intriguing, paradoxical images of Dutch artist M. C. Escher (1902–1972).

rienced in our day-to-day lives: for example, a road seems to narrow as it recedes into the distance, even though we know that it remains the same width. Others are contrived: artists, for example, use a number of optical illusions to convey depth on a two-dimensional canvas.

In all sciences, researchers investigate mistakes and exceptions to shed light on the normal functions and characteristics of a given process. This is why for centuries philosophers, and later psychologists and neurologists, have been trying to understand how visual and auditory illusions – perceptual mistakes – arise. Human beings are storytellers and our brain is equipped for that. It is partly for this reason that amnesia is included in this chapter, because this disorder makes it hard to construct the coherent narratives we rely on to explain ourselves to others – and to ourselves. Another form of evidence comes from looking at what patients with various types of brain damage can and cannot do. Finally, the trivial mistakes of everyday life, such as lapses of memory and the familiar tip-of-the-tongue pheonomenon, described by Freud in his book *The Psychopathology of Everyday Life* (1904), show the ways in which our mind plays tricks on us independently of external stimuli.

Fooling the Senses

Human beings are storytellers with minds designed for this purpose. Our brains constantly strive to make sensory information coherent, to structure it into a form of meaningful narrative. Most of the time, the story that the brain constructs corresponds well with the reality of the outside world, but sometimes the story we arrive at is a fiction. Sometimes, but not always, we know that we are seeing an illusion.

The best-known and most intensively studied illusions are undoubtedly visual tricks, such as the railway-line illusion (see illustration, below right). When I look at this simple illusion, I have an uncanny feeling (shared by most observers, including psychologists specializing in the study of perception): I know that what I am seeing is an illusion and I understand how the illusion has been brought about, but nevertheless I continue to be taken in, no matter how many times I look at it. My intellect and my eyes, therefore, can give me conflicting messages.

Some clues to the origin of this paradox come from studies of human development, notably those conducted by the great Swiss psychologist Jean Piaget (see page 78). One of Piaget's most interesting findings was that until the age of about seven months, an infant has no sense of object permanence. A baby will look at an interesting object – a red ball, for example – following it with its eyes. But if the ball is moved behind a cushion, in full view of the infant, he or she will act as if the ball has ceased to exist. The baby will not try to retrieve the ball and will be surprised if it reappears. Out of sight is not just out of mind, but completely out of existence. Only when the baby is about 12 months old will he or she

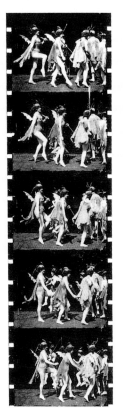

begin to understand that the object has not really disappeared.

Piaget's study emphasizes the extent to which babies learn through experience to perceive. As we learn, we come to rely on certain useful working assumptions (in this case, that an object cannot simply vanish), and such assumptions underlie our perceptual experience. The assumptions become second nature: we never think of them until something goes wrong or looks bizarre; and they are so deeply ingrained that we often continue to see images

There are some illusions in which we are willing participants: when we visit the cinema, we know that we are watching a series of still pictures projected at the rate of 24 frames per second, yet our brains construct from this information a smoothly changing scene. The illusion of cinema is brought about by a physiological phenomenon called persistence of vision, in which the brain continues to register an image on the retina for a fraction of a second after the image has disappeared.

The railway-line illusion (right) depends on the fact that our perceptions automatically compensate for distance. When someone walks toward us, we do not perceive them as growing in height, even though the image cast on the retina increases in size. Here, the converging lines make it seem that the higher horizontal line is farther away than the lower. Although the two horizontal lines are the same length, we perceive the "farther" one as larger.

All our senses are subject to illusions. A small object feels heavier than a large object, even though the two are of exactly the same measured weight.

in a certain way even if we know with certainty that they are based on false assumptions.

We also learn to judge size and distance, although not consciously so. A crucial part of this is learned when a baby's eye guides its hand to an object that it sees, and the baby then confirms the distance by touching the object. By integrating the visual and tactile information, the baby slowly learns that the apparent size of an object depends partly on how far away it is, but that the actual size remains the same. This is "size constancy": we know that a jumbo jet on the ground is the same size as a jet high in the sky, even though the former looks huge while the latter appears to be a tiny moving speck.

There are other crucial visual constancies that we learn early in life. Shape constancy, again unconscious, usually confirms that an object that appears different because it is viewed from different angles does not in reality change its shape; lightness and colour constancy confirm that objects remain the same colour under lighting of varying strengths and colour.

There are many types of optical illusions, with different cognitive or physiological bases, that play against our understanding of these constancies. In a good attempt at drawing

together very different phenomena, the experimental psychologist Richard Gregory has devised a useful classification of illusions that recognizes four main ways in which the mind is fooled – ambiguities, distortions, paradoxes and fictions.

Ambiguities are cases in which the pattern we "see" in one image appears to change before our very eyes, alternating between two possibilities. There are some famous examples: the simple outline of a duck's head that changes into a rabbit; and a vase, the background of which can sometimes become the faces of two people (see page 100).

According to Gregory, our perception switches between two different interpretations of the same object because there is not enough information to confirm either one version or the other: the mind cannot decide between two equally valid "stories". It is a fundamental tenet of this view that at any moment you see either the rabbit or the duck, either the vase or the faces, but never both together. However, occasionally my own perceptions seem more confused. Sometimes I can see both, and sometimes I see neither, as if the image were suspended in a strange sort of perceptual limbo.

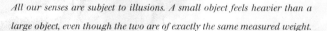

The second of Gregory's categories – distortions

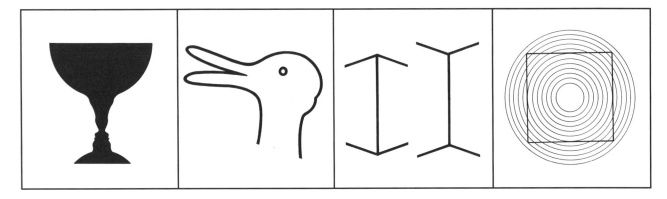

of size, shape and length – are perhaps the most familiar of all visual illusions. Some have a physiological basis, while others are caused by errors of cognition further up the system – more in the cortex than on the retina.

Many of these illusions, such as the distorted square shown above, are geometrical tricks devised in the laboratory by playful psychologists. These tricks are successful because, in the natural world, the eye and brain do not usually encounter precise geometrical arrangements and so have no experience of separating two clear-cut patterns. When viewed under bright light, the pattern of concentric circles appears to affect the apparent shape of the square, but when viewed under dim light (you can simulate this by squinting), the square appears free from distortion, even though the information held in the image is the same as before. According to Gre-gory, this indicates that the illusion is rooted in the physiology of perception rather than in "higher-level" cognitive processes. If the illusion were caused by errors in higher mental processing (see page 52), the brain would be expected to misread information regardless of sensory strength.

Another example of distortion is the Mueller-Lyer illusion (above). Here, two vertical lines of identical length appear longer or shorter depending on the orientation of pairs of terminal "fins". The illusion is clearly exposed as such if you place a ruler next to the lines to measure them, but however much you look, however much you know, you cannot avoid seeing the illusion. It is thought that the "fins" serve as visual depth cues, resembling the corner angles we see in buildings and the corners of rooms – and in drawings and paintings of them. Unlike the square illusion described above, the

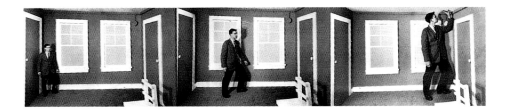

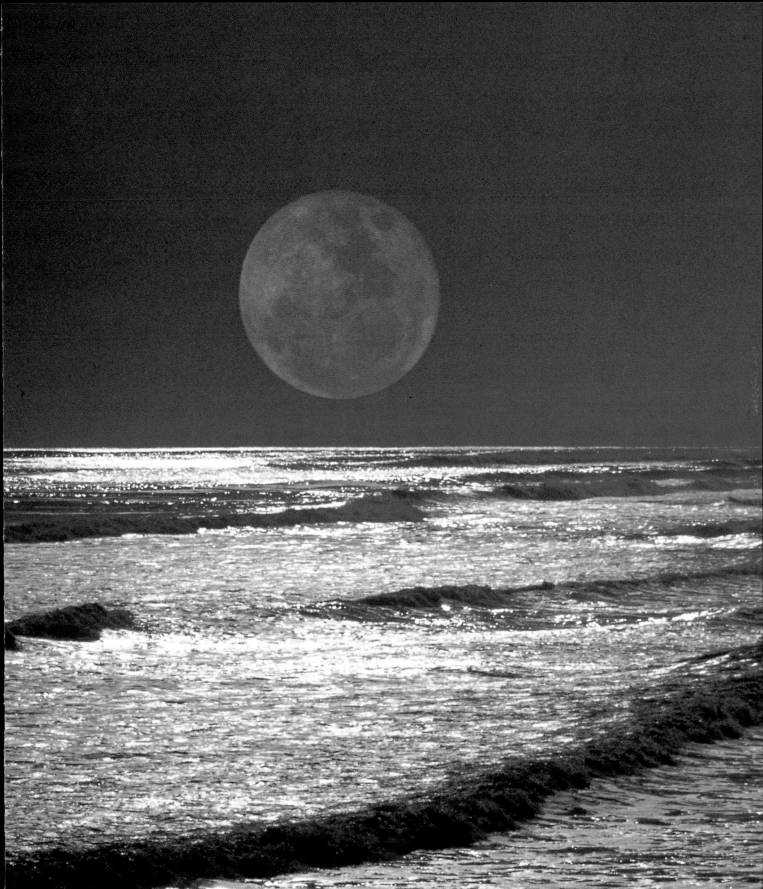

Mueller-Lyer illusion seems to have a cognitive rather than physiological basis. It cannot be neutralized by changing the level of illumination or by other methods in which the sensory information is disassembled (if, for example, the vertical lines and the fins are not touching). Intriguingly, it appears that certain peoples, such as the Bushmen of the Kalahari Desert in southern Africa, are less susceptible to the Mueller-Lyer illusion. Some experts suggest that because the Bushmen of the Kalahari live in a desert environment that lacks the architectural verticals and corners familiar to most people, they have not learned the visual assumptions of right angles and straight lines that underlie the Mueller-Lyer illusion.

The third of Gregory's categories, paradoxes, is exemplified by the "impossible" objects and scenes depicted in the work of M. C. Escher (see page 96) and other artists. We perceive an object regardless of the fact that our intellect tells us it cannot exist because it contravenes the laws of logic. Gregory points out that the ability to perceive improbable images is vital: without it we would be blind to many novel, and possibly even life-threatening, stimuli.

The last of Gregory's four categories of illusions is that of the fictions. These are the cases in which the predictive "storytelling" capacities of the human brain are most in evidence. Our eyes see only part of an object, but our brain

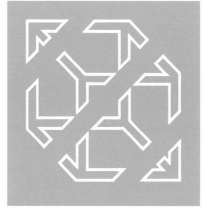

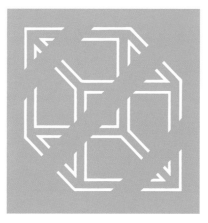

fills in the gaps and we perceive the object as a whole. The gaps are often perceived as "ghostly" surfaces, as demonstrated in the cube illusion (below).

Nowhere is the deliberate use of illusion more noticeable than in an art gallery, where we can admire the repertoire of visual tricks that artists use to convey a sense of depth on a two-dimensional canvas. The techniques for showing depth in a painting were developed in 15th-century Europe. Before this, artists depicted objects and their surroundings independently, as they *knew* them rather than as they *saw* them: so a human figure might have been shown with the most important feature (the face) facing forward, but the rest of the body in profile. This changed at the beginning of the Renaissance in Europe, when artists began to discover the principles of linear perspective. They realized that parallel lines and planes appeared to meet at an infinitely distant point as they receded from the observer, and that this could be simulated on a two-dimensional surface by constructing guidelines that converged on a single vanishing point. The mathematical laws of perspective were formalized by the Italian architect Filippo Brunelleschi (1337–1446) and were taken up by other Renaissance artists. Only late in the 19th century did Western artists begin to move away from the rigours of (by then) conventional perspective.

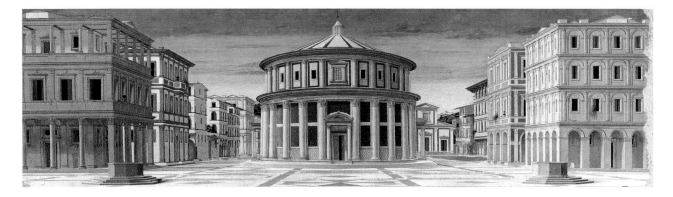

The early use of linear perspective is exemplified in Veduta di città ideale *(View of the Ideal City) by the 15th-century artist Piero della Francesca.*

In addition to linear perspective, there are a number of other depth cues that help us to interpret a flat image as three-dimensional, and that often appear in painting after the Renaissance. These include obvious cues, such as relative size (the fact that closer objects appear larger than distant objects), and less obvious ones, such as texture gradient (the definition of textures is poorer in more distant objects – we may be able to see individual bricks in the foreground, but only more uniform walls in the distance). Location in the picture plane is another essential cue.

Illusions bedevil our other senses as well: although scientists have been studying visual illusions since the 19th century, they have only recently become interested in aural illusions, or tricks of hearing. Work by the psychologist David Deutsch has identified an illusion that affects our hearing. Two tones that are one octave apart are presented one to each ear, so that when the left ear hears the high tone, the right ear hears the low tone, and when the right hears the high, the left hears the low. These vary back and forth in quick succession. Although two tones are sounded at the same time, this is not what the subject perceives. Instead, one ear is only able to hear the high tone, which alternates with silence; and the other ear hears only the low tone alternating with silence.

How can we account for this illusion? The most plausible theory posits that we have two independent brain mecha-nisms involved in the detection of sound, one for judging pitch and the other for locating the source of a sound. The illusion depends on the unnaturally rapid shift of the source of a particular pitch of sound: this confuses the brain's perceptual mechanisms, which simplify the stimuli and (incorrectly) locate each pitch of sound in one place.

But perhaps the most interesting aural illusions are the ways in which we bridge sounds so as to weave them into one story. During a conversation at a noisy gathering, you will concentrate on the person with whom you are speaking and filter out other voices as irrelevant. Psychologists have aptly called this the cocktail party effect, and are able to reproduce it successfully under laboratory conditions. A subject wearing earphones has different messages projected into each ear. In a typical form of this experiment, the subject is asked to "shadow", or pay close attention to, what is coming into one ear and to repeat it aloud, word for word. Subjects could manage to do this, but in the process they seemed not to hear anything that was being fed to the other ear. If they were asked about the contents of the messages given to the other ear, they could not answer. They did not even notice when the message being given to the unshadowed ear switched into a foreign language. This phenomenon is called selective attention. Through such experiments, it has become clear that attention is not an all-or-nothing process.

The Colour of a Trumpet

As a child develops, he or she learns to use all the senses cooperatively. The hand stretches out to touch an object that the eye has seen; the ears register a sound while the eyes focus on its origin. What the child learns from one sense can be transferred to another in a process described as cross-modal transfer. For example, a blindfolded infant allowed to touch and feel an object will subsequently be able to identify the object by sight. Babies are able to do this by the age of about six months, and by 24 months, they are experts.

Although learning to integrate information from different senses is vital, we think of the senses as fundamentally separate – seeing is an entirely different process from smelling, and we do not confuse a sound with a taste. Yet there is evidence, some anecdotal, some more scientific, to suggest that the senses are in fact linked. This idea of sensory unity is an old one. The ancient Greek philosopher Aristotle argued that the five senses were drawn together by a "common sense" located in the heart; and the anatomical drawings of Leonardo da Vinci reflect the 15th-century belief that the senses had a common mechanism. In more modern times, many individuals have reported experiencing what is normally felt through one sense via another, or described occasions when experiences of one sense also trigger experiences of another. This linking of the senses, known as synesthesia, has been reported by many respected scholars. The physicist Sir Isaac Newton wrote that, for him, each note of the musical scale corresponded to a particular colour of the spectrum: when he saw a colour, he sometimes heard the note. And the 17th-century philosopher John Locke (see page 45) reported the case of a blind man who claimed that he had had a revelation of what the colour scarlet looked like when he heard the sound of a trumpet for the first time. More recent studies include the case of a girl who associated colours with the notes of birdsong, and a subject who felt pressure sensations in his teeth when cold compresses were applied to his arms. Among a group of college students it was found that 13 per cent consciously summoned up images of colour when they were listening to music, claiming that this made the experience more enjoyable. When the same students were asked to draw what they "saw" when they heard a note rise and fall on a clarinet, their images included lips, lines, triangles and a house nestling amid hills. It is not suprising that synesthesia has appealed to artists and writers over the years, because it is tailor-made for metaphor.

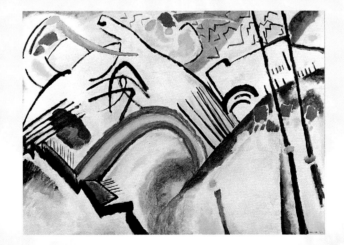

The works of the Russian painter Wassily Kandinsky (1866–1944), such as Cossacks *(1910–11), exemplify the artist's belief that colour could affect the mind. His assertion that "colour is a power that directly influences the soul: colour is the keyboard, the eyes are the hammers, the soul is the piano with many strings" suggests first-hand experience of the condition of synesthesia.*

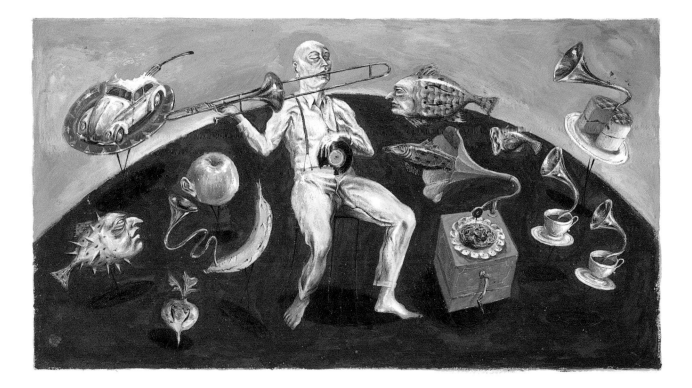

The Symbolist movement, which flourished in Europe in the last years of the 19th century, made particular use of the supposed "correspondences" between the senses. In one of the movement's most famous novels, *Against Nature* (1884) by Joris Karl Huysmans, the dissolute aristocrat des Esseintes hears a symphony when he tastes different types of alcoholic drink: each drink corresponds to a particular instrument in the orchestra.

To neurologists, synesthesia remains a mysterious phenomenon. It is known that information from the different senses is processed in (often widely) separate areas of the brain, and we can hypothesize that people who experience synesthesia have connections between these disparate areas, which in most people are either inhibited or simply do not exist. Moreover, the fact that some drug states can induce "confusion" of the senses reinforces the idea that we all have such connections, although they are normally suppressed.

a	black
e	white
i	red
o	blue
u	green

Amnesia

Even the layperson is likely to know something about amnesia from its depiction in movies and novels. Typically, a character's entire life history is unaccountably blanked out to the extent that he or she has no recollection of his or her own name or family, and the plot is driven by dramatic flashbacks reconstructing a bizarre series of events. In truth, amnesia, or loss of memory, is far less glamorous than the movies suggest – it is one of the most distressing of all neurological conditions. But it is of great scientific interest because it sheds light on the structure of memory and, also, on how we learn.

Although some cases of amnesia appear to have psychological causes – an individual responds to extreme stress by becoming unable (or unwilling) to recall past events – many have tangible physical origins. Damage to the brain, a stroke, drinking too much alcohol and surgical intervention can all bring about memory loss, and given this diversity of causes, it is likely that the term amnesia describes not one but several neurological dysfunctions.

Psychologists describe two main types of amnesia. In retrograde amnesia, a trauma (frequently a head injury resulting from a road accident) induces loss of memory of events that happened in the years before the accident. Most patients begin to recover their memories within weeks or months, with earlier memories returning first. Gradually the "lost" period shrinks until the patient can fully recall all but the few minutes immediately preceding the trauma. This information, it is thought, did not register in short-term

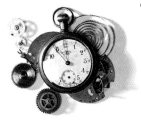

Cases of anterograde amnesia are frequently associated with damage to the hippocampus, suggesting that this part of the brain is involved in converting short-term into long-term memories.

TYPES OF KNOWLEDGE

In the 1950s, Canadian neurosurgeons began a study of a 29-year-old man known as H. M. who had undergone surgery for uncontrollable epilepsy. After surgery, unfortunately, H. M. suffered extreme anterograde amnesia with the usual symptoms – most markedly, the inability to transfer information from short-term to long-term memory, although existing long-term memory remained unaffected. Curiously, although H.M. was unable to transfer new facts into long-term memory, he was able to learn some complex new tasks, such as reading mirror writing and tracing a path through a maze. This finding suggests that our memories of procedural knowledge (knowing

how to do something, such as riding a bicycle or solving a puzzle) are organized in the brain in a different way from declarative knowledge (knowing a particular fact).

memory strongly enough to pass into the long-term store (see page 87). The gradual recovery of memory suggests that there is considerable redundancy in the brain. If one neural network is knocked out by the trauma, another establishes itself (by the activation of new connections between cells) and is able to access the "old" memories.

The second type of memory loss is anterograde amnesia. Sufferers have little trouble in remembering material learned prior to the trauma (unless, as is often the case, this condition is accompanied by retrograde amnesia) but find it very difficult to learn anything new. While their intelligence and short-term memory are largely unaffected (they can, for example, remember a telephone number for a little while), these

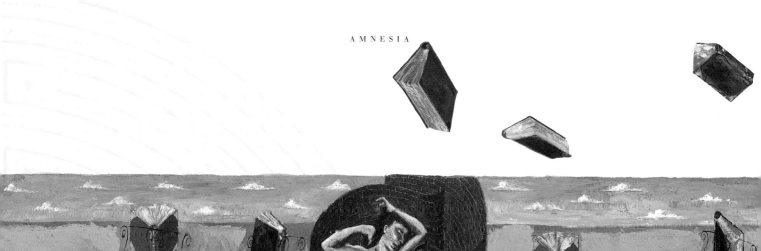

patients seem unable to transfer information into long-term memory. Anterograde amnesia makes for a poor quality of life: although patients feel that there is something wrong with them, and consequently suffer persistent unease, they cannot pinpoint the problem or compensate in any way for the flaws in their brains. They may become angry or exhibit other changes in personality.

If the patients recover, they become their old selves and regain their former personalities, but extensively-studied cases like H. M. (see box opposite) and J. reveal the agonies of long-term amnesia. I filmed J. for a television documentary, *Memories are Made of This* (1993). An hour after we had filmed him talking to his psychologist, who had been treating him for eight years, he did not remember who she was and had no idea that he had been filmed. J. lives in a perpetual present. He cannot structure his life through the sort of narratives that we normally construct about ourselves, our relationships, our past and our hopes. He is bitter about being trapped in the here and now: he complained that it was unfair that there was no medicine to cure him.

Although neurologists are still a long way from a full understanding of amnesia, studies of patients have helped to unravel some of the mysteries of memory. They have persuaded psychologists that there is a distinction between short-term and long-term memory, and provided information about the ways in which our memories are consolidated.

Slips of the Mind

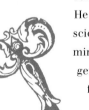

We all make mistakes. Fallibility is part of the human condition. The ancient Greek tragedian Euripides wrote: "Men are men, they needs must err." The mind can be fooled in many different ways, and while the consequences of our errors are sometimes dire, more often they are just irritating or comic.

We have all experienced "unconscious" errors – slips of the tongue, the inability to put a name to a familiar face, losing an object that we know we have just this second put down – and thought them too trivial to worry about. But a number of experts believe these tiny errors to be highly significant. Sigmund Freud, for example, explored unconscious mistakes, which he called parapraxes, in one of his early books, *The Psychopathology of Everyday Life* (1904). Freud accepted that some apparently random errors are caused by fatigue, but he believed that most "mistakes" have hidden meaning, revealing our forbidden wishes, hostilities and fears. He claimed that parapraxes showed that the unconscious mind could take control of the conscious mind. One famous "slip" was when a polite Viennese gentleman told Freud he had had dinner with a friend "*tête-à-bête*". The correct phrase is *tête-à-tête*, but the man thought his friend a fool, and *bête* is French for stupid. Although he was too discreet to express it directly, the gentleman's hostility came out

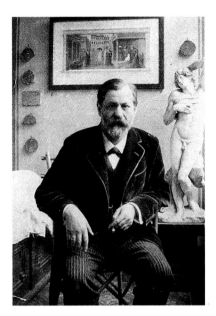

Born in 1856 in Freiberg, Moravia, Sigmund Freud qualified in medicine at the age of 26. His work with the neurologist Jean-Martin Charcot at the Salpêtrière Hospital in Paris aroused his interest in "functional" nervous diseases – those for which no physical basis had been established. Freud's studies of the causes of these disorders (especially hysteria) led him to develop his controversial theories of personality, which stressed the role of psychosexual development in early infancy (see pages 38 and 88). He believed that these infantile wishes and desires could be accessed by examining material from the unconscious, which surfaced in dreams, in everyday errors or slips of the tongue (parapraxes), and in psychoanalysis. The latter technique, which was developed by Freud, relies on a trained analyst interpreting material that emerges while a patient free-associates. Freud developed and popularized his ideas, practising psychoanalysis in Vienna until the Nazi invasion of Austria in March 1938, which forced him to flee to London where he died in 1939.

in a slip of the tongue. On another occasion, Freud himself argued with a friend about the number of hotels at a particular resort. Although Freud had taken his holidays close to the resort for seven summers, he insisted that it had only two hotels, when in fact it had three. Why had he forgotten this information? Freud theorized that it was because the third hotel was called "Hochwartner" – a name closely resembling that of a rival Viennese doctor – and maintained that he had repressed the name owing to his jealousy. In a similar vein, Freud noticed that his medical colleagues would sometimes try to open their clinics using their house keys. His explanation was simple: the doctors would much rather be at home than at work.

Other recorded parapraxes include the case of a woman under analysis by the Hungarian psychologist Sandor Ferenczi. On one occasion, the woman could not recall the name of the psychoanalyst Carl Jung (see page 41), with whom she was certainly very familiar. Ferenczi concluded that this lapse of memory was caused by the woman's bitterness at having been widowed at the age of 39, an age at which she felt too old to remarry. Jung, in German, means "young", so the inability to recall Jung's name was a way of avoiding thoughts about her lost youth.

Freud liked to collect slips of the tongue and pen, gathering a remarkable collection of humorous and embarrassing errors – what many people now call Freudian slips. A Viennese newspaper, for example, once referred to "His Highness the Clown Prince", rather than "Crown Prince"; and another had to print an apology after calling a group of ex-soldiers "battle-scared veterans" rather than battle-scarred veterans". Unfortunately, the printer's devil still dogged the apology, in which the soldiers were renamed "bottle-scarred veterans".

Freud said that jokes involved the invasion of the unconscious in a similar way, providing a channel through which aggressive or dangerously erotic material could force its way out of the unconscious in the stuffy, formal society of early 20th-century Vienna. Jokes possessed what Freud called "psychic economy" and so could slide through the barriers of repression. Humour provides relief by diverting energy from unpleasant emotions, and rather than being an "emotional response of the unsophisticated adult" (a view held by some psychologists in the 1950s), it represents an important psychological defence mechanism.

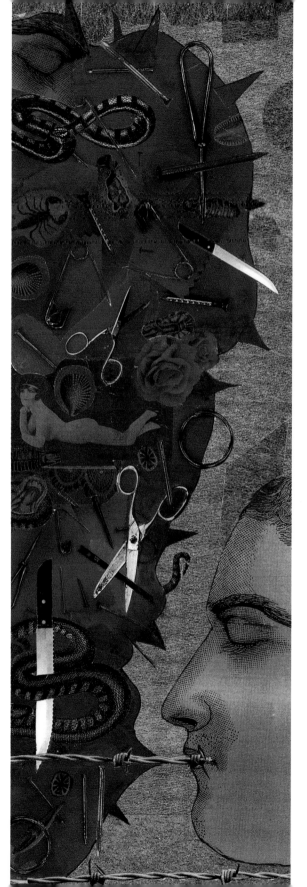

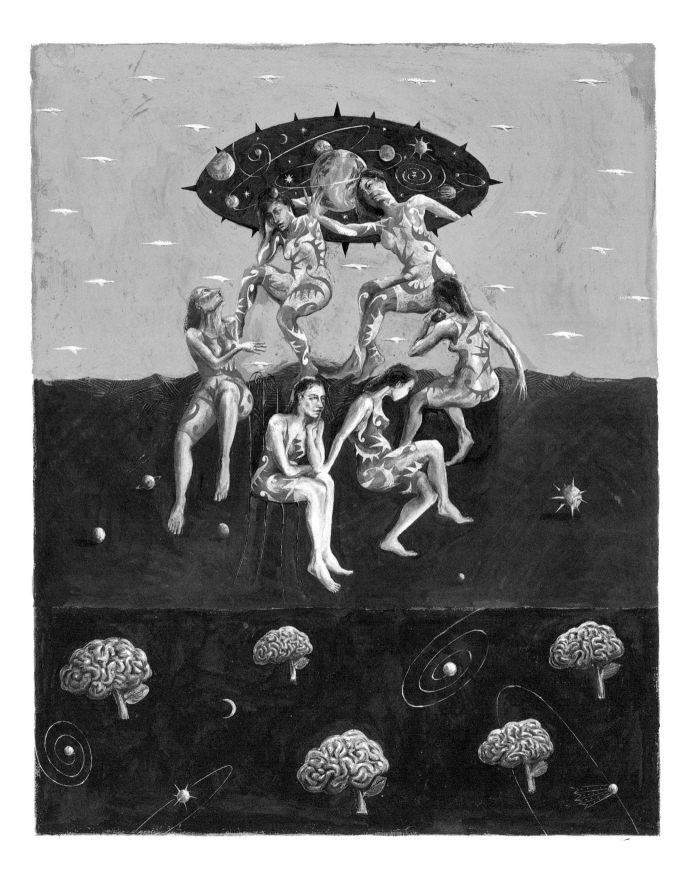

Altered States

It is not possible to divide states of being into the neat categories of consciousness and unconsciousness. Too many curious and interesting states lie between, challenging a simple definition. These altered states of consciousness defy objective description because they are intensely personal. Nevertheless, these experiences, which range from the mild distraction of a daydream to wild, drug-induced hallucinations, can have certain common characteristics. Perceptions of the self and of the outside world may change – some drugs, for example, radically alter perception of space and time. Scientists and artists have long been fascinated by altered states of consciousness and many, such as the British author Aldous Huxley (1894–1963), experimented with drugs partly to see what they would do to the workings of the mind: Huxley's experiences with mescalin are recorded in his book *The Doors of Perception* (1954). Drugs – legal and illegal – can make the mind both less and more critical as users become less inhibited but also sometimes paranoid.

In his provocative book *The Origins of Consciousness in the Breakdown of the Bicameral Mind* (1976), the psychologist Julian Jaynes argues that altered states are a throwback to our primitive past. Jaynes maintains that until around 4000 BC, human beings were not conscious as we are today but

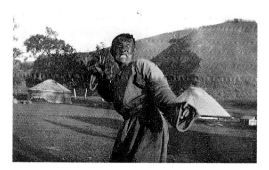

The shaman or "medicine man" was (and in some cases, still is) a key member of societies in the Arctic regions and central Asia. But he or she is more than just a doctor, acting also as priest and psychopomp, able to escort the souls of the dead to another world. The shaman can accomplish feats of healing and spiritual guidance through self-induced trance states, often accompanied by convulsions and protruding eyes, in which he or she leaves the body and gains wisdom from the spirit world. Whether or not we believe this account, it is clear that the shaman is able to enter an altered state of consciousness at will.

existed in an almost hypnotic state, hallucinating, hearing voices and carrying out instructions that seemed to come from the gods. Only slowly did humankind throw off these shackles, and the altered states that we experience now are no more than relics of our preconscious past.

Jaynes' ideas remain controversial, but it is certainly true that a common thread runs through many, though not all, of the phenomena examined in this chapter. In an altered state of consciousness, we have a sense of touching on truths usually denied us in normal consciousness, and of exploring more fundamental aspects of the self. Although it is fanciful to suggest that these truths are antique echoes of the gods, the work of both Jung and Freud has legitimized the view that there are valuable insights into the self buried beneath consciousness, waiting to be excavated.

The term "altered states" covers a number of phenomena. Some arise naturally and automatically (dreaming, for example, is thought to be common to all mammals). Others are attained through learned techniques such as meditation. Some are induced by drugs. Others still – the paranormal states – are highly controversial, and many people doubt their existence. The diverse nature of these states of consciousness raises many questions about the operation of the human

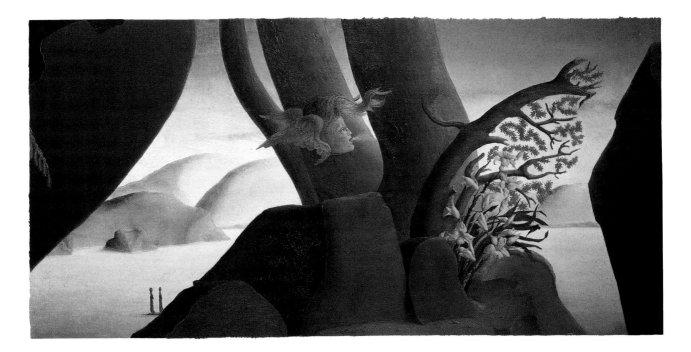

The artists and writers of the Surrealist movement, which flourished in Europe in the 1920s and 30s, explored altered states of consciousness to gain access to "higher truths", striving to unite conscious and unconscious realities into one "surreality". Some experimented with "automatic" writing, in which the writer's hand is guided by an unseen force; others used self-hypnosis; and others still simulated states of madness. The above painting, The Breeze at Morn (1930), by the British artist Thomas Lowinsky, uses the Surrealist "trick" of depicting an irrational landscape in a realistic style.

There is one altered state of consciousness that we have all experienced – dreaming sleep. Dreams are so different from our normal state of awareness that they were once seen as supernatural in origin, and sometimes as vehicles for prophecy. In the account of Pharaoh's dream in the book of Genesis, for example, the appearance of seven fat and seven thin cattle is interpreted by Joseph as predicting the advent of seven years of plenty followed by seven years of famine (below). Sigmund Freud set in train modern research into the psychology of dreams, claiming that the dream was the "royal road" to an understanding of the the unconscious.

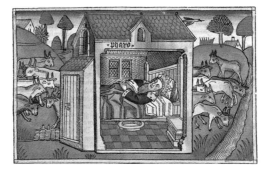

mind. For example, one of the most distinguished physiologists of the last 30 years, Michel Jouvet of the University of Lyon in France, argues that "intuitively the dream is of no use" – so what are the biological or psychological reasons for dreaming? Many psychologists and psychotherapists – not only Freudians – would disagree vehemently with Jouvet's statement: Freud considered dreams to be essential maintenance for the mind, and some psychologists today see dreams as devices that help to consolidate long-term memories.

The issue of the paranormal is more complex because it is even harder to document than other forms of altered state experiences. However, if paranormal states, such as telepathy and psychokinesis, can be shown to have any substance, then it will be virtually impossible to discount non-material theories of consciousness (see page 38).

To understand altered states one must assess subjective accounts of what it is like to "be in" these states, along with objective research that tries to identify their physiological basis and effects. These subjective and objective realities can be very different. For example, the Mekeo, a New Guinea tribe, have a concept of the soul that is very unlike the Christian one. In their view, when a person dreams, the soul issues forth and has adventures in the landscape of sleep. The soul belongs to a particular body, but the physical brain has no control over its nocturnal doings. When a Mekeo wakes up, he is often worried about what his soul has got up to, because the consequences of its activities may return to haunt his waking self. To a physiologist, this model of different levels of

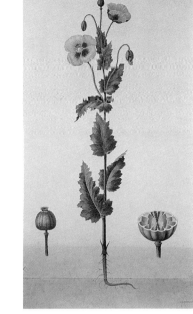

For millennia people have used drugs, such as opium (extracted from the poppy Papaver somniferum, *left), to achieve altered states of consciousness. Many artists have believed that drugs could unleash creative forces. The British poet Samuel Taylor Coleridge (1772–1834) reputedly wrote his mysterious short poem "Kubla Khan" in an opium-induced haze. The French poets Arthur Rimbaud (1854–1891) and Charles Baudelaire (1821–1867) both became addicts. In the 1960s, Timothy Leary and other beat gurus claimed that drugs such as LSD could take them to otherwise unreachable parts of the psyche. Those who fear the effects of drugs, however, maintain that these romantic claims are delusions, and that most people who take drugs do so because they cannot cope with reality.*

consciousness seems to be mere superstition; yet to the Mekeo it feels like experiential truth. In addition, because the mind becomes less critical during the experience of an altered state, it is difficult, if not impossible, to explain it in language that can be understood by someone who is not in that state.

The more we learn about altered states, the more it becomes apparent that the boundaries between conscious and unconscious, voluntary and automatic, awake and asleep, are blurred at the edges. For example, recent research by Peter Hampson and Peter Morris questions the long-accepted view that "unconscious" behaviour is outside of "conscious" influence: they found that subjects can control the content of hypnagogic hallucinations – the vivid images that we tend to "see" during the transitional state between sleep and waking (see page 119).

Sleep, Dreams and Symbols

For centuries, people have believed that their dreams are significant. In ancient Egypt, the gods were thought to speak through the dreams of the Pharaohs, and in other cultures, too, dream experiences were given supernatural significance, often being seen as night-time visits of the soul to other worlds. In the Judeo-Christian tradition, angels often arrive in dreams, bringing revelations. Dreams seem to promise an understanding of the universe, the gods or the self; and decoding the often bizarre streams of events and symbols that populate our dreams has always been a preoccupation of inquirers into the nature of the mind.

Freud's theories of dreaming did not invoke supernatural causes. In his *Interpretation of Dreams* (1899), Freud proposed that dreams are expressions of material that is too frightening or guilt-laden to find a conscious outlet and so becomes repressed in the unconscious (see page 41); they provide a means of fulfilling our repressed infantile desires. Through interpretation, dreams become a "royal road to a knowledge of the unconscious".

Rather than appearing in our dreams in a literal

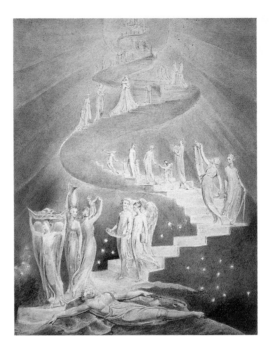

The content of our dreams has traditionally been thought to reveal a higher spiritual order. Jacob's Ladder *(above) by the artist and mystic William Blake (1757–1827) portrays the dream of Jacob from the Book of Genesis: "And he dreamed that there was a ladder set up on the earth, the top of it reaching to heaven; and the angels of God were ascending and descending on it."*

form, the repressed material (what Freud called the latent content of dreams) was woven into complex symbols (the manifest content) that disguised its true nature. Protected from having to confront our unconscious desires and anxieties, we can enjoy the psychological and physiological benefits of sleep. The dream, therefore, was for Freud "the guardian of sleep".

Freud relied on the technique of free association to discover the latent content of dream symbols. He believed that the symbols that appeared in dreams are influenced by personal experiences and by what is current in the culture of the time. Those that do not depend on personal associations and are wholly the result of cultural influences are the classic Freudian symbols, the source of endless comment and jokes. For example, anything that can penetrate or be erected, such as a sword, pistol or tower, symbolizes the male genitalia, while anything that can contain or be entered, such as a purse, jewelry box or cave, is a symbol of the female genitalia. At the same time, everyone has a personal history and that creates its own symbols. For example, my mother used to have a crocodile handbag. If I dream of caressing

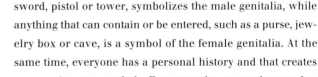

an alligator, I may be expressing my desire to stroke my mother – a repressed Oedipal wish

The dream theories of Carl Jung (see page 42) owe much to the work of Freud. Like Freud, Jung believed that dreams were expressions of unconscious material, but he differed sharply when defining the meanings and origins of dream symbols. His theories, although interesting and influential, are also essentially impossible to prove or disprove.

Jungian therapists recognize three "levels" of dreams. Level 1 dreams have no deep symbolic meaning, and are just remnants of the recent thoughts and feelings of the conscious mind. Level 2 dreams use symbols to express material in the personal unconscious (see page 42) – material that relates primarily to our physical and sexual preoccupations – and in this sense they employ symbols in a similar way to that proposed by Freud. Level 3 dreams, or what Jung called "great dreams", are qualitatively different. They contain emotionally-charged and powerful symbols that express the innate qualities and behavioural predispositions that make us human – what Jung called archetypes. The archetypes reside deep in the collective

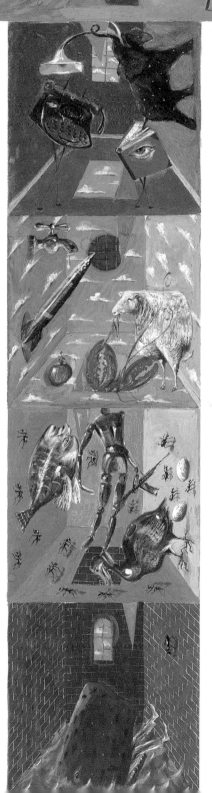

unconscious of every person, and can emerge only in symbolic form because they evolved before humankind acquired speech; and because they are so ancient, archetypal symbols are common to all humans. Many believe that Jung's concept of the collective unconscious has no basis in fact: how could these ancient symbols, they ask, be passed on over the centuries? To these sceptics, the only explanation – infinitely less mystical than Jung's – is that cultural influences have been brought to bear on our dreams.

Freud and Jung both maintained that there was a psychological "purpose" in dreaming, but other theorists dismiss dreams as trivial, seeing them simply as mental by-products of the mind's daily business.

This possibility seems unlikely, however, especially since studies have shown that dreaming sleep occurs in a wide range of animal species: its long evolutionary history strongly suggests that it is of some biological importance. Moreover, experiments on sleep deprivation show that when people are finally allowed to sleep after a long period of wakefulness, they catch up first on their *dreaming* sleep, which again suggests that dreams are somehow necessary.

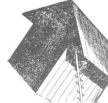

The first edition of Freud's *Interpretation of Dreams* sold fewer than 1,000 copies – a bitter disappointment to its author – but by around 1905 the book had gained a serious audience and sparked off considerable interest in dream analysis. However, it was not until the 1950s that dreams attracted the attention of experimental psychologists, who began to unravel their physical and neurological properties.

Some early experiments on dreams were carried out by William Dement and Nathaniel Kleitman. In their dream laboratory, the researchers awakened subjects at different stages of sleep and questioned them about their dream activity. They found that those woken during the periods of sleep characterized by rapid eye movements (REM) almost always reported particularly vivid dreams, while those woken during non-REM periods of sleep reported far less colourful dreams (which more closely resembled "normal thought"), and only then about 25 per cent of the time. These findings have led some researchers to the conclusion that REM and non-REM sleep are as different from each other as sleep is from wakefulness: each is a distinct state of consciousness.

During REM sleep, the heart rate increases and the brain's activity, as measured by electroencephalography (EEG, see page 72), closely resembles the activity of conscious attention (this is one reason why REM sleep is also known as paradoxical sleep). Although the eyes move while we dream (note that this does not necessarily mean that the dreamer is "watching" his or her dream events), the rest of the body's voluntary muscles are virtually paralyzed. So during REM sleep, the brain is very active but is kept prisoner within an inert body. Its motor areas cannot communicate with the muscles and its sensory areas receive no input from the body. So when we dream that we are walking, the experience seems "real" because we are using the same areas of the brain that we would use if we were consciously taking a

WHAT DO CATS DREAM ABOUT?
In one of the most startling of dream experiments, Michel Jouvet surgically removed the pons of a cat – the brain structure that suppresses movement of an animal's body during REM sleep. When the cat fell into REM sleep following the operation, it was able to move and literally "act out" its dreams. Jouvet observed the cat's behaviour and, to the dismay of cat lovers, reported the following: "What you see in the cat is nearly always aggressive behaviour. Very stereotyped, extremely monotonous. Cats that are very nice normally become vicious tigers when they are dreaming and throw themselves at imaginary prey. I used to have one in my office that would terrify people when it was dreaming."

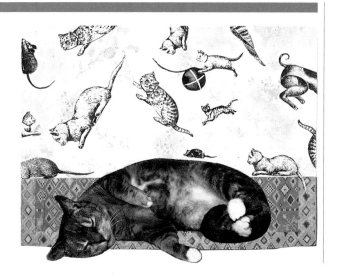

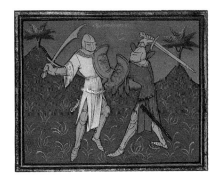

stroll, but without using the muscles and without sensing that we are not using them. The French neurologist Michel Jouvet performed a remarkable series of experiments on cats to explore this phenomenon. They revealed that the muscular and sensory inhibition in REM sleep was mediated by the pons in the reticular formation of the brain (see box opposite).

None of the above findings answers the basic question of why we dream, and indeed there is at present no convincing biological explanation for our dream life. There are, however, a number of rival theories: these include the notion that dreaming allows the consolidation of memory traces; that it helps the renewal of proteins in the brain; and that it is somehow associated with maintaining the integrity of the personality. This last theory is supported by Michel Jouvet, who argues that it is during REM sleep that an individual's DNA (genetic material) has time to reprogram itself. Jouvet sug-

Carl Jung believed that unconscious archetypes broke into our dreams, often appearing as characters from myth or legend. The animus, for example, which Jung held to be the male energy in the female unconscious, could emerge in the form of an idealized man, such as a knight in shining armour (above). The trickster, the rebellious, mocking energy of the collective unconscious, appears as a jester or fool (below).

gests that "[if] you use drugs to suppress dreams in an individual … then his genetic reprogramming to be aggressive, to be himself, to be free-willed may disappear". If he is right, dreaming is not simply an altered state of consciousness but rather one upon which our normal, conscious behaviour depends. Jouvet's ideas remain controversial, adding to the many debates on the subject.

For now, we can can only dream of an end to these debates about dreaming.

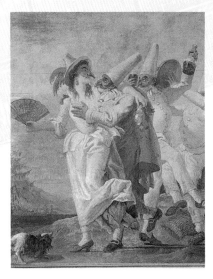

Daydreams

Few psychology texts examine daydreaming in detail. Yet many surveys suggest that ordinary men and women, who are neither disturbed nor neurotic, spend a large part of each day in some sort of fantasy, reverie or daydream. In an unusual British study, the psychologist E. J. Dearnley recorded what he was thinking and doing whenever a buzzer sounded at random times during a number of 24-hour periods. Dearnley found that fantasies or daydreams accounted for an astonishing 11 per cent of his waking hours.

Even individuals doing work that requires a high degree of concentration can lapse into daydreams. Michael Czikzent-mihalyi of the University of Chicago found that even surgeons have been known to slip into financial or sexual fantasies while performing operations. These types of quick fantasy rarely have a structured narrative. They are moments when we stop paying attention to what we are seeing and hearing and switch into an inner theatre of the imagination where we can play at wish fulfilment. Many of Dearnley's day-dreams, for example, centred around sitting in the local pub.

But there are other fantasies qualitatively different from these "wouldn't it be nice if ...?" stories. These are sustained fantasies, which often seem to have been crafted, worked and reworked to meet some more profound psychological need. Sustained fantasies usually take the form of longer, more coherent narratives, and are typically clearer and more easily interpreted than dreams. In *The House of Make Believe*, Jerome Singer of Yale University traces the links between childhood fantasies and those of later life. Singer claims that sustained fantasies, which may run longer than 60 seconds, are a way of coping with deep-seated childhood anxieties and fears. Indeed, it is Singer's view that all fantasies are healing and creative: even guilty fantasies are a way of purging guilt. Psychiatrists who deal with certain kinds of offenders would disagree. When one daydreams, normal inhibitions are bypassed: for many criminals, this provides a mental theatre in which to rehearse violent scenarios. The evidence of the rather macabre biographies of serial killers shows that they had frequently recurring violent fantasies before they turned to murder.

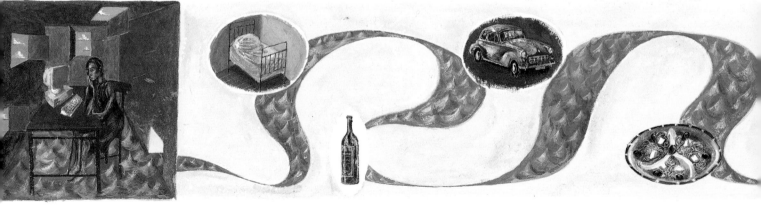

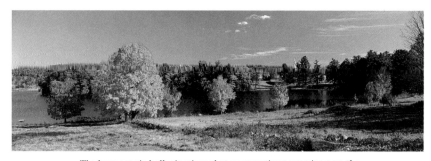

The hypnagogic hallucinations that we sometimes experience on the verge of waking are vivid, colour-saturated images.

A third type of daydream is the hypnagogic hallucination. This type of vivid image may be experienced on the edges of consciousness when one is either just falling asleep or, less frequently, on waking up. Hypnagogic hallucinations are often said to possess an exaggerated sense of reality combined with super-saturated colour. They are particularly fascinating because, unlike dreams, they are subject to the control of the will. The Belgian psychologist Jon Varendock tried hard to bring the phenomenon of hypnagogic hallucination within the field of psychoanalytic theory in the same way that Freud had shed light on the content of dreams. However, many of the images that were presented by his subjects were confused, proving extremely difficult to interpret in terms of wish fulfilment, and could not be "read" as easily as the stories that we tell ourselves in daydreams.

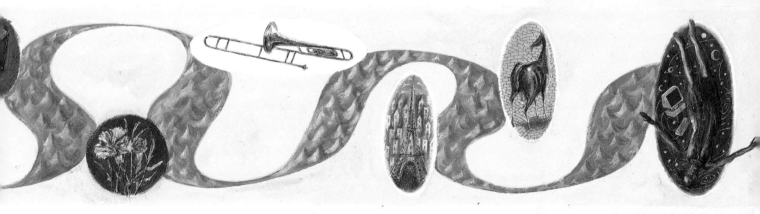

Fantasy and Sex

Our ability to use our imaginations erotically is extraordinary, and over the course of the 20th century there has been more and more freedom to explore fetishes and sexual fantasies both in private and in public. Cultural attitudes to sexual fantasy have changed enormously. In the 19th century, sexual subjects were unacceptable (some commentators believe that is the reason that pornography flourished), but today in the West we live in a perma-sexual (permanently, pervasively, permissably sexual) culture. In place of the puritanism of Freud, who believed that fantasies were a sign of immaturity, many therapists now consider that it is perfectly normal to have sexual fantasies, and some even believe that they can be used to achieve a more fulfilling sex life.

Alfred Kinsey, in his pioneering surveys of sexual behaviour begun in 1938, found that most of his subjects had sexual fantasies, beginning just before the onset of puberty, and that these fantasies continued throughout adulthood, even among people who had fulfilling sexual relationships. In fact, he found that people spend a surprising amount of time thinking about sex, and this has been confirmed by other studies: a survey in Chicago in the 1970s suggested that people had sexual fantasies about eight times a day.

There are vast cultural differences in what

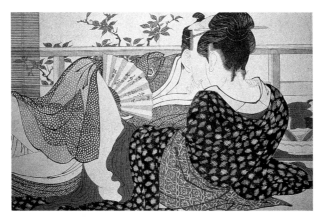

Erotic art has served a deep-seated human need in many cultures. This Japanese print, Lovers, *is from the series "Poem of the Pillow" by Kitagawa Utamaro (1753–1806).*

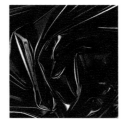

different societies consider acceptable material for sexual fantasy and fetishes. Many fetish objects have lost much of their mystique because we are so widely exposed to them. Some once-forbidden thrills, such as rubber suits and body piercing, are today marketed not only as fetish objects, but also, with a dash of irony, as high fashion. The Victorians would not have understood that – for them, the fetish was shocking and dangerous, the true dark side of sexuality. Freud saw fetishism as the result of linking unresolved childhood drives to objects that seemed "safe": you could not lust after your mother, but you could lust after her high-heeled shoe.

But the line between what society accepts and does not accept is not always clear. Most people would say that they disapprove of fantasies that revolve around inflicting serious harm on oneself or somebody else – but at the same time, renowned sex researchers Masters and Johnson found that one of the most common themes in the sexual fantasies of both men and women is being forced to have sex (others include making love to a different partner from the usual one and watching others have sex). There is also a legal debate as to the degree to which people should be allowed to harm themselves, or to harm others even with full consent. Research into sexual fantasies is complicated

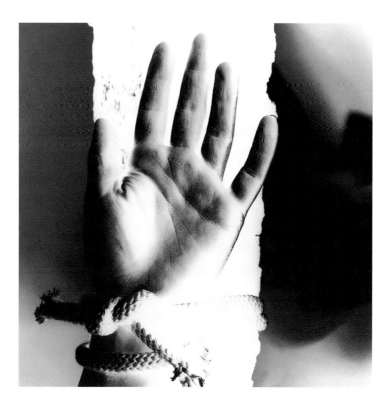

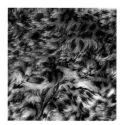

and must rely on what patients report to their therapists, but some studies have found links with childhood events – either sexual violence or a strict, repressed upbringing. There is an obvious distinction between fantasy and action – a fantasy does not harm others. However, some people who have fantasies that involve serious harm to themselves or others claim that they feel compelled to act them out.

People with less extreme fantasies sometimes choose to turn them into reality. Generally, four factors influence whether or not people try to do this: how powerfully erotic the fantasies are; how receptive the partner is; how confident the fantasizer is; and how bizarre the fantasy is. Many dramatize only a small aspect: for example, a woman who dreams of bondage may wrap scarves loosely around her partner's wrists. Some sex therapists use the acting out of fantasies as part of their treatment, arguing that one of the causes of anxiety about sex is not knowing what one's partner enjoys, but they warn that the process may cause the fantasy to lose its ability to arouse: the fantasy may sometimes turn out to be more fulfilling than the reality.

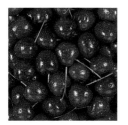 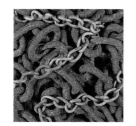 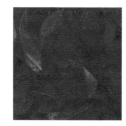 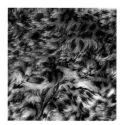

Hypnosis

Hypnosis has had a checkered history. Ever since the Austrian physician Franz Anton Mesmer took Paris by storm with his demonstrations of "magnetic influence" in the 1780s, its reputation has suffered at the hands of entertainers and fraudsters. Yet the evidence strongly suggests that hypnosis is a genuinely altered state of consciousness, with real clinical applications.

The word "hypnosis" was coined in the early 19th century by the British surgeon James Braid, who was the first to subject the phenomenon to serious examination. Braid originally proposed that hypnosis was a form of "nervous sleep", similar to natural sleep, caused by brain fatigue resulting from sustained concentration on the voice or actions of a hypnotist. But in his later studies, Braid noticed that subjects would continue to hold on to objects after hypnosis: their muscles did not relax as in normal sleep. In the light of such evidence, he played down the importance of physiology, and suggested that hypnotism was essentially psychological. Modern studies show that the brain waves of hypnotized subjects are much like those of the waking state.

When subjects are hypnotized, they can speak, walk and carry out instructions. Yet there are some noticeable changes from normal consciousness: attention becomes very selective, with the subject ignoring everything but the hypnotist's

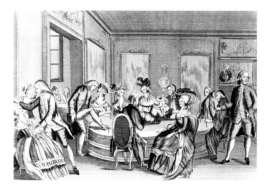

The Austrian physician Franz Anton Mesmer was the first person to experiment with hypnotism (hence the word "mesmerize"). Mesmer believed that he could cure ills by using his hands to channel a patient's "animal magnetism". This force was thought to be related to physical magnetism, so the patients would sit around a large magnetized tub while Mesmer practised his strange art. The magnetic theory soon proved to be false, and it was concluded that Mesmer's successful cures were effected in some way by his direct interaction with the patient.

voice; the subject rarely initiates thought or activity, but waits for suggestions from the hypnotist; and fantastic ideas or situations are more readily accepted as reality. So what then is the curious state of hypnosis? American psychologist Arnold Waxman defines it as "an altered state of consciousness effected by total concentration on the voice of the therapist": it is almost as if the willing, relaxed subject relinquishes control over part of his or her consciousness to the hypnotist. Others argue that hypnosis is no more than a form of role playing, the result of social pressure to cooperate with the hypnotist. However, they struggle somewhat to explain either post-hypnotic suggestibility or the way in which hypnosis can evoke valid memories, two phenomena that suggest that the hypnotic trance is an altered state of consciousness.

The "classic" method of hypnotism is to put a subject into a relaxed frame of mind and ask him or her to concentrate on an object, such as a swinging pocket watch. But even this is not necessary. One of the early researchers into hypnosis, George Estabrooks, made a recording of the verbal instructions usually given to hypnotize subjects, intending to play them to a group of volunteers. Unfortunately, Estabrooks played the wrong record, exposing the group to Swiss yodelling. He found to his amazement that one of the subjects fell

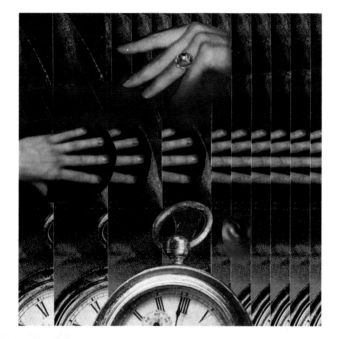

into a deep hypnotic trance. This story reveals that some people are far more easily hypnotized than others. There are no measurable differences between the susceptibility of men and women, or between people of different ages (except children aged between 8 and 12, who are particularly easy to hypnotize). But there is some evidence to suggest that individuals who readily accept fantasy, and are able, for example, to empathize with characters in books or films, are more likely to be susceptible.

There are three phenomena associated with the hypnotic state that are especially intriguing. Two – the use of hypnotism to control pain, and post-hypnotic suggestion – have been proved in hundreds of experiments. The mechanism by which hypnotism brings about pain relief is a mystery. Unlike other psychological methods of pain control, such as visualization, hypnotism does not cause the body to produce endorphins, the neurotransmitters that block pain receptors. Pain relief and other messages have been shown to persist after the hypnotic session has ended.

Post-hypnotic suggestion is another startling phenomenon. The hypnotist can make two types of lasting suggestions to a subject during the trance: negative suggestions, such as not to feel pain or not to remember what transpired during the session; and positive ones, improving the subject's overall mental state.

The third phenomenon – the use of hypnosis to recover memories – remains more controversial. Although some subjects have been seen to relive childhood experiences and to recall details of events witnessed fleetingly, some experts say that this results from eagerness to please the hypnotist.

Meditation

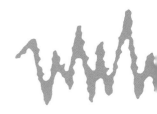

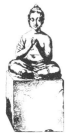

One function of consciousness is to knit together our sense of self-identity. But many religious traditions believe that enlightenment can be achieved only by breaking the shackles of self and attaining "purer" states of consciousness through meditation.

Although meditative techniques are most often associated with Eastern systems of belief, they are also a feature of the Christian faith and are increasingly used in a secular context. For example, transcendental meditation, which gained popularity in the West in the 1960s, is largely free of religious connotations. Many top athletes also use techniques akin to meditation to fine-tune their performances; and practising psychologists report that meditation allows people, whether religious or not, to improve their self-esteem and come to terms with previously suppressed feelings.

As well as its psychological benefits, the meditative state has marked physiological effects – these phenomena are measurable and reliably repeatable, and thus are a suitable object of scientific study. Such studies have revealed some remarkable effects: meditation can lower a subject's metabolic rate, decreasing blood pressure, pulse rate and muscle tension. Studies of one Indian guru, published in the highly reputable science journal *Nature*, showed that the subject could reduce his oxygen intake to one-third of the normal

resting state – an extraordinary feat, given that respiration is controlled by the autonomic nervous system, over which we ordinarily have no conscious control. Other studies suggest that meditation can help to alleviate bronchial asthma, hypertension and insomnia, and reduce stress – indeed the brain waves produced during meditation are similar to the alpha waves that characterize the state of relaxation in the early stages of sleep (see page 72).

There are a number of meditative techniques, which can be divided into two broad categories – concentrative and opening-up meditation. Concentrative meditation, in

The Indian meditative technique of yoga (right) dates back to at least the 2nd century BC. In its purest form, it is an eight-stage journey to enlightenment, which is achieved only when the meditator perceives himself or herself as one with the object of meditation. Yoga exercises are designed to increase relaxation, stabilize the rhythm of breathing and encourage steadiness of posture. Today, meditative methods developed by sports psychologists are an integral part of an international athlete's training. The athlete is encouraged to visualize in detail each part of a race in order to prepare the body for the experience itself (below).

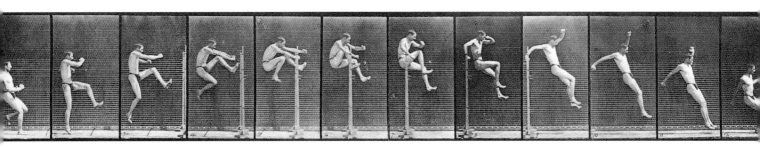

which a single object or thought provides a focus that helps the meditator to remove all else from consciousness, has been formalized in numerous meditative traditions. In Zen Buddhism the focus may be a simple, repetitive activity, such as the meditator's own pattern of breathing or heartbeat, the ticking of a clock, or a *koan* (paradoxical thought) such as: "What is the sound of one hand clapping?" Christian meditators, such as the 15th-century scholar Thomas à Kempis, would focus on the image of Christ crucified, while practitioners of yoga use a mantra, or set of words, as the focus of concentration. In the Tantric traditions, body posture acts as the focus. In the symbolic language of Tantra, the Kundalini or serpent energy slumbers at the base of the spine: the meditative posture helps to rouse this energy, giving the adept access to higher states of consciousness.

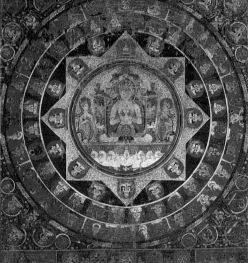

The regular geometric form of the mandala (above) is a meditative focus in some Eastern spiritual traditions. The mandala is a visual representation of the universe, and by mentally moving toward its centre, the meditator becomes aware of progressively deeper levels of meaning. Interestingly, some psychologists note that patients with no grounding in Eastern mysticism may spontaneously draw mandala-like symbols in the course of therapy.

The psychologist's interpretation is that a person's body image is intimately linked with his or her sense of self. Body image – the visceral sense of being – is shaped by the constant barrage of sensory information reaching the body. Maintaining the same posture for long periods of time sends a uniform, continuous input to the brain's perceptual and sensory systems, and the resulting habituation reduces awareness of body image, and so is said to loosen the shackles of self.

Opening-up meditation, in contrast, uses the techniques of concentrative meditation, but moves beyond them. The meditator is told to become aware of what is happening without actively focusing, to become open to all the perceptions that constitute the buzzing confusion normally filtered out by the brain. This should result in an expanded awareness and greater mental clarity.

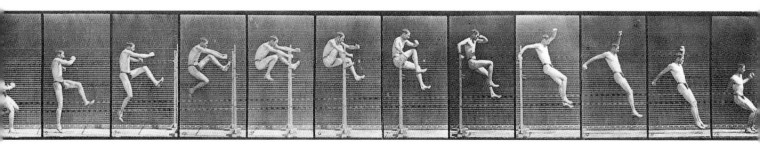

Vision and Trance

Throughout human history, people have sincerely reported seeing visions, and even some fairly sceptical psychologists have accepted their claims as genuine. The 19th-century psychologist William James was fascinated by visions, and in his book *The Varieties of Religious Experience* (1902) he recorded a number of them. It is virtually impossible to carry out research into visions in the laboratory, because they do not happen on demand; as a result, the only evidence that visions do exist is the accounts of those people who have experienced them.

Often visions may occur in response to stress. People stranded in the desert often "see" the oasis for which they have been searching, and victims of shipwrecks believe that they have spotted the rescue boat. Similarly, widows and widowers often report that they either see or sense the presence of their spouses shortly after their death; but this occurs less frequently as the pain of the bereavement and the need for comfort subside.

Visions are often central to religious experience. Many conversion experiences have involved visions or other

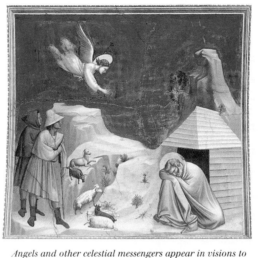

Angels and other celestial messengers appear in visions to communicate divine messages. In this painting by Giotto (1276–1337), The Vision of Joseph, *an angel tells Joseph that Mary will give birth to the son of God.*

sorts of divine revelations. Some religious practices foster atmospheres conducive to this: periods of meditation, for example, seem to predispose some people to visions, although the mechanism for this is unknown. Other religious practices use different sorts of mind-altering substances, ranging from wine and incense to hallucinogenic drugs, to inspire mystical visions.

In some cultures, shamans are priests who, while in a trance state, allegedly receive visions from other levels of the cosmos. In many traditions, the shaman's soul is said to leave his or her body to travel to the spirit world. This trance state is different from that achieved through meditation: whereas people who are meditating are focusing their minds on one image to achieve a great calmness, shamans remain intensely concentrated but at the same time extremely active as they travel between worlds and meet with spirits. Some psychologists have seen similarities in state of mind between shamans and schizophrenics. However, while a schizophrenic's mind is typically disordered, a shaman's is coherent; and the shaman's integral role in his or her community contrasts with the isolation of schizophrenia.

Out-of-body experiences are not restricted to religious practices: they seem to occur in reponse to some kind of emergency situation. This is the case with near-death experiences. There have been thousands of reports of near-death

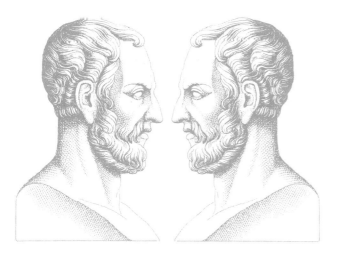

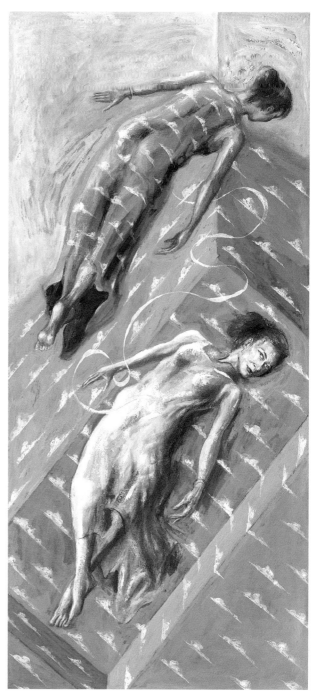

experiences, many noting the same types of sensations. Subjects feel as though they have left their bodies, and many look on as doctors operate or family and friends mourn – but despite this, they feel only inner peace and happiness. Some people report travelling down a tunnel toward a bright light, where benevolent presences wait; some make contact with long-dead friends or family members, or with a stranger who urges them to return to their bodies. Many also report that their out-of-body experiences reinforced the value of their own lives and the lives of others.

Although reports of out-of-body experiences are not uncommon, scientists have been unable to explain them conclusively. They may be triggered by a physical cause: some physiologists have suggested that hypoxia, or low oxygen levels in the brain, might cause a consistent pattern of hallucination in all sufferers. Other experts believe that out-of-body experiences are purely psychological, a way of denying death. Still others see them as an alternative state of consciousness, a bridge between life and death.

Drugs

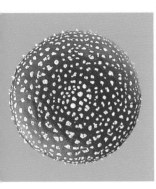

At the end of the 17th century, the famous English physician Thomas Sydenham wrote: "I cannot forbear mentioning with gratitude the goodness of the Supreme Being who has supplied afflicted mankind with opiates for their relief." Many powerful hallucinogens are of natural origin: bufotenine is present in the fly agaric toadstool (*Amanita muscaria*, above left); LSD was originally derived from ergot, a fungus that infects wheat and rye; and mescalin is present in the peyote cactus (*Lophophora williamsii*).

A modern Sydenham who praised opium might lose his licence to practice medicine, and recent studies have revealed cases in which dying patients were denied doses of morphine for fear of turning them into addicts. This comparison is instructive because it demonstrates our love-hate relationship with mind-altering drugs: on the one hand, they can relieve pain or transport us to new levels of awareness; and, on the other, they are feared and demonized as causes of mental and physical degradation.

It is curious that we should be so confused about drugs, because as a species we are very experienced in their use and misuse. Drugs have been recruited to achieve altered states of consciousness since the beginnings of recorded history. Sumerian tablets dating from *c.*4000 BC refer to opium; the effects of cannabis were known to the Chinese around 2700 BC; and in Central America, species of mushrooms and cacti have been eaten for their hallucinogenic properties since at least 1000 BC. For the ancients, drugs usually served ceremonial or ritual functions or were taken

in preparation for battle. According to some historians, the battle-fury of the Vikings was partly due to their habit of consuming fly agaric, and the word "assassin" has the same Arabic root as hashish, a form of cannabis: the assassins, a group of warriors in 12th-century Persia and Syria, were rumoured to use cannabis before they killed, perhaps to give them courage, or to allow them to distance themselves from their actions.

Many drugs are used in similar ways today: to escape reality, lose inhibitions and touch the untouchable. In the last 50 years, we have been exposed to an enormous array of psychoactive drugs that affect mood, behaviour or conscious-

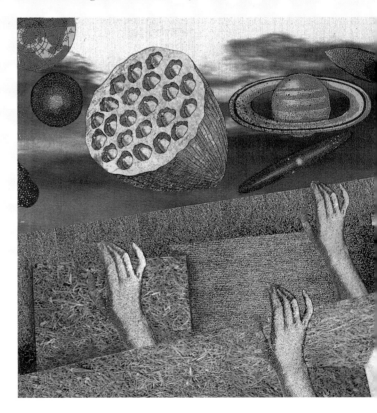

ness. Some people have come to see these substances as providing a quick fix for physical and psychological problems. The medical profession has helped to create this view of drugs: in the 1970s in particular, doctors would prescribe antidepressants and tranquillizers to people who were depressed or anxious, helping to normalize the routine use of psychoactive drugs. For these and other social reasons, drug use – legal and illegal – has proliferated in recent years, and we must accept that we now live in a drug culture.

Drugs that affect consciousness can be classified into four main groups – opiates, depressants, stimulants and hallucinogens – which act on the brain in different ways and have dif-

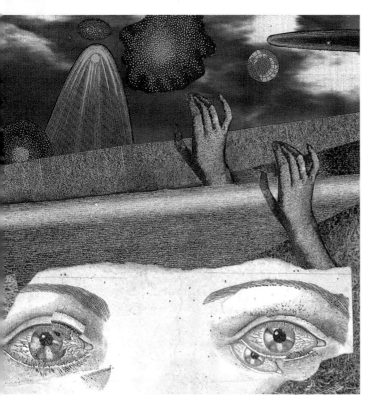

ferent psychological impacts. Opiates are drugs derived from the dried resin of the opium poppy, or synthetic versions of these chemicals, such as heroin, codeine and morphine. All have been used medicinally at some time for their pain-killing properties, and codeine and morphine are still prescribed today. They are used illegally for similar reasons: heroin gives the user a "high", reducing anxiety and producing a sense of temporary well-being.

Opiates mimic the brain's natural painkillers, endorphins. Endorphins are neurotransmitters (see page 27), molecules that pass from one neuron to another. Endorphin molecules are the correct size and shape to bind to opioid receptors, and when they do so, the net effect is to block pain and produce sensations of pleasure. Opiate drugs also bind to the opioid receptors of the neurons and thus increase the user's sense of well-being.

Repeated use of opiates, however, produces a cascade of painful and psychologically disturbing effects: the brain becomes accustomed to receiving an external supply of painkillers, and so progressively cuts down on its own production of endorphins. The user compensates by taking larger and larger doses, risking a lethal overdose. When the effects of the opiate wear off, the brain finds itself short of painkillers, natural and artificial. The result is that the user suffers painful withdrawal symptoms, including stomach cramps, vomiting and intense headaches, which can be most easily alleviated by another chemical "fix". The initial "high" of the drug is soon replaced by the self-sustaining cycle of opiate addiction. Thomas de Quincey, a 19th-century writer, was the first to

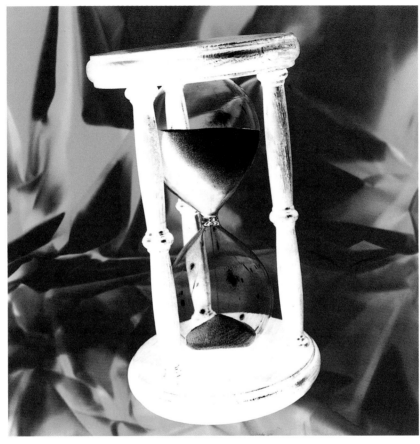

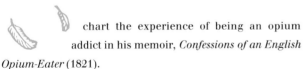

chart the experience of being an opium addict in his memoir, *Confessions of an English Opium-Eater* (1821).

Depressants include prescription tranquillizers, such as Valium, and barbiturates, such as Seconal, which are used to reduce anxiety and treat insomnia. But by far the most widely used depressant is alcohol.

Because it is consumed, tolerated and even actively marketed in many countries, it is easy to forget that alcohol is also addictive and a drug, and for various reasons, we often choose to ignore the enormous range of physical and social problems that it directly causes. The psychological effects of alcohol on the brain are fairly complex: moderate drinking seems to reduce our tensions and inhibitions, making us feel "up", but heavier consumption often produces irritability and mood swings and makes us feel "down". A 1995 study of murders showed that most murders of strangers were committed under the influence of either drink or drugs.

Our normal, sober state is maintained by a delicate balance between the excitation and inhibition of neural activity in the brain. Alcohol suppresses both of these processes, but the first to be affected is inhibition: this is why, when we have a few drinks, we at first feel stimulated. Only later does alcohol begin to suppress the excitatory action of our neurons. It is at this point that we begin to feel "down", and this effect will often last for a longer period of time.

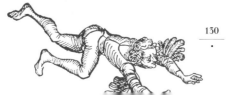

Stimulants are drugs such as amphetamines, cocaine, nicotine and caffeine. To greater or lesser degrees, these substances produce euphoria, increase alertness and stamina, and enhance the user's self-confidence. There is even some tenuous evidence that they might improve our performance in cognitive (thinking) tasks. Stimulants work either by promoting the release (or prolonging the activity) of neurotransmitters such as noradrenaline (norepinephrine), dopamine and serotonin in the brain, or by interfering with the brain's natural depressants (caffeine, for example, suppresses the activity of adenosine, one of the brain's natural "downers").

Cocaine, which is extracted from the leaves of the coca plant, is the most powerful natural stimulant, and has been used since earliest times. It produces not only a feeling of well-being but is also something of an aphrodisiac, especially for men. But it has its perils: cocaine is highly addictive, and the user develops a tolerance to the drug, consequently requiring progressively higher dosages. The cocaine "high" is followed by periods of irritability and depression, and prolonged use may cause hallucinations because the user's sensory neurons are firing uncontrollably (the hallucinations reported include that of cocaine "bugs", the terrible feeling of insects crawling beneath the skin).

Hallucinogenic drugs profoundly change the way in which the user sees his or her inner and outer worlds. Sounds and colours may be altered or intensified (users of mescalin, for example, often report seeing in soft focus) and perception of time may be seriously affected, with hours condensed into minutes. Users of hallucinogens, such as LSD (lysergic acid diethylamide) or Ecstasy (MDMA), often report feeling a diminished sense of self, almost as if they were merging with their surroundings, or claim to have profound, meaningful insights into self and spirit. "Trips" are not always pleasurable; some users become disoriented and paranoid, and their panic may also become dangerous.

Although psychedelic drugs such as LSD are generally considered to have adverse psychological effects, some psychiatrists believe that they allow access to parts of consciousness that are normally blocked, and that they may therefore have some therapeutic value. The last doctor to be licensed to use LSD in Europe was Jan Bastiaans, professor of psychiatry at the University of Leiden. Bastiaans treated Dutch soldiers returning from action in a vicious war in Indonesia in the 1950s. Many of the veterans found it hard to integrate back into normal life because in their unconscious they had repressed, or buried, memories of the atrocities they had witnessed. Bastiaans administered LSD in an attempt to free up these repressions: in a number of cases he believed that the drug lowered the soldiers' defences and made it possible for them to be healed. However, the medical profession no longer condones the use of hallucinogenic drugs in psychiatric treatment, because the risk of negative effects is great.

TWELVE-STEP PROGRAMS

Twelve-step programs, such as Alcoholics Anonymous (AA) and Narcotics Anonymous, offer help to many people with substance abuse problems and other addictions, including gambling. These are self-help groups: people work together to create a supportive environment in which they can come to terms with their addictions and move beyond them. Typically people attend three to five meetings a week. The 12 steps refer to stages of self-knowledge one has to achieve in order to learn to control an addiction.

The Power of Suggestion

The way we think is influenced by the social context in which we operate. This is not simply a question of our consciously picking up information and knowledge from the people around us. In some cases, pressure from other people can make us see things from their point of view, or can make us behave in ways that we would not previously have done, as though we had surrendered up part of our consciousness. To an extent, every one of us is suggestible. We all yield to some of society's norms; and the behaviour of people working in large companies is frequently shaped by some kind of corporate "ethos". Psychological studies of suggestibility indicate that there may be more than one process at work.

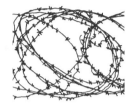

Two simple experiments reveal the power of suggestion in different contexts. The first looks at an individual's reponse to someone who is in a position of authority. An experimenter repeatedly gives the subject the same suggestion: for example, she tells the subject that his body is swaying. Soon his body will begin to sway. Not everyone is susceptible to this form of suggestibility (sometimes known as primary suggestibility), and neurotic people succumb more easily than "well-balanced" individuals. In another famous experiment from the 1950s, the social psychologist Solomon Asch looked at group dynamics. He presented a group of seven to nine subjects with a card showing three lines of different lengths: the subjects were asked in turn to identify the one line that was the same length as a reference line shown on another card. The correct answer to the question was obvious – one line clearly matched the length of the reference line – but all the members of the group, except one, were experimental "plants": they had been briefed by Asch to give an incorrect answer. The point of the experiment was to determine how far the true subject, the one "innocent" member of the group, would go along with the others. The researchers found that only one in four individuals held out consistently against the view of the group, proving that the power of suggestion can sometimes override the evidence of our own senses. Pressure to conform weakens if the group is not unanimous, even if there is only one other dissenter; and even if that one other dissenter is wrong, the subject will still feel more free to express his or her own opinion.

Asch's experiment may be artificial, with few direct parallels in real life – but if what we see can be undermined by pressures to conform, it seems almost certain that our everyday moral and social judgments (about which we are usually less certain) will be subject to the same or greater pressures.

Suggestibility can have grave consequences, especially in the setting of the police interrogation room. Forensic psychologists became interested in the power of suggestion in the 1970s, following a series of high-profile cases in which the police were accused of unfairly extracting confessions from suspects. Individuals were convicted on evidence from confessions that were elicited by dubious means, and spent years in jail before their convictions were quashed on appeal. At the root of these appeals was the state of mind in which confessions were made. The subjects were told time and time again that they had committed these crimes, and eventually a few of them started to wonder if it really might be true. On some occasions suspects were allegedly also deprived of sleep, light and food and were beaten up. Had the suspects been so suggestible that they just parrotted what the police wanted to hear? In certain cases, this appeared to be true. The suspects later reported that they were no longer sure exactly what they had done or where they had been at the time that the crime was committed.

Police interrogators know how to exploit the situation. Barrie Irving of the UK Police Foundation noted: "The principal psychological factor contributing to a successful interrogation is privacy – being alone with the person under interrogation." (A successful interrogation in this context is one that ends with a confession.) Under such conditions some suspects become more suggestible, even though they know that eventually they may be convicted of a crime. But not all suspects buckle under the pressure: Gisli Gudjuddson, author of *The Psychology of Interrogations, Confessions and Testimony* (1992), has shown that there are a number of factors that tend to make people confess to having done something that they have not done, including low intelligence, a high degree of anxiety and an inability to remember. There may also be a personality factor present: a tendency to comply and an unwillingness to confront.

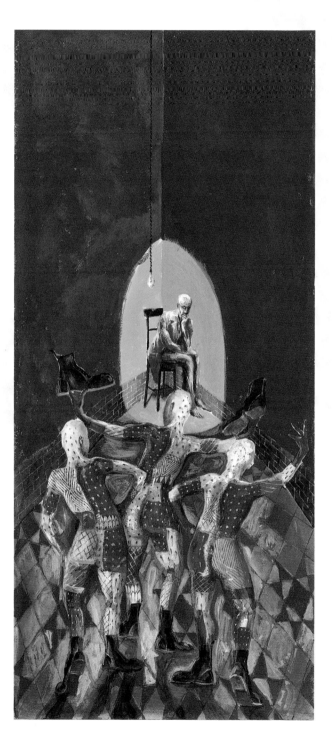

Body Language

It is hardly a revolutionary insight that words can hide our real feelings. This is not just a question of lying: it may be that one is too tense, frightened or embarrassed to utter the truth. Under such circumstances, the truth often emerges in non-verbal forms, such as changes in posture, gestures, twitches or facial expressions.

Some commentators have drawn parallels between human body language and displacement activity in animals. Displacement activity is a concept developed by ethologists (students of animal behaviour) such as Konrad Lorenz and Niko Tinbergen: basically, it is a behaviour that an animal performs to discharge sexual or aggressive energy, often when the animal is in the grip of conflicting instincts. It wants to fight for a new mate but when it sees that its rival is large, it wants to flee. So instead it hops or pecks the ground. Human beings also show displacement activities. Instead of hitting someone, I clench my fists or I bite my nails. When I feel anxious but do not want it to show, or perhaps when I am not even aware of my own anxiety, I may repeatedly touch my face (it is there so I must exist) or I click my heels.

One of the most important channels for non-verbal communication is eye contact. Intense eye contact has measurable physiological effects – increased pulse rate and changes in skin resistance (the measure of stress used in lie detector

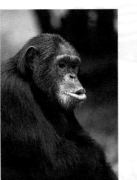

The human face can be very expressive, and capable of communicating subtle shades of emotion and feeling. Despite the fact that facial expressions are crucial clues in social interactions, it is likely that they are largely innate, because the ability to form recognizable expressions is shared with other primates (left). Charles Darwin argued that facial expressions originally served a real biological function: frowning shaded the eyes from intense sunlight, widening of the eyes improved vision during times of stress, and so on.

tests) – but has different connotations in different social situations. In a hierarchical system, such as the workplace, intense eye contact can signify superiority or hostility, and looking away signals weakness or evasion. But in romantic situations eye contact is a prelude to further intimacy. A number of popular books have explored issues such as the mirroring of postures – when two people imitate each others' gestures. As people become more informed about the impressions that their body language can convey, they may start "putting on" certain kinds of body language and attempt to conceal others.

Much of the grammar of body language is culture-specific: people in western Europe and the United States, for example, expect others to respect a "personal space" of around 2 ft (60 cm) during face-to-face conversations. They may feel threatened when speaking to well-intentioned South Americans, whose private space is smaller. Similarly, the Japanese prac-

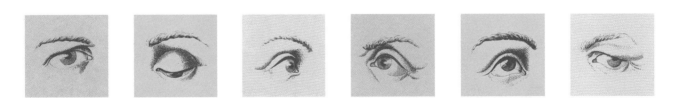

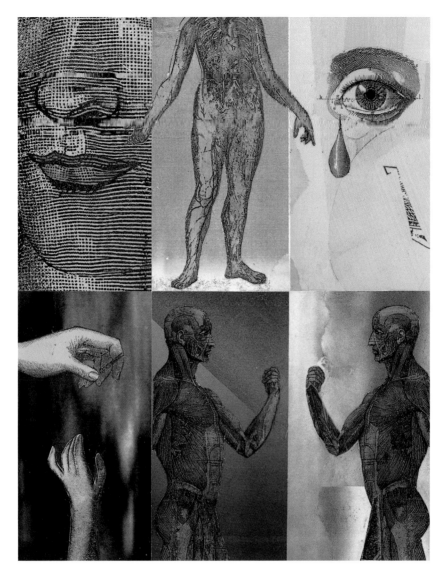

tice of *omoiyari*, or empathy, which focuses on trying to understand implicitly the desires of others, is sometimes interpreted by Westerners as diffidence. Other types of non-verbal communication, however, appear to be more international. For example, different forms of both threatening and benevolent facial expressions are consistently recognized across cultures.

The study of non-verbal behaviour is older than one might think. Charles Darwin studied the grimaces and gestures of many species, and in 1872 published *The Expression of Emo-* *tions in Animals and Men*, in which he argued that human characteristics such as laughter had developed from the expressions of our ape-like ancestors. In 1960, the study of non-verbal communication was still restricted to university psychology departments. But today people are no longer naive about the significance of gestures and body posture. Our awareness of this concept affects the way we behave and the way we think, illustrating an interesting quirk of post-modern life – that our knowledge of psychology could actually be leading to changes in consciousness.

The Mind and the Paranormal

In our normal waking state, we cannot predict the future, move objects without touching them, or tell what is inside a sealed envelope without opening it. Yet there is some, albeit highly controversial, evidence that we can enter paranormal states of consciousness in which we can perform such extraordinary feats by channelling information or energy in ways that defy all known physical laws. These supposed mental phenomena, which include telepathy, precognition, clairvoyance and psychokinesis, have been given the collective label "psi".

Mystics have long made claims about the hidden powers of the mind, but it was not until 1882 – the year of the foundation of the Society for Psychical Research in England – that psi phenomena were subjected to any kind of scrutiny. The Society, whose members included the respected physicist Sir Oliver Lodge, psychologist William James, and Sir Arthur Conan Doyle, the creator of Sherlock Holmes, used scientific methods to investigate the paranormal, hoping to find evidence of survival after death and of "souls" sending signals from the "other side". Given their aims, it is hardly surprising that many scientists doubted their findings. It did not help that some of the mediums studied by the Society turned out to be brazen frauds. Nevertheless, the Society has since then succeeded in maintaining high standards of research, and the last century of experimentation has occasionally yielded some remarkable results.

The "best" evidence in the field of psi investigation is for telepathy, a phenomenon in which thoughts are transferred directly from one individual to another, and for psychokine-sis, the ability to move objects at a distance with the power of the mind or the supernatural.

The first and perhaps still the most influential experiments on extra-sensory perception (ESP) were those carried out by the biologist Joseph Rhine, who headed a department dedicated to the study of ESP at Duke University in the United States in the 1930s. Rhine's method was simple. He put the subject – the receiver – in one room, while in a second room another person dealt cards one by one from a deck of 25. The cards, known as Zener cards, were printed with one of five simple geometric designs: there were five cards of each type in the deck. The receiver had to guess or in some way "know" which cards were being revealed. Rhine's early results were astonishing because they revealed a strong positive result, with the receivers consistently scoring more than the five "hits" that would be expected from pure guesswork. And in one series of tests, a subject called Hubert Pearce correctly "guessed" every card in the sequence of 25. Rhine's experiments were criticized by sceptics who believed that clues about the cards had been passed on deliberately or unwittingly to the receivers. But whether or not this was the case, Rhine's positive results could not be reproduced by other experimental psychologists in their own laboratories. Scientists see repeatability as a critical test of any experimental finding, and failure inevitably raises serious doubts about the validity of the results. One argument used by supporters of

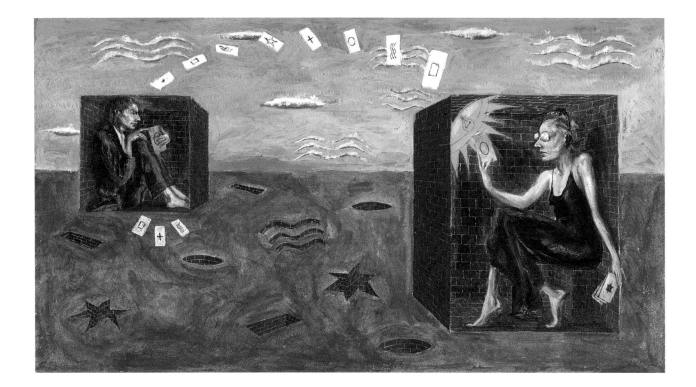

ESP is that such criticism is invalid, precisely because psi phenomena are not repeatable at will and may be triggered by emotional intensity or personal crisis. Supporters subscribe to a technique known as meta-analysis. Rather than insisting upon the replicability of each individual experiment, they treat all the studies on a given subject as a unit. As long as a statistically significant number of studies in a particular subject area are replicable, then advocates of meta-analysis maintain that they make their point with scientific validity.

There are many anecdotal accounts of telepathic happenings, although since they cannot be confirmed, these accounts can-

not be considered serious evidence. This one is typical. In 1955, Joicey Hurth was washing dishes in Cedarburg, Wisconsin. Her son and her husband went off to catch the latest Disney film. A few minutes later, her daughter came back from a party. She too had wanted to see the film. Her mother told her to catch up with the rest of the family, warning her to be careful crossing the street. A few minutes after her daughter had gone, Mrs Hurth reported that she felt a terrible chill. Somehow she knew her daughter had been hurt. In a panic, she called the movie theatre and was told that a little girl had just been run down by a car immediately outside. Is it possible that the daughter's fear and emotions were so strong that they were somehow transmitted to the mother? Or did Mrs Hurth unconsciously construct the story after she had found out about the accident?

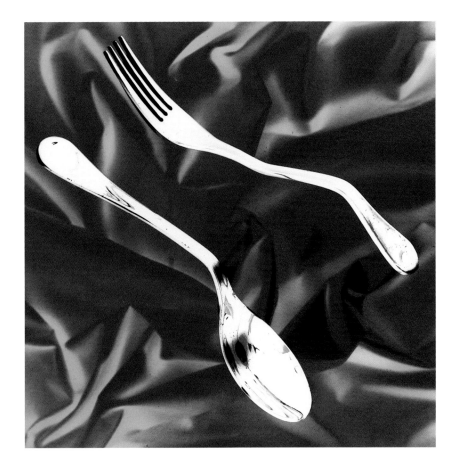

The psi phenomenon of clairvoyance is related to telepathy in that it involves knowledge that is not acquired by traditional methods. In the case of clairvoyance, however, the knowledge is not possessed by any other person either. For example, if a deck of cards were shuffled, I then looked at the top card, and you "read my mind" to discover what was on that card, that would be telepathy. However, if the cards were shuffled, nobody else saw them, and you knew the identity of the top card, that would be clairvoyance.

The experimental evidence for psychokinesis (the moving of objects by mental force) is as susceptible to doubt as that for telepathy: in many cases the methods, statistical analyses and, occasionally, the honesty of the experimenter is questionable; and all too often the results are not reliably repeatable. However, again the anecdotal evidence is strong – Uri Geller's alleged ability to bend spoons without touching them is internationally known, and there are hundreds of stories of poltergeist phenomena in which objects move for no apparent reason and a child or a young woman is said to have "unconscious" telekinetic power. But the results obtained by Dr Helmut Schmidt of the Mind Science Foundation in San Antonio, Texas, still await satisfactory explanation. Schmidt used the decay of a piece of the radioactive isotope strontium 90 to drive a random number generator. (Physicists have established that it is impossible to influence the rate of radioactive decay by any chemical or physical means.) The random number generator was connected to a circular array of nine light bulbs. When the generator produced a positive number, the lights would illuminate in a clockwise sequence; negative numbers would have the reverse effect. When no subject sat in front of the machine, the pattern of illumination was, as expected, entirely random. But this was not the case when subjects were asked to concentrate on trying to make the lights move either clockwise or counterclockwise around the circle. Many subjects seemed to have the ability to move the lights, but in the direction opposite to the one intended. Some parapsychologists have claimed that this experiment shows that the mind can influence subatomic particles. Even critics of the experiment cannot explain this result.

Precognition is the phenomenon of knowing what is going to happen before it does. Again there is much anecdotal evidence for this phenomenon – in fact, most of us have experienced a feeling of precognition at one time or another. Frequently, people report having dreamed of an event that later happened. In the popular press, psychics make annual predictions of what the year ahead will bring, most of which turn out not to be true. Precognition has yet to be tested in a satisfactory way under laboratory conditions.

Despite widespread scepticism, experts from many fields find it difficult to dismiss claims of ESP and other

RABBIT TELEPATHY

A bizarre experiment was reportedly conducted by the Soviets during the Cold War years concerning telepathy in rabbits. Young rabbits were taken away from their mothers, who remained on land as their young sailed with the Soviet submarine fleet. At a preordained time, the young rabbits were killed, hundreds of feet beneath the sea. Thousands of miles away, parapsychologists were monitoring the brain waves of the mother, and they reported extraordinary distortions in the patterns at the time that her offspring died. This experiment reveals one of the contradictions of Marxist psychology. According to Marxist doctrine, human beings are social animals with no souls, and yet psi phenomena cannot exist if one denies the non-material aspect of the mind.

psi phenomena outright. One reason is that it is hard to prove a negative – that psi phenomena do not exist – although many scientists are so prejudiced against the idea that the debate is not always reasonable. However, psi phenomena continue to capture the public's attention, and some law enforcement agencies bring in psychics claiming to know the whereabouts of stolen goods or kidnapped people and follow up assiduously on their leads.

Scientists resist claims of the paranormal for both good and bad reasons. Many claims certainly do stretch credulity, and many others depend solely on anecdotal evidence. In addition, magicians, such as James Randi, have shown that many psi triumphs can be achieved by the familiar techniques of stage magic. But it is also true that irrefutable evidence for psi phenomena would require many of the existing theories of the mind to be rewritten completely, challenging current orthodoxies about the biology of the brain. As a result, most scientists tend to be highly critical of paranormal studies, demanding more proof from them than they would for "conventional" experiments that elaborate on current trends.

Despite a century of experimentation and many strong claims, there has been no conclusive proof that psi phenomena do – or do not – exist. We should remain open-minded but properly sceptical.

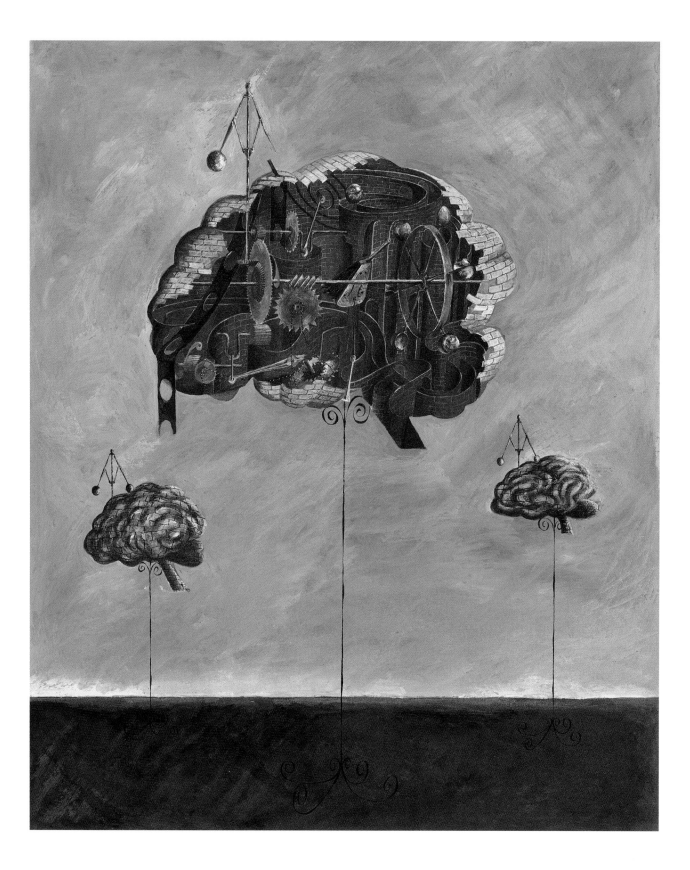

The Mind under Siege

Human beings are fascinated by madness. Themes of obsession, insanity and violence are standard Hollywood material. But this interest in madness is nothing new. More than 2,000 years ago, Aristotle noted that genius is nearly always tinged with madness, and in the 1st century AD the physician Areteaus of Cappadocia produced, in his book *De Causis et Signis Morborum* (On the Causes and Signs of Disease), a remarkable classification of mental illnesses that would be recognized by modern psychiatrists.

Our fascination with mental breakdown has two main causes: first, our love of horror; and second, our fear of, and fascination with, losing control of our "real" selves. In the madness of others we see a mirror. Anyone's wits could "turn". This is more true than ever before, because people are living longer and statistics show that 20 per cent of those who are over 85 suffer some form of dementia. But there are less sinister reasons too. We are touched by the plight of the mentally ill; and some cultural traditions believe that there may be a message in madness, because the gods speak through those afflicted.

Many great artists have been interested in madness and what it can reveal about the human condition. A surprising number of Shakespeare's protagonists – Hamlet, Ophelia, King Lear, Lady Macbeth and Macbeth – come close to madness. Shakespeare's apparent belief that madness is touched

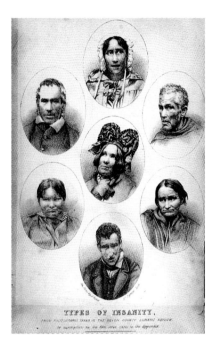

In the 19th century, there was great interest in the classification of mental illness. Some psychologists proposed typologies (above) based on the physical appearance of sufferers.

with truth was shared by many writers and artists of the Surrealist movement, which flourished in Europe between the First and Second World Wars. Influenced by the work of Freud and the psychoanalytic movement, artists such as Salvador Dali (1904–1989) feigned states of madness in order to unite the conscious and unconscious minds in a "surreality".

Despite interest in madness on many levels, society has treated the "mad" punitively. This has been true regardless of whether the official belief is that the mad are possessed by demons – the view of Christian scholars until 1650 – or the victims of disease.

The insensitive treatment of psychiatric patients over the years reflects both society's fears and misunderstandings. For centuries, people believed that madness was caused by demonic possession, and that the appropriate treatments involved drastic means: these ranged from cutting holes in the skull to create an exit, to starvation and whipping, all creating conditions that the demonic spirit would find intolerable. An alternative school of thought held that mental illness had an organic cause and that there was no way of remedying the imbalance of humours, or bodily fluids, that was the at the root of disease. Mentally ill people were considered incurable and dangerous, and they were often subjected to appalling cruelties. In addition, the definition of mental illness has been broad in most societies, taking in any individual who did not conform with the social norms of the time, ranging from unmarried mothers to criminals and political dissidents.

The first dedicated psychiatric hospital was the Hospital of St Mary of Bethlehem – better known as Bedlam – in London, established in 1402. During the 18th century, the public was allowed into the establishment to look at the patients, a bizarre form of entertainment that attracted thousands of people each year. The term "bedlam" came to mean terrible chaos and uproar, probably reflecting the atmosphere in the asylum during the 15th and 16th centuries. Patients were often beaten and kept in chains, in a gloomy, dank place that was more like a prison than a hospital.

In the history of psychiatry, much credit is due to the Parisian doctor Phillipe Pinel (1745–1826), who worked in La Bicêtre and La Salpêtrière, asylums for men and women respectively. He removed the shackles from mental patients, arguing that they were not so dangerous as to require chains, and he found that many improved as a result of this more humane treatment. He inspired other doctors to develop what came to be called "moral treatment", a relatively liberal regime under which asylums were built in the countryside

and patients were allowed to work in the open air: although they were still confined for decades, they were at least kept in better environments.

Although demand for specialized treatment for mental patients led to a rapid growth in the number of asylums in both Europe and in the United States, standards of treatment did not improve, and many patients continued to be restrained. A variety of restraints was invented, partly in the belief that patients were suffering from over-stimulation, and if they were kept still, their spirits would settle down.

In the first half of the 20th century, conditions had only marginally improved on those described in Bedlam. Books such as Albert Deutsch's *The Shame of the States* (1948) painted a horrifying picture of the conditions that thousands of American patients suffered. They were kept in vast asylums, they were often beaten, and they rarely saw a doctor, although they were supposed to be sick.

In the 1930s, two new forms of therapy were invented, which many people condemned as cruel. One was electro-convulsive therapy (ECT). Patients are strapped down, electrodes are placed on the left and right temples, and an electric shock is applied to the head. Films of this procedure

The debate continues over the roles of genetics (right) and environment (far right) in the causation of mental illness. Many experts now recognize that while our genes can predispose us to illness, social factors play a crucial role.

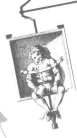

are horrifying. Patients are jolted into long convulsions and can suffer memory loss. Although the treatment has some value in countering extreme depression, psychiatrists have not tried to refine it beyond administering muscle relaxants to patients before the procedure; and despite the fact that studies have shown that the same curative effect could be achieved by shocking only one hemisphere, resulting in less memory loss, many psychiatrists still shock both hemispheres. ECT remains widely used – in 1994, there were 5,000 instances of the treatment being administered in the UK without the express permission of patients. The second therapy was lobotomy, in which some of the connections from the cortex to the frontal lobes were cut. Although some patients did become less disturbed, most became vegetables. The treatment has been discredited, although some neurologists have studied these sad cases to further the understanding of the frontal cortex.

Many people feel that this eclectic mix of cruelties reflects our lack of a mature understanding of mental illness. It remains mysterious, and even now, with sophisticated drug treatments available, we do not have enough insight to devise effective, humane cures. Our emotional response to mental illness is still primitive – we fear losing our minds and so we punish those who seem to have suffered that fate.

Some experts argue that certain forms of mental "illness" are, in fact, merely convenient labels for those of whom soci-

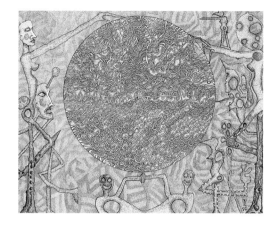

Many people who are mentally ill find it possible to express visually the complex nature of their illness, as in this painting, People Trying to Reach Me, *by David Chick.*

ety disapproves. The school known as antipsychiatry, which includes the Scottish psychiatrist R. D. Laing and the American Thomas Szasz, claims that the diagnosis of schizophrenia is far too imprecise, and that many people diagnosed as schizophrenic were really suffering what Szasz called "problems in living" and Laing called "the family nexus". In his book *Cruel Compassion* (1994) Szasz claims that, far from being helped by being diagnosed as sick, "patients" were made worse.

Arguments like these are less influential now than they were in the 1960s and 1970s, both because of the work been done to refine the diagnosis of schizophrenia and the biochemical advances in understanding the condition. But curiously, the more we understand about the biochemistry of the brain, the harder it is to maintain a crude biological position. For years, there were bitter debates between those claiming that mental illness was genetic, and critics who argued that breakdown was a result of social and emotional deprivation. Perhaps it is part of the maturing of psychology and psychiatry that the zealots are admitting that even the most biologically-susceptible person is unlikely to have a schizophrenic episode unless it is triggered by stress.

Schizophrenia

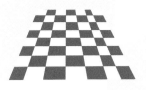

As late as the 19th century, visions and voices that some people experienced were believed to have prophetic meaning. It was only with the advent of Western empirical psychological investigation that they came to be seen in a different light. In 1897, the eminent German psychiatrist Emil Kraepelin described the mental disorder schizophrenia (from the Greek words for "split mind") as one in which the sufferer experienced hallucinations and a sense of being controlled by "alien forces", often accompanied by withdrawal and lack of emotion. Kraepelin believed schizophrenia to be an organic disorder, caused by detectable changes in the structure of the brain, and interpreted visions and voices as "the mangled garbage of a sick mind".

Today, definitions of schizophrenia are less clear cut. In the 1960s, radical psychologists, such as the Scottish psychiatrist R. D. Laing, questioned orthodox perceptions of the illness. Laing pointed out that almost any form of behaviour could be taken as a symptom of schizophrenia, allowing psychiatrists to give a medical label to individuals who refused to conform to the expectations of their family or society. He observed: " ... psychiatrists do often diagnose people as psychotics who don't seem to me to have anything intrinsically the matter with them. In that case the diagnosis comes to be like the positioning of someone on a social chessboard." He also analyzed the messages that some schizophrenics heard, concluding that far from being "mangled garbage", they reflected real traumas in the lives of the sufferers. Recently,

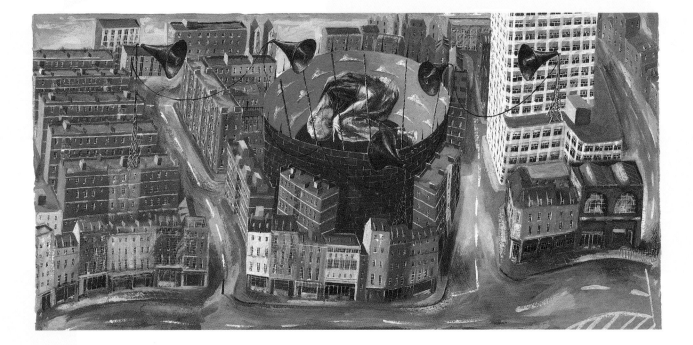

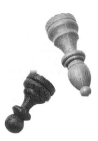

work at the University of Leiden in the Netherlands has concentrated on teaching patients how to listen to these voices – a development that would have astonished Kraepelin.

Schizophrenia is one of the most feared and misunderstood of all mental disorders, affecting up to 250 million people worldwide. Despite popular belief, it has little to do with "split personality". Psychiatrists have identified the "first rank" symptoms of schizophrenia, which include sufferers feeling that they are out of control of their minds, generally seeing visions and hearing voices – this is the typical layperson's impression of "madness". Schizophrenics become disordered and illogical in their thinking, and they also become very withdrawn and have difficulty communicating. If patients do not have these symptoms then, by definition, they have some other form of mental illness. Some withdraw to the point of becoming catatonic, but it is wrong to believe that all schizophrenics enter this state. Many of the misconceptions about the disorder come from inconsistencies in its diagnosis: this problem is being addressed by the World Health Organization, which since 1979 has been running a project to ensure that psychiatrists around the world follow uniform criteria when they apply the diagnosis.

Schizophrenia fascinates psychiatrists, psychologists and neuroscientists because the thoughts and feelings of sufferers are so extraordinary. The disease is frequently accompanied by paranoia and delusions: patients can think that they are

COLD WAR MEDICINE
The Soviet government used to apply diagnoses of schizophrenia in order to remove political dissidents from the public eye. Soviet doctors devised a bizarre rationale, saying that their patients suffered from "sluggish schizophrenia and that their decision to fight against the injustices of a totalitarian regime was one of the symptoms of the illness. It did not take much to be diagnosed – all one man did was to run on stage during a concert, grab a cello and yell, "Long live Reagan!"

God, Robert de Niro or the Queen of Sheba. Some may experience extremely bizarre hallucinations – for example, one sufferer believed that the golf scores in the British Open were coded messages for him, coming directly from God. And sometimes the messages that sufferers "receive" urge them to violence, and sometimes to murder. Such cases are exceptional, but help to promote widespread public fear of the disease.

Many schizophrenics are not permanently "out of their minds", and many have calm, lucid episodes in which they can relate to others what the crippling condition feels like. Typical is the case of an American woman who describes "the people inside my head who sometimes come out to haunt and torment me". She is unable to shake off these "people", who always surround her, making her life a fearful nightmare.

Research on the neurological and biochemical aspects of schizophrenia in the United States, Japan, Germany and the United Kingdom has revealed several structural abnormalities in the brains of schizophrenics. Some, but far from all, have much larger ventricles – areas in the prefrontal cortex of the brain. In about 15 per cent of sufferers, these areas are atrophied (literally dead), and PET scans (see page 183), which can produce pictures of brain function, show that many schizophrenics have low activity levels in the prefrontal cortex.

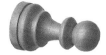

Ironically, while some areas of the schizophrenic brain may be dead, in other ways the sufferer's brain is overactive. Most schizophrenics appear to have an excess of dopamine in the brain. This neuro-transmitter smooths the passage of messages from cell to cell, but if dopamine is present in excess, the cells become "overlubricated" and relay inappropriate messages.

This theory fits the chaotic way in which schizophrenic patients think, but raises the question of why dopamine levels are elevated in the first place. Is it heredity or the product of a disturbed home environment? Although schizophrenia undoubtedly runs in families (relatives of a schizophrenic are ten times more likely to develop the illness than the average person), many psychiatrists now accept that stress also has an effect. A patient may be fine until something in the family environment goes wrong, causing stress, which then triggers a new episode of schizophrenia. Obviously, families with a schizophrenic member are likely to become more disturbed and stressed, creating a spiral of cause and effect that makes it difficult to identify the root cause of the illness.

In addition to the family connection, studies around the

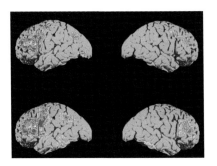

These PET scans (see page 183) compare brain activity during speech in a normal person (above) and a schizophrenic (below): the schizophrenic's brain is much more active.

world have noticed that schizophrenia is far more prevalent in the lower classes than it is in the upper or middle classes, and that the highest incidence of schizophrenia is among the urban poor. There are two possible explana-tions. One is that the predisposition for schizophrenia is evenly distributed across the population, but that greater environmental stress due to socioeco-nomic circumstances causes a higher incidence of the disease in a particular social stratum. An alternative explana-tion suggests that people who suffer from schizophrenia have difficulties in school and in work and therefore drift downward in society. It seems likely that both theories are true.

Today, it is possible to use our increasing knowledge of the role of dopamine in the brain to design drugs that are effective in suppressing hallucinations in schizophrenics. Drugs such as haloperidol and depixol block the dopamine receptors, and with less dopamine awash, schizophrenic patients appear to calm down. Their thoughts do not flash uncontrollably from cell to cell, and they stop hearing voices. However, like all drugs, these have side-effects. They can produce involuntary movements and twitches in the body; and many patients have

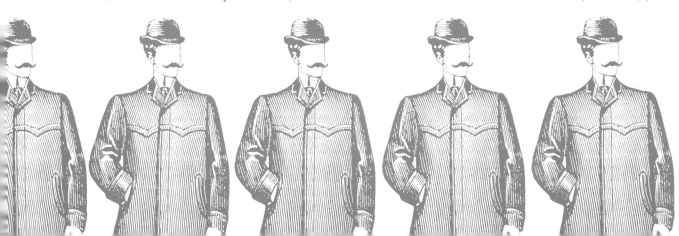

complained that the drugs make them feel like zombies, because of the tranquillizing effect. Often schizophrenics discontinue their medicine because they find the side-effects so distressing. When this happens, the result is a paradox. To suffer from schizophrenia is not to be in control of yourself, not to be normal. The drugs suppress these symptoms, but they leave patients feeling that, having been doped into quietude, they are no longer themselves: they feel that they have been robbed of their minds.

Over the last 20 years, the treatment of schizophrenics has changed as many Western countries have closed psychiatric wards, in response both to budgetary concerns and to reformers who have claimed that long-term institutionalization was counterproductive, making patients helpless and dependent. Because schizophrenia can be effectively controlled by drugs, and because in many patients the symptoms are either mild or not constant, manifesting themselves only during psychotic episodes, some schizophrenics are able to function in the "outside world".

However, although many schizophrenics have been released into the community, it is unclear whether this has been beneficial for all: it has been estimated that more than one-third of the people who live in homeless shelters in New York City are mentally ill, as is a high proportion of the prison population. For some, the return home presents just the sort of environmental stress that provokes episodes of the disease; still others have no homes to which they can return. Others still, as we have seen, find it difficult to remain on their med-

ication. There is also a risk that schizophrenics will commit violent acts, and this has led to demands for more supervision once sufferers have been released. However, forensic psychiatrists, who specialize in the treatment of people with criminal tendencies, argue that schizophrenics are no more violent than any other group of mentally-ill people, and that it is extremely difficult to predict which individuals will commit acts of violence. It is unfortunate that provisions for community care have not met the targets that were established when the strategy of deinstitutionalization was adopted.

Depression and Mania

It is estimated that one in nine men and one in six women will become clinically depressed at some time in their lives. To be clinically depressed is more than just being sad as a result of life's knocks. Indeed, it is a normal reaction to feel "down" if you lose your job, get divorced or suffer a bereavement. Most people recover from such traumas within a few months, but in cases where recovery is extremely slow, or the despair experienced is extreme, clinical depression may be diagnosed. Its classic symptoms include feelings of dejection and low self-esteem, and a loss of interest in work, leisure and relationships. Sufferers find it difficult to feel motivated, and the consequent lack of achievement in their lives merely reinforces their feelings of inadequacy, trapping them in a downward spiral. Even getting out of bed can become impossible. Other symptoms include loss of appetite and sex drive, early waking and fatigue; and because depression causes one's thoughts to turn inward, trivial ailments may become exaggerated, contributing to the subject's symptoms. For a minority of sufferers, depression is a chronic problem, but most depressive episodes last no more than six months, and they have a less than 50 per cent chance of recurring.

The roots of depression have been

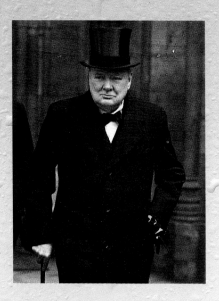

Depression is debilitating, but it need not be crippling. The great British statesman Sir Winston Churchill was a depressive, describing his moods of despair as his "black dog".

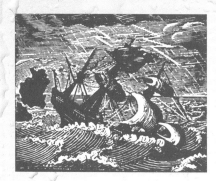

studied from ancient Greek times onwards. In one of the most comprehensive accounts, the *Anatomy of Melancholy* (1621), the English clergyman Robert Burton proposed a number of factors, sometimes bizarre, that can provoke melancholy – bereavement, immoderate passions, bad air, gambling and too much food, among others. He made some sharp points. For example, he considered that not all people are equally susceptible to depression: "That which is but a flea biting to one causeth insufferable torment to another." And he reported that someone who has a basic "moderation" (who is what today we would call well-adjusted) can sustain many setbacks, while "a second is no whit able to sustain, but upon every small occasion of misconceived abuse, injury, grief, disgrace, loss, cross rumours yields so far to passion that his complexion is altered, his digestion hindered, his sleep gone, his spirits obscured, his heart heavy."

Psychologists now know that individuals have different susceptibilities to depression, and that their susceptibility depends in part on their "stability". Burton's catalogue of the causes of depression seems improbable, but we are not much closer today to understanding what triggers depression, or even whether all depressions are of the same type. In the 1950s, the success of drugs such as imipramine (which works directly on the central nervous system) in treating some depressives led theorists to recognize two distinct types – endogenous and reactive. Endogenous depression did not appear to have been triggered by external events and responded well to drug therapy: it was therefore assumed to be biochemical in origin. In contrast, reactive depression was a reaction to life problems such as poverty, divorce, bereavement or other woes. Many psychiatrists now consider this divide to be simplistic because it is so difficult to disentangle psychological and physical causes.

The biological component to depression is still poorly understood. It appears that the condition is associated with decreased levels of the neurotransmitters noradrenalin (norepinephrine) and serotonin in the brain, and most anti-depressant drugs work by stimulating this complex neurotransmitter system. However, it is difficult to say whether it is the chemical changes that cause the psychological distress of depression or the psychological distress that triggers changes in brain chemistry: this is why many psychologists argue that, in looking for the true cause of depression, it is unwise to focus on neurons at the expense of neuroses.

There is also a debate over the relative roles of genetics and social influence. Take the case of someone for whom the psychological causes of depression are clear: he was neglected by his parents and suffers from feelings of rejection. Did his parents pass on to him a poor genetic inheritance? And did they themselves inherit traits that made them poor parents? Or was his childhood experience the sole cause?

PROZAC

Sometimes referred to as the miracle drug of the 1990s, Prozac (fluoxetine) has been widely prescribed for depression. It has a reputation as a "happy" drug, improving mood with very few side-effects – and one of the side effects is weight loss, which many people actually consider a benefit. Prozac also increases the concentrations of serotonin and noradrenalin (norepinephrine), but in an indirect way. It begins to work after about three weeks, a shorter timelag than with conventional antidepressants. Although it may have fewer side effects, around 10 per cent of patients in early trials did suffer from anxiety. Prozac has also been found to be effective in people who suffer from obsessive-compulsive and panic disorders.

Psychoanalytic theory argues that a depressed person is really in mourning for an "internal object" – for example, the love of a parent or the mother's breast – lost during childhood. A trauma later in life reawakens the fear experienced during the first loss and the sufferer regresses into a state of helplessness – that is, depression.

Cognitive theories argue that depression is caused by faulty thinking rather than by a faulty brain. People believe themselves to be worthless, and blame misfortunes on their personal inadequacies, interpreting events in a uniformly negative light. These cognitive distortions reinforce their own lack of self-worth, and they become depressed.

Another theory, that of learned helplessness, was developed in the 1970s by American psychologist Martin Seligman from studies on animal behaviour. When animals find that no course of action they undertake will produce a positive pay-off – that is, if nothing that they do improves their situation – they become lethargic, passively accepting their fate. Similarly, when people are confronted by a negative situation that they cannot change, such as death of a loved one or being made unemployed – they become depressed. This theory has been used to explain why some individuals are predisposed to depression. The suggestion is that people who have had childhood experiences in which they failed to control their environments have "learned" to be helpless, thus developing the sort of "attributional styles" – the ways in which we explain events to ourselves – that will lead to depression. They will believe that negative events are always their own fault and that there is nothing they can do to change that; this explanatory style is characteristic of depressed people.

The cognitive explanations for depression have one essential shortcoming in common – it is the chicken and the egg question over again. That is, they beg the question whether the negative mental attitudes precede the depression, or the depression generates the negative attitudes.

Not surprisingly, the treatments available for depression reflect the theories of its origins: numerous therapies address its psychological causes (see page 160), and anti-depressant drugs can be successful in treating its biochemical effects. By alleviating some of the symptoms of depression chemically, therapists can often begin to treat the psychological causes more effectively. Another, controversial,

MANIC DEPRESSION

One of the most dramatic of all mental disorders is manic depression, or bipolar disorder, in which the sufferer experiences profound mood swings. In the manic state, he or she bubbles with energy and enthusiasm, makes ambitious plans and can often convince strangers that these plans are realistic. Manic patients can be very sociable, although they often lose touch with reality – for example, going on profligate spending sprees with their credit cards. Some claim that mania unleashes reservoirs of creativity, indeed that it is a prerequisite of what we call "genius". The "up" mood can last several weeks, but is nearly always followed by a rapid down-swing into a depression that may be more severe than ordinary depression. During this phase, there is a high risk of suicide attempts in some patients. The disorder can, to some extent, be controlled by drugs, although patients may mourn the loss of their vibrant "other" personality. The drugs also have many physical side-effects, and may cause kidney damage in the long term.

treatment for depression is electroconvulsive therapy (ECT; see page 142) in which an electrical current is passed through the brain via electrodes on the scalp, causing the patient to go into a type of spasm. No one really knows why ECT works, but it can be effective. Improvements are reported in 70 per cent of patients, and many psychiatrists claim that ECT is sometimes the only effective treatment for severely depressed individuals who do not respond to drug therapy. However, it has extreme side-effects, including long-term memory loss.

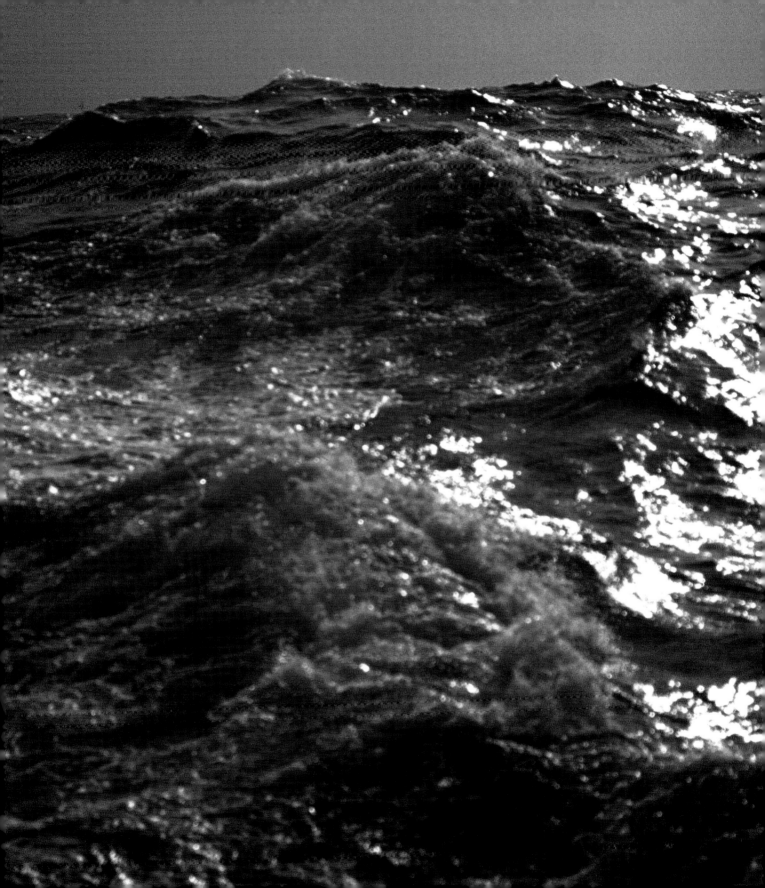

Phobias and Anxieties

We all suffer from anxiety at certain times. Stress – a feeling of tension and worry – is often accompanied by physical symptoms such as sleep loss, headaches and a racing heart. There is a difference, however, between normal anxiety in response to a real or perceived threat and what Freud called neurotic anxiety, which may not be tied to a specific source of stimulus, or is out of proportion to the stressful stimulus. Such anxiety can be extremely disruptive, intruding into almost every waking moment. In some cases it may become a panic attack, in which sufferers experience severe physical distress including nausea, palpitations and breathlessness to the extent that they believe themselves about to die. While in some individuals the irrational anxiety is "free-floating" (liable to surface at any time in any situation), in others it is provoked by specific situations.

One particular form of anxiety tied to specific stimuli are phobias. These fascinate psychiatrists and psychologists partly because, although there are common phobias such as claustrophobia (fear of enclosed spaces) and arachnophobia (fear of spiders), many are highly individual. One psychologist, for example, told me of a client who was phobic about using a toilet outside his own home.

Phobias can be crippling. Perhaps the most common of these is agoraphobia, fear of open spaces. This can be induced by very different kinds of spaces, from supermarkets and streets to open fields. In extreme cases, the agoraphobic can become a virtual prisoner in his or her own home. Other phobias are inconvenient: an arachnophobic can hold down a job and keep his or her marriage in good shape despite an irrational fear of spiders. However, any phobia can start to interfere with daily life – if,

for example, the arachnophobic were to become frightened of corners, because he or she knows that spiders can often be found lurking in them.

There have been a number of attempts to explain the causes of phobias. The two classic explanations are based on the psychodynamic theories of Sigmund Freud (see page 40) and the learning theory (see pages 20, 30). Freud argued that phobias result from the repression of fear in the unconscious, and its subsequent symbolization. A real fear, experienced early in life, may be taboo, or too terrifying to come to terms with, so it becomes attached to an apparently trivial stimulus. One of Freud's early case histories – that of Little Hans, a five-year-old boy who would not leave his house for fear that he would be bitten by a horse – is the classic illustration of this theory. According to Freud, Little Hans was not really afraid of horses: he was afraid of castration. This fear was rooted in

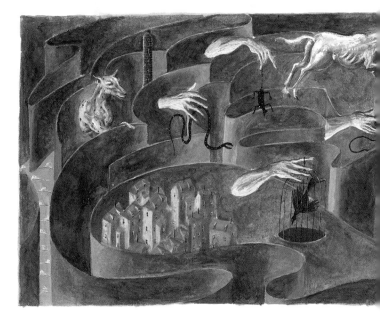

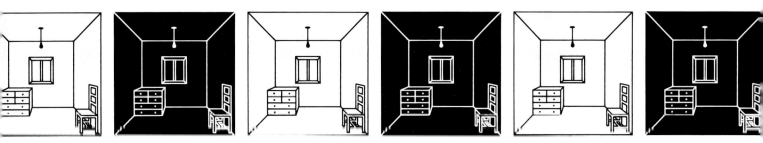

"Oedipal" conflict – Hans' unconscious desire for his mother and jealousy of his father. Hans (again unconsciously) feared that he would be punished for those forbidden feelings by castration; and having noticed in the street a horse with a particularly large phallus, Hans shifted his fear of castration on to the innocent animal.

The second main approach to understanding phobias comes from learning theory. This argues that phobias are the product of association produced by classical conditioning (see page 30). The key experiment is the much discussed "Little Albert" experiment carried out by the founder of behaviourism, John B. Watson, and his wife. Watson banged a steel bar behind Little Albert's head while the infant was looking at a rat. Little Albert cowered in terror at the loud noise. Because the noise had been presented together with the rat, Albert associated fear with the neutral stimulus – the

rat – and two years later became extremely agitated when shown a rat. Watson wrote: "... the instant the rat was shown, the baby began to cry. Almost instantly he turned sharply to the left, fell over, raised himself on all fours and began to crawl away so rapidly that he was caught with difficulty before he reached the edge of the mattress." (Historians of psychology have raised some doubts about the details of the Little Albert experiment, but its basic points stand.)

Neither Freud nor learning theory, however, can explain all the facts about phobias. Why is it that phobias of flowers and armchairs are rare, while spiders, heights and the dark are often the basis of irrational fears? Conditioning would predict that phobias should develop equally for any neutral object. Some experts have argued that we are biologically predisposed to fear objects and animals that could pose a real threat – this makes it easier to condition fear of these things. Others point to studies that suggest that we learn our fears and phobias by observing the fears and phobias of others, especially our parents.

While there are many disputes about causes, there exist well-tried ways of curing phobias through desensitization and behaviour therapy. The essential element in each is relaxation. While in a relaxed state, the subject imagines, step by step, the stimuli that create the fear and panic. So, for example, someone who is terrified of travelling in an elevator may first be asked to imagine themselves in a long corridor at the end of which there is an elevator door. They are then asked to imagine approaching the door, opening it and entering the elevator, letting the door close, and finally going up a floor. The idea is simple: for most, but not all, people, the physical relaxation and the gradual mental conquest of what is most feared eradicates the learned associations between the stimulus and the fear.

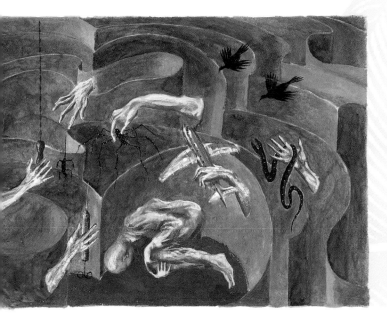

Ageing and Dementia

Between our late teens and early 80s, we lose up to eight per cent of our brain weight. But this does not translate directly into a loss of "brain power", because as we age, the interconnections between our neurons continue to increase in number and complexity (as long as we remain mentally active), and experience compensates for speed. Brain processes do slow down with age, however. Signals sent from one part of the brain to another are weaker, and there is more interference from "noise" generated by the spontaneous firing of neurons, so the signals will take longer to "register" at their destinations.

In many people, ageing is often accompanied by the deterioration of short-term memory and of the efficiency of its conversion into long-term memory. As well as making people more forgetful, this means that tasks that require material to be "held in mind", such as mental arithmetic, may become more difficult.

These normal effects of ageing, however, are very different from senile dementia. In the popular definition of the word, to be demented is literally to be out of one's mind, but in psychiatry the word dementia has a more precise meaning. Until the 1940s, dementia praecox (precocious dementia) was the term for what we now call schizophrenia; but today dementia is used to describe the organic deterioration of the brain that affects the elderly. The main, but not sole, form of dementia is Alzheimer's disease, and 25 per cent of people who live to be older than 85 will show some symptoms. Understandably, fear of the disease is growing as life expectancy in the West continues to increase.

The early effects of Alzheimer's include simple loss of memory, but the symptoms can get much worse, affecting both personality and intellect. Sufferers often lose their ability to write and speak – postmortem examinations show that the language areas of the brain are frequently badly affected – and have psychological problems. As far back as 1948, the neurologist Kurt Goldstein described the "catastrophic reaction" of profoundly demented people. Unaware of the true nature of the decline of their mental faculties, dementia

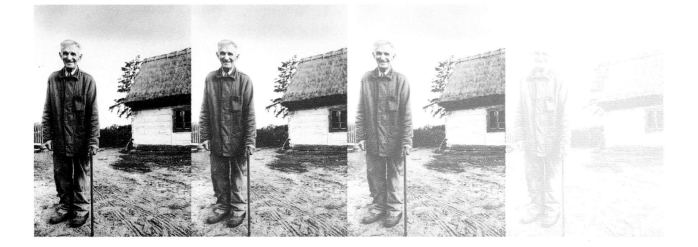

sufferers realize that they cannot respond to the demands of everyday life, and may react by crying uncontrollably, or becoming angry or restless. Some patients manage to keep up appearances of normality, but many become violent or sexually embarrassing, losing the inhibitions that held these urges in check earlier in life.

The underlying neurology of Alzheimer's has been known for about 20 years. Nerve cells in the brain die, and once they die they are never replaced (see page 29). In Alzheimer's, the dead nerve cells are converted into structures called plaques and neurofibrillary tangles, in which the dead cells coalesce into webs of material that interfere with the proper functioning of the surviving brain cells. This pattern of degeneration is variable: in some sufferers it is localized, causing only one particularly severe symptom; in others it is widespread, causing a more general deterioration.

Although Alzheimer's is organic rather than psychological in origin, and in the majority of cases is inexorable in its progress, there is evidence that stress can make it worse. However, there are strategies that can help, at least in the early stages of the disease. Faced with the deterioration of his memory owing to Alzheimer's disease when he was in his 70s, the prominent psychologist Donald Hebb set little "traps" for himself so that he could not step outside his own front door without finding a message reminding him to perform some act or other. Hebb believed that by using such tricks he could "outsmart" the disease, keeping it at bay even though his brain was degenerating.

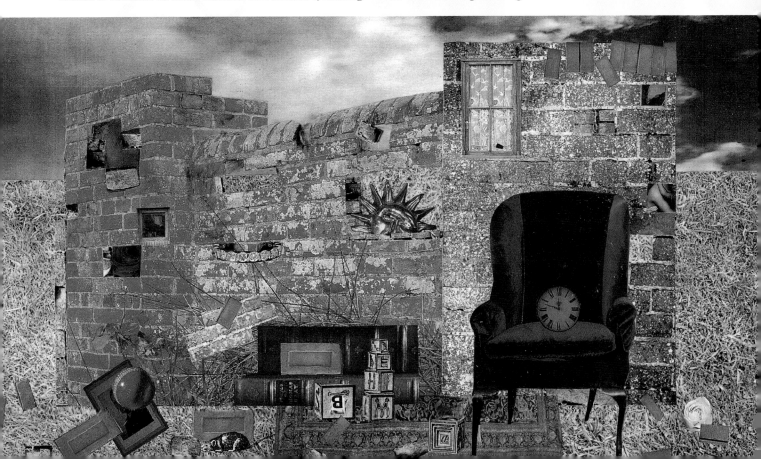

Mind and Environment

For centuries, it has been maintained that the moon can have a profound effect on human behaviour. There has been much theorizing about the coincidence between the 28-day menstrual cycle in women and the 28-day cycle of the moon. Men, too, have been supposedly affected by the phases of the moon, which have been thought to cause outbreaks of violence – the root of the werewolf legend. A correspondence has also been proposed between lunar phases and depression.

Other natural cycles also affect the human condition. In the 5th century BC, Hippocrates saw that people suffered from agues and fierce sweats – maladies associated with anxiety – in the summer. Current statistics show that people are more likely to become violent in the summer and depressed in the autumn or winter. Often the depression lifts as spring arrives – this is known as seasonal affective disorder, or, appropriately, SAD, for short.

Some psychologists believe that SAD is caused by tampering with the natural body clock, known as the circadian rhythm, which closely follows the patterns of day and night. It controls a number of physiological changes in the body, including variations in some hormone levels and in body temperature. Interestingly, if subjects are deprived of all the normal external stimuli that would help them to determine the time of day or night – such as sunlight or clocks or regularly scheduled events – and are allowed to create their own timetables, they tend to exist on a 25-hour clock, rather than the usual 24-hour one.

SAD is triggered by exposure to less light: as the days become shorter in the autumn, the depression begins, often accompanied by disturbed sleep patterns. Although found in many countries, SAD is more common in Alaska, Norway, Siberia and Finland, the lands of the midnight sun. Episodes tend to be short: only rarely do they last more than three days. In a few sufferers, however, the depression can last from late autumn to early spring. There also seems to be a relationship between SAD and suicide: although suicide statistics are notoriously unreliable, some experts claim that there are more suicides in winter.

There is a relatively simple explanation for SAD: our evolution has made us enormously sensitive to light. We are largely ruled by the pattern of day and night as our ancestors were: individuals in conditions of sensory deprivation desperately try to keep track of whether it is day or night, and if they are unable to do so, they become confused and distressed. SAD seems to be related to the lack of natural light in the winter months. Therefore, there is a relatively simple treatment. The deluxe therapy is to head for warmer, sunnier climes. Far more practical is the use of artificial light, either ordinary lightbulbs or in some cases ultraviolet lamps however, exposure to ultraviolet light carries its own risks): this often begins to lift the depression within 72 hours. Although the external stimulus for SAD and a reasonably effective treatment are both known, the biochemical mechanism remains a mystery. It is also unclear why certain individuals are more vulnerable than others.

Appetite and Exercise

Contemporary experts talk as if they had discovered the psychological benefits of exercise, but the relation between body and mind has been known for centuries. It is true that in the 1980s, exercise became an integral part of a fashionable lifestyle, and modern gurus preached its many therapeutic benefits. However, as with many other fads, there is a reverse side of the coin. Some commentators have noted the downside – an obsession with idealized body images – linking exercise and eating disorders, such as anorexia nervosa and bulimia, as well as other forms of uncontrolled eating.

Despite our modern obsession with weight, there is good evidence that we consume fewer calories than our 19th-century ancestors did, although we weigh more – our greater weight is certainly ironic, considering that to be fat was a status symbol in the 19th century. At the same time, however, Victorians took substantially more exercise in the normal course of a day than we do: they were not the car-bound couch potatoes that we have become.

Exercise does more than simply tone the muscles. Strenuous activity stimulates the release of both hormones and neurotransmitters such as adrenalin and endorphins. After completing 30 minutes of strenuous exercise, people rate their state of well-being higher than they did beforehand; controlled studies have shown that individuals who follow a three-month-long exercise program report feeling less depressed and having an improved sex drive. Some studies also claim that exercise can enhance cognitive performance. But there are limits – some people

pursue an idea of fitness too far, damaging their health by forcing the body to be too lean, with the same physiological effects as starvation causes.

Hunger is regulated by the brain as well as by the digestive system. The stomach, small intestine and liver all send messages to the brain about the amount of nutrients remaining to be used by the body; at the same time, the brain monitors the amount of fat stored in the body. This information is processed by the hypothalamus, which tries to maintain steady biochemical levels, particularly of glucose (which is needed to produce energy) and fat (which represents energy reserves). When either glucose or fat levels fall, the brain triggers hunger messages, whereas when these levels are adequate, hunger ceases. If fat stores fall below normal level, the body does all that it can to conserve them, slowing the metabolism and reducing non-essential functions: this is why, for example, the menstrual cycle often ceases in female athletes.

The body's self-regulatory mechanism can go wrong, however – as it does with eating disorders. In the case of obesity, it is not yet known whether internal or external factors, or a combination of the two, are the cause. Advocates of the "setpoint" theory support an internal hypothesis: they believe that the body has a set number of fat cells, determined either at birth or in infancy, and this number either remains constant or increases throughout life. Although it is possible to lose weight, by decreasing the size (rather than the number) of the fat cells, the brain will always want to trigger the body to return these fat cells to their normal size, which means that the weight will be put back on. Other scientists advocate a behavioural point of view, according to which obese people simply have different eating habits from people of normal weight: one theory says that obese people are more responsive to external appetite stimuli, such as the presence,

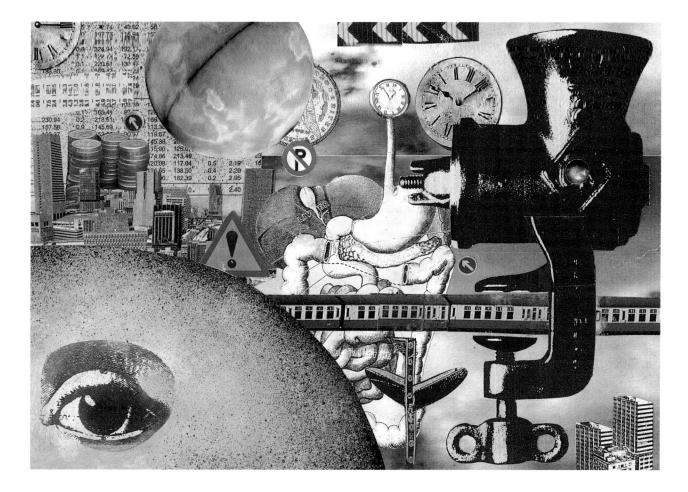

taste or aroma of food, while thinner people are more responsive to internal stimuli, such as levels of glucose.

Social pressure to be thin affects us all, and can be destructive. Fad dieting, which causes rapid weight loss, is dangerous to health, increasing the risk of a range of diseases, including cancer and heart disease. Teenage girls and young women are more vulnerable to the pressure to diet than anyone else, sometimes with destructive results, as in the case of two disorders in particular: anorexia nervosa, in which a person undereats, often to the point of starvation; and bulimia nervosa, which involves a constant cycle of binging (eating massive amounts of food), then purging by vomiting. The causes of these disorders are not known. Susie Orbach, in her book *Fat is a Feminist Issue* (1979), maintains that girls and women can use anorexia as a protest (almost certainly unconscious) against the sexual role that women are meant to play. Around 80 per cent of people with anorexia are hospitalized, and up to 30 per cent ultimately die from the disorder. Bulimia is even more insidious: because sufferers are generally of normal weight, it can be impossible to detect unless the sufferer actually seeks help.

Psychotherapy

Not even Freud's angriest critics would deny his influence – his ideas have changed the way in which we think of ourselves. Freud was deeply influenced by the ideas of the Enlightenment, an intellectual movement in 18th-century Europe – the celebration of reason, the pursuit of truth through objective inquiry – and the notion, nicely summarized by the American philosopher John Passmore, of the "perfectibility of man".

Freud's great legacy is psychoanalysis and, more broadly, psychotherapy – the treatment of mental disorders by psychological rather than by biological or chemical means. Therapy aims not merely to heal but to help you realize your true potential, to find the real you. In the words of therapist Carl Rogers: "In general the evidence shows that the process [of therapy] moves people away from fixity, remoteness from feelings and experience, rigidity of self-concept, remoteness from people, impersonality of functioning, and moves toward fluidity, changingness, immediacy of feelings and experience." D. W. Winnicott, the child psychiatrist and psycho-

analyst, gave a rather more whimsical description, suggesting that therapy consists of "two people playing with each other".

These two quotations underline the difficulty in defining psychotherapy: indeed, in 1978, a British Joint Working Party on the "caring" professions concluded that it was impossible to arrive at an acceptable definition. In 1973, J. D. Frank defined psychotherapy as a social influence exerted by a trained and sanctioned healer on someone who seeks help. Even this broad definition, however, is flawed, because many psychotherapists have only the most minimal training. In general, psychotherapy stresses the importance of emotional and social factors. In this it differs from the medical model, which sees psychological distress as an illness with physical and biological causes – too much dopamine causes schizophrenia; too little acetylcholine causes dementia. (In practice, however, few psychiatrists today maintain quite such an extreme position.) Also, the medical model emphasizes cure rather than change. Its aim is to dispose of distressing symptoms rather than to help patients to be more themselves, or to find their "authentic I".

Today, therapy is a major industry. There are no accurate figures on how many therapists work, for example, in the United Kingdom, because one does not need any formal qualification to practise legally, but best estimates point to a figure of over 50,000. In the United States, there are many more. There are also many different schools of therapy, ranging from the totally respectable to the scarcely credible, so that it would be impossible to give an exhaustive list.

Most schools of psychotherapy, however, stress either a historical approach, as did Freud, who claimed that understanding the truth about the past would relieve problems in the present; or a here-and-now approach, in which the

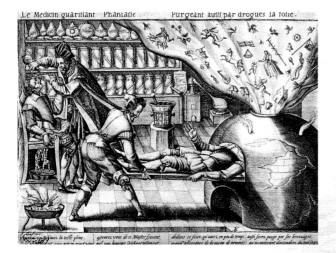

Le Medicin guarissant Phantasie.   Purgeant auffi par drogues la folie.

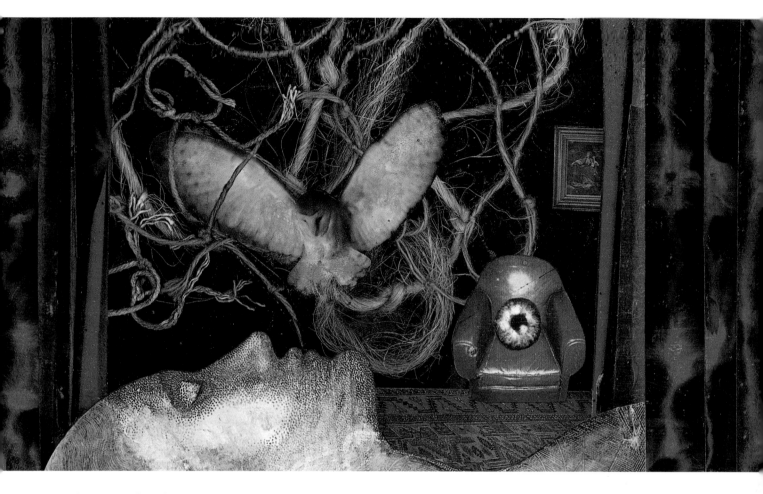

emphasis is on the information that the client presents at the time of therapy as the basis for diagnosis and treatment, rather than looking to the past. The techniques of some of the most important schools are outlined below.

Psychoanalytic therapy is based on Freud's conviction that most neuroses and emotional problems derive from motives and anxieties repressed in the unconscious during childhood. The therapist aims to help the client to understand what can be done in the present to correct the damage done in the past. Insight and introspection are essential to elicit a cure.

Behaviour therapy does not believe in insight, concentrating instead on treating behaviour through the techniques of conditioning championed by psychologists such as Watson and Skinner (see page 30). It is very effective in treating anxieties and phobias such as agoraphobia and fear of flying. In effect, the therapist helps the client to learn a desirable behaviour, or unlearn an undesirable one.

Cognitive behaviour therapy was developed by Aaron Beck for use particularly with depressed patients. Beck claimed that thinking and reasoning processes affect behaviour, and wrote: "An

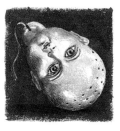

individual's affect and behaviour are largely determined by the way in which he structures the world." By pointing out distortion and inconsistency in thinking, the therapist teaches patients to take a different view of themselves and their experiences.

Rational emotive therapy, founded by Albert Ellis, is somewhat similar to cognitive behaviour therapy in that it claims that an individual's faulty thoughts and ideas lead to dysfunctional behaviour. Ellis suggests that there are three

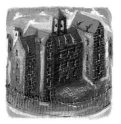

particularly destructive kinds of irrational belief. These are: "I must be competent in everything and approved by everyone"; "Others must treat me properly and when they don't they are worthless"; and "I must have everything I need easily and immediately." The therapist attempts to introduce the patient to a more rational and attainable set of beliefs.

Gestalt therapy, founded by Fritz Perls, stresses the need to help patients to become self-supportive and responsible for themselves by becoming aware

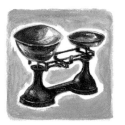

of their whole personalities (*Gestalt* is the German word for "whole"). Perls did not believe in delving into the past. Instead the Gestalt therapist emphasizes awareness of the here-and-now, paying attention to non-verbal

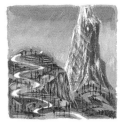

behaviour. Patients are encouraged to take the hot seat and to act out the roles that they perceive others may be playing in their lives, as well as suppressed aspects of their own personalities.

Client-centred therapy was founded by Carl Rogers, who spent years dealing with problem families in Rochester, New York. Rogers argued that there was no need for the therapist to remain the mysterious figure that he was in analysis. Instead, he should give "unconditional personal regard" to his clients (it was Rogers who started the fashion of calling people "clients" rather than "patients"), which meant accepting them and all their faults. This acceptance would allow the client to develop a sense of confidence and worth, and would help him or her to confront negative feelings about themselves – the key to any progress. Rogers had a remarkably positive personal presence and considerable influence, but his methods have been criticized as being too naive and optimistic. He also pioneered studies that looked at the effectiveness of psychotherapy. His daughter Natalie started a related school called person expressive therapy.

Humanistic therapy, founded by Abraham Maslow, whose ideas became popular in the 1960s, argued that once people had satisfied their needs for food, shelter and sex, they needed new goals – goals of self-actualization, of becoming complete. Unlike many other forms of therapy, humanistic therapy does not try to interpret or alter a client's behaviour, but merely attempts to clar-

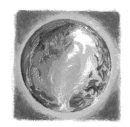

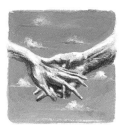

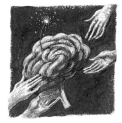

ify his or her feelings and emotions. Its aim is to achieve "peak experiences" – moments of intense joy and insight that are seen as steps on the path to self-actualization. Maslow was a highly influential cultural commentator, and he inspired many different schools of therapy in his time.

Transactional analysis was founded by Eric Berne. Life is a series of social transactions, Berne argued, and these often go wrong because of lies and subterfuge. By analyzing our behaviour in terms of three aspects of our personality – termed the parent, adult and child – the truth behind our oppressive and destructive social interactions is revealed.

Confrontational therapy was founded by Frank Farrelly. The belief here is that too much therapy mollycoddles the patient, who should be made to face the truly inadequate nature of his or her being. So if someone comes in claiming that his wife does not love him, the therapist should point out that the patient's behaviour is so selfish and obnoxious that it is hardly surprising.

Psychodrama techniques were pioneered by Jacob Moreno, who used to get his patients to act out situations that troubled them. Often these were encounters with parents and

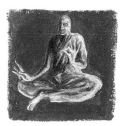

loved ones. Patients were encouraged to gain insight into their dilemmas by taking one of these roles, so that they could see how they behaved from the perspectives of others.

Research into different forms of therapy shows clearly that the personality of the therapist, and the degree of rapport with the client, are at least as important as the choice of particular therapeutic technique used. Some notable critics of therapy, such as the British psychologist Hans Eysenck, have questioned whether therapy has any value at all. In 1952, Eysenck challenged the psychotherapeutic movement by suggesting that its "successes" would have occurred even without the intervention of therapists – in other words, that most neurotic conditions will resolve themselves spontaneously. To prove or disprove Eysenck's assertion, however, is not so simple, because any assessment of the success of therapy requires agreement on a number of points. First, what is the purpose of therapy? Is it to allow people to be functional – able, as in Freud's famous phrase, to love and to work – or is it to get them to develop to their full potential and allow them to feel happier within themselves? Second, who is to judge whether improvements have been made – the subjects themselves, the subjects' partner or close family, or the therapist? Nevertheless, a number of credible studies that take account of these variables have confirmed that psychotherapy is clearly more effective than no treatment at all for a number of different conditions.

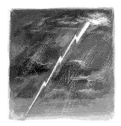

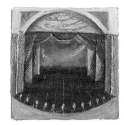

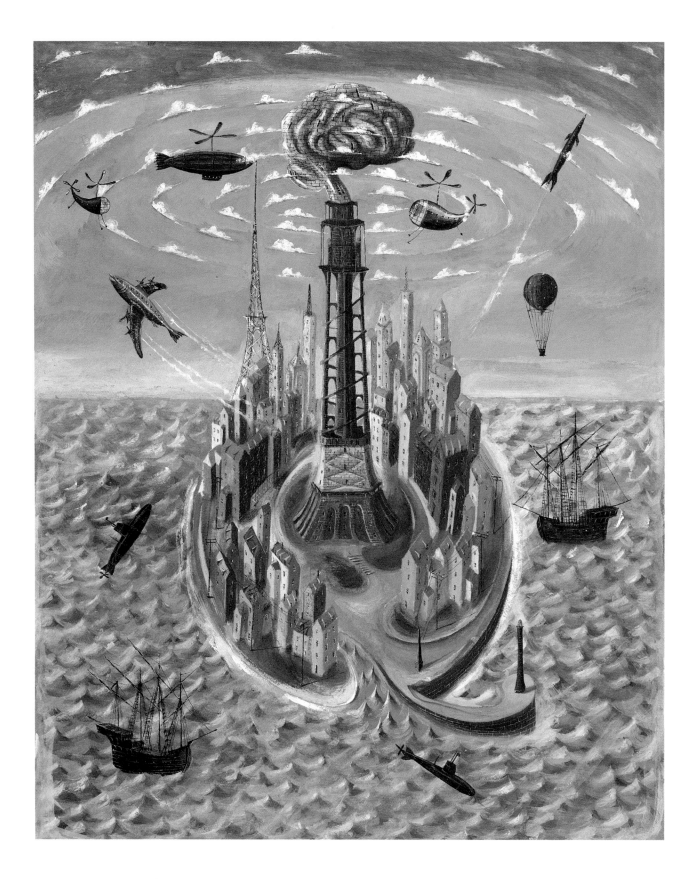

The Ascent of the Mind

At first glance, the colour-ful shape at the centre of this page appears to be nothing more than an amorphous inkblot. But a longer look is likely to reveal patterns, shapes and faces that were previously undetected – forms that we ourselves project onto the design. Such blots are the basis of a psychological test devised by the Swiss psy-chiatrist Hermann Rorschach in 1922. Rorschach asked patients to look at 10 such patterns and allow their minds to make associations, which he believed would reveal the patient's needs, problems and overall personality. There are still many debates about whether or not the Rorschach test measures anything at all, but what is significant is that any normal person can understand the nature of the test. It comes easily to us because, in everyday life, we are constantly searching for associations or links between one idea or object and another. We naturally invest stimuli with many layers of meaning.

Humans seem to be unique in this respect, for although a rat, chimpanzee or dolphin can be taught (or, more accu-rately, conditioned) to recognize a pattern and distinguish it from a triangle or square, most of us presume that such shapes do not trigger a chain of associations; others would argue that this line of thinking reveals human arrogance.

The human brain is often described, in language borrowed from computer science, as an information-processing device. This description conjures up images of a number-crunching machine driven by the laws of logic. Such an impression is misleading. A computer reduces every item to its logical components, making no distinction between a problem that, for example, involves counting apples and one that involves counting oranges, as long as the logical operation is the same in each case. It can only see "yes" and "no" or black and white: there is no "maybe" or shade of grey. Human reasoning, on the other hand, is profoundly influenced by the "content" of thought. To solve a problem we rely on inference, we build mental models and, as in the Rorschach test, we look for sim-ilarities with objects or situations that we have dealt with in the past. We look for theories to unite our experiences, to account for similarities and, more philosophically, to give our lives meaning. The way in which we think is based on this desire for extended meanings, and our creativity and intelli-gence are the tools that we use to find them.

Creativity and intelligence are the greatest accomplish-ments of our species. One cannot easily define the qualities that mark out a product of human endeavour as a work of genius. Nonetheless, psychologists have tried to define or quantify the nature of creativity and genius. Just as works of genius are products of their time, so the explanations of cre-ativity and intelligence put forward over the years have reflected prevailing cultural and political concerns and have aroused intense feelings. To this day the study of these higher thought processes continues to be surrounded as much by controversy as mystery.

Intelligence

It is probably not very smart to attempt a definition of intelligence. The word has too many meanings and is used to describe too many different types of thinking. The cunning of a detective, the wisdom of a judge and the analytical powers of a scientist are undeniably all forms of intelligence. Moreover, different cultures identify widely divergent mental skills as intelligence: a tribesman's proficiency at tracking animals and a philosopher's dexterity with abstract concepts are regarded as pinnacles of intelligence in their own societies.

None of this, however, has prevented the psychologists from seeking an all-encompassing definition. As long ago as 1921, a respected psychological journal solicited the views of 14 eminent researchers in the field. Their definitions of intelligence had two common themes – the capacity to learn from experience, and the ability to adapt readily to new conditions and challenges. This assumes that the many different forms of intelligence alluded to above have only one or two foundations, and it also implies that these can be measured and therefore compared between individuals.

The analysis of intelligence cannot be divorced from the long and controversial history of intelligence measurement – what we now call the IQ test. For some, these tests provide a good predictive measure of educational and occupational success, but for others they have little value. The issue is neatly summarized in the words of Edwin Boring (1886–1968), professor of psychology at Harvard University, who, when asked to define intelligence, replied that it was "what intelligence tests measure".

Others still criticize IQ tests as being sexist, racist and, consciously or unconsciously, designed to favour white middle-class males. This is because IQ tests measure convergent thinking, which involves focusing in on one idea, because they ask questions that have only one correct answer. Con-

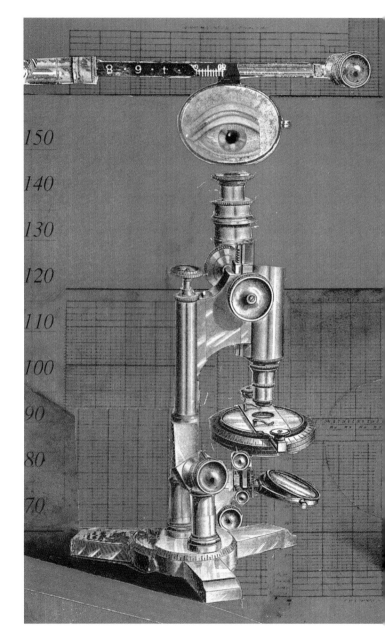

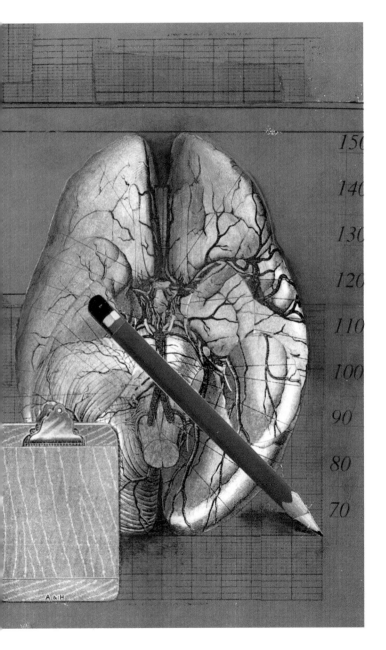

vergent thinking, in which men are sometimes said to be more skilled than women, is particularly prized in Western cultures, even though the solutions to many everyday problems are reached by different problem-solving strategies. For example, the question, "What is the best itinerary for a two-week tour of Greece?" allows for many answers. Some will be wrong – for example, spending 14 days in Athens and ignoring every other site – but many will be right, and the most appropriate solutions will take into consideration many highly varied factors. Critics say that IQ tests do not touch on that kind of thinking, even though it is more applicable to the skills developed in day-to-day life; and some extend their argument along Boring's lines, asserting that IQ tests and other standardized tests assess only the subject's aptitude for test-taking – this is why IQ tests do not accurately predict academic, personal or professional success.

In addition, the tests often assume, either explicitly or implicitly, a degree of general knowledge, which is inevitably culturally loaded. Consider this question: "The following words are all anagrams: LAID, GRITMETA, THERATCH, SITMASE, SAPISCO. All of them, except one, are famous artists. Name the one." The answer is THERATCH, which unravels into Thatcher: the others are Dali, Magritte, Matisse and Picasso. To be able to answer the question, one needs some basic knowledge of Western art history.

The first attempts at measuring intelligence were made in Victorian England by Sir Francis Galton, a brilliant, if eccentric, natural scientist. Following in the Darwinian tradition (Charles Darwin was his cousin), Galton believed that the ongoing evolution of our species could be understood according to the rules of natural selection, and duly set about quantifying human characteristics, both physical and mental, in a scientific analysis of human diversity. His belief was that this

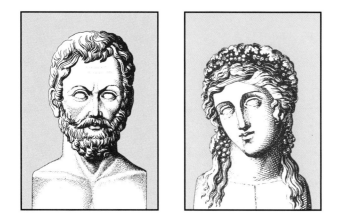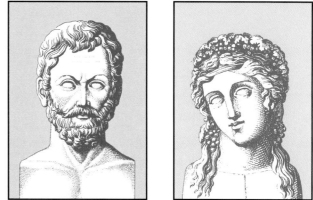

accumulated knowledge could one day be used to direct the course of human evolution – a theory that he called eugenics. Though now shocking, Galton's idea was not out of step with the climate of the time – the new status of science as the principal motor of human progress, and the desire to believe in the innate superiority of Indo-European races over others.

To measure intelligence, Galton used a number of simple psychophysical tests – including tests of speed of reaction to stimuli, and of sensitivity to stimuli applied to the skin. These tests have since been recognized as measures of sensory acuity rather than of intelligence, but some experts have built on Galton's ideas, arguing that intelligence is essentially quickness of mind. Intelligent individuals are simply able to process information more quickly.

After Galton, there was some very systematic work on the nature of intelligence, which was motivated more by practical social concerns than a desire to uncover a biological basis for intelligence. In 1904, the French psychologists Alfred Binet and Theodore Simon were commissioned by the Parisian educational authorities to devise a test that could distinguish between "normal" children who could be placed into ordinary schools and those who needed remedial help. The basis of the test was simple: Binet and Simon first determined what children at different ages could achieve over a range of different skills. They learned, for example, that a typical four-year-old could count to five and recognize letters of the alphabet and simple shapes, and argued that a ten-year-old unable to complete these tasks was probably not very intelligent, while a three-year-old able to do so was probably highly intelligent.

Binet and Simon emphatically rejected the notion of a fixed, innate intelligence independent of environmental influences: their test, which allowed a comparison between the "mental age" and chronological age of a child, was a useful diagnostic tool that could help teachers to remedy weaknesses in their pupils. But the testing method was soon appropriated by those of the deterministic Galtonian school. The concept of intelligence quotient (IQ) was introduced (the figure is calculated by dividing mental age by chronological age, and multiplying by 100), and has been used to measure the intelligence of children and, in an adapted form, adults ever since, although many psychologists are now moving toward testing systems that measure the degree to which an individual's score varies from the mean.

Many believed a person's IQ score to be genetically fixed – a label that remained constant throughout life – and this notion became enshrined in the laws of some countries. The "national origin quotas" of the 1924 US Immigration Act, for

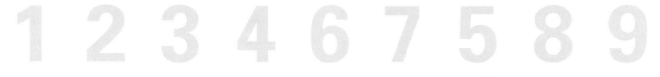

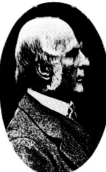

example, set limits to the numbers of "geneti-cally inferior" southern and eastern European immigrants admitted, while encouraging admis-sion of "superior" Nordic peoples (interestingly, later studies have found that the children of some of these "inferior" immigrants actually show slightly above-average scores on IQ tests).

Few psychologists today believe that intelligence is solely determined by genetics, admitting that environment and con-ditioning play a substantial role. Even biological determinists point out that IQ tests are poor predictors of success.

The nature-versus-nurture argument has had a troubled history and is yet to be satisfactorily resolved. Strong support for a genetic basis to intelligence came from the work of Cyril Burt, the chief educational psychologist in London from 1911. Burt measured the intelligence of 53 sets of identical twins who had been separated at an early age and reared apart. Burt found that the twins had almost perfectly identical IQ scores – at face value, conclusive proof that environment played no part in determining intelligence and that genetics was all that mattered. Nature, not nurture, was important. But reviews of Burt's work, such as *The Burt Controversy* (1995) by Norman Macintosh, argue that it is likely that Burt falsified some of his data. If this is true, all that his studies show with any degree of certainty is the highly-charged nature of the intelligence debate.

Since Burt, other investigations, including other twin stud-ies, have shown that there is a large hereditary component to intelligence, but many studies have also acknowledged an environmental effect. For example, studies that were part of Robert Plomin's Colorado Twin project in the 1980s, one of the most extensive psychological investigations into twins, have found that children of different biological parents reared

Sir Francis Galton (1822–1911) was a pioneer in the measurement of human intelligence. Endowed with an independent fortune and a keen mind, he devoted his life to scientific studies, including meteorology as well as psychology, but his primary interest was in discovering the relative roles of heredity and environmental factors in human development. In all his investigations, he emphasized quantitative studies, searching for measurable characteristics and statistically verifiable trends. While many of his studies led nowhere, some initiated forms of investigation still used today, such as the technique of free association.

in the same home tend to have closer IQ scores between the ages of seven and 14 than later in life. It is as if environmental influences are at their strongest during childhood and early adolescence, after which, on average, children revert to being closer to the score of their biological parents. In terms of brain structure, this suggests that certain neurological develop-ments that start around the age of seven are stalled or even reversed around the age of 14. This is just one illustration of the always complex relationship between nature and nurture in the matter of intelligence.

We know that our "brain power" depends in part on the intricacy of the connections between neurons, and that some of these connections are the product of experience – our exposure to the environment. In theory, therefore, it should be possible to boost these connections by appropriate condi-tioning or learning. John B. Watson (1878–1958), the founder of behaviourism, claimed that if he were given a child up to the age of seven, he could shape him or her in endless ways, conditioning him to act intelligently or like a perfect fool. For-tunately, perhaps, Watson never tested his claim, and he later qualified his bold statement. The degree to which our intelli-gence can be shaped by learning is still debatable.

Creativity and Genius

A survey of genius by Hans Eysenck, Emeritus Professor at the Institute of Psychiatry in London, examined the nature of creativity in the world of music. Among his findings was the fact that around 250 classical composers have their music played today, and half of all performances are accounted for by the work of just 16 composers. This figure underlines the common-sense observation that people who produce great and enduring works of art, or who make significant breakthroughs in science and philosophy, are few and far between. So what is it that separates the innovators from the journeymen? This question is often addressed by psychologists eager to unearth the seeds of creativity. But like the search for intelligence, their quest can be criticized on the grounds that there may be more than one, or more than a few, basic types of creativity that require very different types of analysis.

The Victorian polymath Sir Francis Galton (see page 169) argued that genius was a matter of heredity, and believed that the best families, sending their children to the best schools, were bound to produce the best, most creative brains. Galton's élitism (he used his own family tree as evidence) has been proved to be groundless. Genius does not run in families, but rather surfaces in the unlikeliest of places, or to paraphrase Shakespeare (whose own family was undistinguished), genius is not of genius born. This point was underscored by E. T. Bell in his book *Men of Mathematics.* Bell examined the family backgrounds of 28 of the world's greatest mathematicians and found little evidence of inherited ability. Fermat's father was a leather merchant; Pascal's was a minor civil servant who forbade his son to look at mathematics books; Gauss's father was a peasant; Monge's was a pedlar; and Srinivasa Ramanujan, widely acknowledged as one of the most intuitive mathematicians ever to have lived, came from peasant stock. You can breed champion racehorses, but it seems that you can't breed composers, writers, painters, scientists or mathematicians of genius.

Are creativity and genius simply aspects of intelligence? The answer again appears to be No. Psychologists who study creativity agree that one has to be reasonably clever to be a genius, but simply being clever is not enough. There are many thousands of people worldwide who have IQ scores of at least 150 but show little sign of creative thought: indeed, above a (relatively low) minimum score, there is little correlation between IQ and achievement. And many individuals now recognized as geniuses were only average academic achievers. Creativity, it would seem, relies on a different cognitive factor than does intelligence. In 1930, the psychologist Charles Spearman called this factor "fluency". Others have called it divergent thinking (which produces many varied ideas) in order to distinguish it from convergent thinking (see page 167), which is the type of thinking measured by conventional IQ tests.

A peculiar phenomenon known as incubation gives some clues to the characteristics of the creative process. When faced with a new problem, the creative individual typically

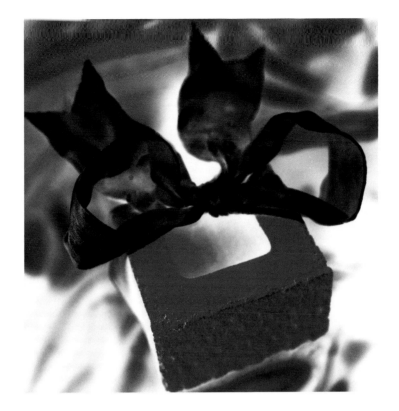

approaches it from a number of angles, but if a solution is not forthcoming, he or she temporarily shelves the problem. A surprising number of gifted people report that often this is when the solution emerges, as though it were incubating in their unconscious while they were daydreaming, playing cards or visiting friends. It has been suggested that other, apparently trivial, activities provide the creative mind with a fresh set of "retrieval cues" that trigger an entirely new approach to the problem – an approach that yields the correct solution. True geniuses are also marked out by their great motivation: unlike the majority of people, they do not rely on

the normal incentives, such as money or peer recognition: rather they find the work itself intrinsically rewarding. This is just as well, because the work of geniuses frequently subverts orthodox thinking, overturning established paradigms; and for this reason, a work of genius may be ignored or ridiculed by the intellectual establishment, and its achievement recognized and acclaimed only in hindsight.

There are a number of tests that purport to be able to detect the particular cognitive style of highly creative individuals. One of the best known, and most amusing, is the Uses of Objects test. The basic question is this: How many uses can

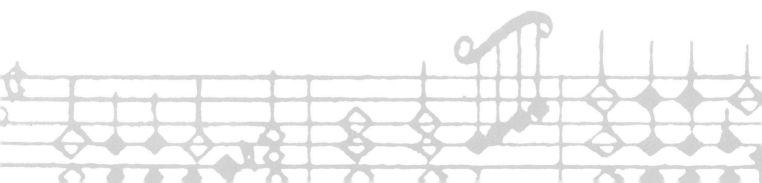

you think of for a brick? Highly creative individuals can think up more bizarre uses than building walls or houses – a brick may, for example, be the perfect missile to sling through the windows of the Research Council that has turned down your application for funding.

In another test, the Remote Associates Test, subjects have to solve riddles along the lines of: "What connects the words mice, wine and blue?" The theory is that the answer (cheese) can only be arrived at by divergent thinking.

But fluency alone is not enough to make a genius. The capacity to make new and unexpected associations is of limited value if one is at their mercy. The ability to discriminate, to know which associations to keep and pursue, and which to reject, is equally important, and it is this ability that differentiates the genius from the "madman".

Over 2,000 years ago, Aristotle observed that genius was nearly always tinged with madness. It seems now that he may have been right. There is evidence to suggest that many great artists and writers – including van Gogh, Nietzsche, the American poet Robert Lowell and possibly Wittgenstein – were very disturbed, and a number of studies have established a link between madness and creativity. In 1994, Felix

Post used the American Psychiatric Association's Diagnostic and Statistical Manual (DSM) to diagnose 291 world-famous scientists, composers, artists and politicians. Post found that a surprisingly large number suffered from psychiatric problems: 31 per cent of composers, 38 per cent of visual artists, 46 per cent of writers and 18 per cent of scientists showed signs of psychopathology and had experienced periods when they could not work at all and needed rest; some had sought treatment in hospital.

Hans Eysenck believes there to be a fundamental biochemical link between madness and genius. Like creative individuals, schizophrenics make bizarre associations. We have seen that one of the causes of schizophrenia may be an excess of the neurotransmitter dopamine in the brain (see page 146): this allows thoughts to slip too easily from one cell to the next without normal inhibition, making for chaotic thinking. Eysenck argues that high dopamine levels in the brain may also be a precondition of genius. But while schizophrenics are not able to use their chaotic associations and are overwhelmed by perceptions, sensations, associations and voices, creative people can manage a level of control.

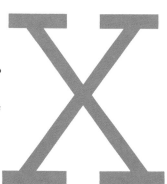

When presented with a stimulus, such as the large X (right), most people are unlikely to pay it much attention; moreover, they are just as unlikely to pay attention if the X is presented to them again. Creative people and schizophrenics, however, are less "rational". *If the X is presented repeatedly, they will sometimes attend to it, sometimes not. This common factor, called flexibility of cognitive inhibition, is another line of evidence for a link between madness and genius.*

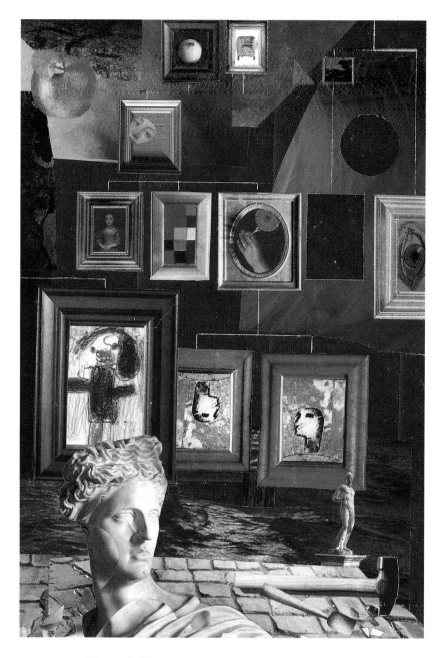

The complex biochemistry of genius, according to Eysenck, has an
equally complex genetic origin. Genius is not an inherited trait, and
cannot be manufactured. It is a genetic freak that will periodically
emerge, sometimes in the most surprising circumstances, as it has done
since before the days of Aristotle.

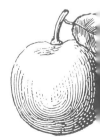

The Evolving Consciousness

Throughout this book I have stressed that the discourse about the nature of the human mind has been conducted in two different languages – the subjective language of thought, emotion and experience, and the objective language of anatomy, physiology and experiment. Each of these approaches has its own pitfalls. The subjective language of the therapist can make us obsessed with becoming perfectly self-conscious. For example, the British therapist John Rowan encourages his clients to discover their own "sub-personalities" in order to learn who they really are and to become more like that person (or should it be persons?). Is this a path to insight or to self-indulgence? On the other hand, the objective language of the scientist can lead us to ignore important aspects of the workings of the mind. The behaviourists, for example, totally spurned the notion of consciousness in the mid-20th century (see page 77); and today, many biologists dismiss as rubbish the ideas of Jung and Freud because they are incapable of being scientifically tested.

There clearly exists a political and intellectual divide in the study of mind, a divide that was dramatically revealed by the split within the American Psychological Association (APA). The experimental psychologists (who had founded the APA in 1893) left the Association in the 1980s, claiming that it had been taken over by the "therapists". They felt that the APA was no longer speaking their language, and that the issues that concerned clinical psychologists and therapists were not really scientific. Faced with these disagreements, some commentators wondered whether it made any sense to pretend that psychology was really one subject, and whether it was worth even searching for a grand theory to unify its different languages and sub-disciplines. I want to suggest that it would be fatal to abandon this quest, because we will never really understand ourselves, our potential and our limits if we dismiss certain kinds of knowledge as peripheral, or if we fail to integrate information from every available source.

It is no good disguising the enormous differences between the two languages of psychology, and finding a way to bridge the divide remains the great challenge. However, given the huge advances in brain science made in the last hundred years, I believe that it is dangerously pessimistic to think that the human mind is incapable of meeting this challenge.

One hundred years ago techniques such as EEG (see page

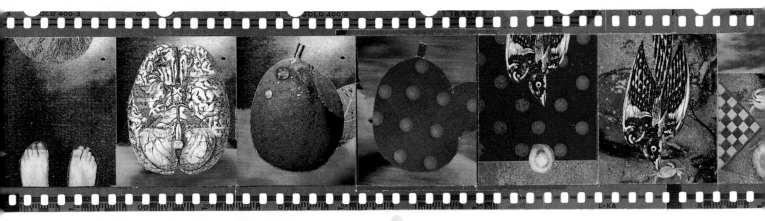

72) and PET scanning (see page 183), which today allow scientists to correlate thought with physiology (albeit on a modest scale), were unheard of, and it is very likely that we will continue to make similar technological advances. If I look into the crystal ball, it is possible to foresee a time when imaging technology will be able to show how different areas of the brain interact when engaged in a particular task, revealing in real time the different neural networks that are brought into play, and the synapses that become active. Where might this technology take us? Let us explore this question using a thought experiment. In one room is a group of scientists provided with state-of-the-art brain scanners. In another (soundproof) room is the subject of the experiment – an actor called Harold. Harold alternately recites a passage from Shakespeare, says it silently to himself, and speaks the passage as he believes a schizophrenic might speak it. Using current brain-imaging technology, the scientists could say only that the language centres in Harold's brain are active; in 25 years time, they may be able to distinguish between the three performances; and in 50 or 100 years, the scientists may well be able to "see" exactly what Harold is thinking – to

know exactly what passage he is reciting, whether his thoughts are straying to his plans for the evening, and whether or not he feels an itch on his arm.

This last scenario raises an intriguing question. Suppose that the 22nd-century scientists, using their sophisticated scanners, determine that Harold is thinking about his holiday in Bermuda. Harold, on the other hand, swears that he is thinking about dinner. Who would we, as objective observers, believe? In certain circumstances, we might believe the scientists. If, for example, Harold were mentally ill, we might favour the scientists' analysis of brain activity, patterns of synapse firing and biochemical imbalances over the report of the subject. But if Harold were sane, with no signs of psychosis, most of us would believe him. The scientists' information does not seem – as we can imagine it now – to permit the final leap into someone else's consciousness. Harold has privileged access to his own brain: his consciousness is out of bounds to others, and his reports are authoritative.

I suspect that this will always be the case. The more scientists learn about brain biochemistry and physiology, the more we will resist their scientific analyses of our consciousness. In

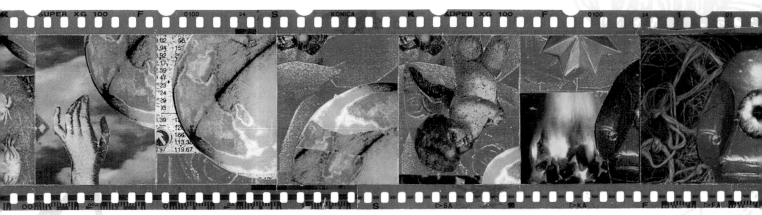

order to remain stubbornly human, we will insist upon the primacy of our insight and we will refine it, becoming better at understanding why we have certain thoughts and ideas. At the same time, we will protect our humanity – our minds – from the incursions of hard science by wrapping it up in cocoons of consciousness and self-consciousness, making our subjective lives so subtle and complicated that they will confound the most sophisticated of scanners.

This idea that we may be able to consciously manipulate the workings of the mind to protect them from scientific investigation seems like an implausible science-fiction fantasy. But we have already seen that human consciousness is not immutable: it evolves, and can be shaped by changes in culture, scientific advances and the extent to which we understand ourselves.

As scientists increase their knowledge of the functioning of the brain, and perhaps the mind, and as we grow in self-knowledge, all of us becoming fluent in both the objective and the subjective languages of the mind, will the nature of consciousness change as a result? Will science fiction become the new reality?

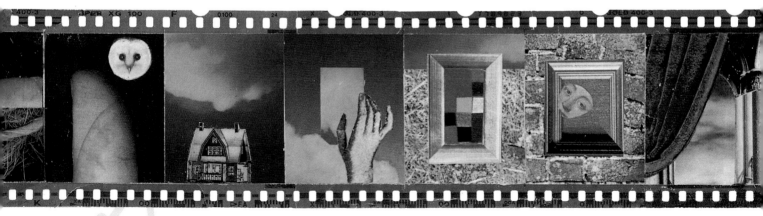

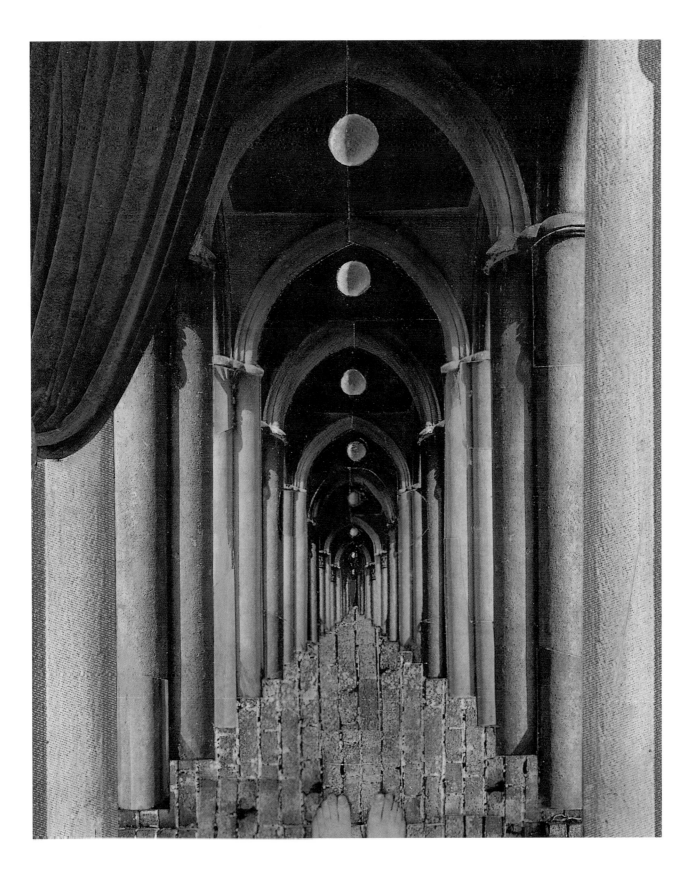

Glossary

Words in *italics* have their own entries in this glossary.

adrenalin A *neurotransmitter* secreted by the adrenal medulla above the kidneys, which increases heart activity and muscle action, preparing the body for "fight, fright or flight".

Alzheimer's disease Senile dementia; a degenerative brain disorder, whose symptoms include increasing loss of memory followed by increasing disorientation and eventually death.

anterograde amnesia A condition in which a person cannot recall events that occurred after a traumatic experience.

archetype A universal human tendency to perceive and act in specific ways. After studying myths, legends and religious customs across many cultures, Carl Jung defined "archetypal" concepts such as the anima (the feminine side of a man's personality) and the animus (the male side of a woman's personality).

artificial intelligence (AI) A branch of research into computer programs that can "think". By combining computer technology and cognitive psychology, scientists try to recreate the human brain as closely as possible in order to learn more about how it works.

autism A psychiatric disorder first apparent in childhood. Symptoms include lack of responsiveness, speech difficulties, stereotypical behaviour patterns and the inability to make normal social contact.

automatic behaviour Behaviour that does not require moment-by-moment willing; examples are breathing or walking.

axon The long tube in a *neuron* that transmits information received by *dendrites* to other neurons.

behaviourism A psychological theory that focuses on the study of an observed stimulus and an observed response.

bipolar disorder Another name for manic depression, in which patients swing between the poles of depression and elation.

Broca's area Part of the *left hemisphere* of the brain, involved in the processing of language.

central nervous system The brain and *spinal cord*.

cerebellum Part of the *hindbrain* that regulates *automatic behaviour*, such as breathing, coordination and the sense of balance.

cerebral cortex The outer layer of the brain, associated with sensory perception and the higher mental functions.

cones *Receptors* in the *retina* specialized for colour vision and concentrated in the *fovea*; they are shorter and less numerous than *rods*.

corpus callosum A bundle of nerve fibres connecting the *left* and *right hemispheres* of the brain.

dendrite The branching part of the *neuron* at the end of the *axon* that receives and carries messages to and from other cells.

ego According to Freudian theory, a crucial part of the personality that represents the conscious self (see also *superego* and *id*).

endogenous depression Depression with no apparent cause.

endorphins A type of *neurotransmitter* produced in the brain. Endorphins have often been called the brain's natural pain killers and have a similar chemical structure to *opiates*.

fetish A form of sexual behaviour that focuses on an unusual object or sexual practice.

forebrain The upper section of the brain, consisting of the *cerebral cortex*, the *thalamus*, the *hypothalamus* and the *limbic system.*

fovea In the eye, a small central region of the *retina* that has a high concentration of *cones.*

frequency The number of sound or light waves occuring during a specific period.

frontal lobe One of the four lobes of the *cerebral cortex*, believed to be involved in movement and higher thought processes such as abstract reasoning.

grammar In research on language, experts differentiate between "deep" grammar and "surface" grammar. Deep grammar is the basic structure of meaning; surface, or prescriptive, grammar refers to the rules of verbs, punctuation and so on.

hindbrain The section of the brain at the base of the head, consisting of the *medulla oblongata*, the *pons*, the *cerebellum* and the *reticular formation.*

hormones Substances secreted by one or more glands that regulate many physiological processes.

hypnosis A technique that induces a state of deep relaxation in a subject, who remains able to respond to suggestions and commands on an unconscious level.

hypothalamus A small but very important structure at the base of the *forebrain* that regulates many *automatic behaviours* (including balance and appetite) and interacts with other areas of the brain to control, among other things, consciousness, survival behaviour, emotions and pain reactions.

id According to Freud, the most basic level of personality. It is made up of instinctual urges such as sexual and aggressive impulses, and operates on the "pleasure principle" without consideration of external reality or rationality (see also *superego* and *ego*).

left hemisphere One of the two sides of the *cerebral cortex*; it controls the right side of the body and is critical for language processing and speech.

limbic system The system in the *forebrain* involved in emotional behaviour, learning and adaptability. It consists of the hippocampus, the amygdala and the septum.

long-term memory (LTM) Memory that lasts longer than a few days; contrasted with *short-term memory*, which lasts only a few minutes.

medulla oblongata The lowest section of the brainstem at the top of the *spinal cord*. It is involved in controlling the heartbeat, respiration, digestion and swallowing; also the place where nerves from the right side of the body switch over to the left side of the brain and vice versa.

midbrain A small section of the brain that is a continuation of the *reticular formation* in the *hindbrain*; it is less important in humans than it is in other mammals.

neural pathway A route along which neural impulses travel.

neurons The nerve cells that are the basic structural components of the nervous system.

neurotransmitter A chemical messenger that is released by a *neuron* and relays a message across the *synapse* to the receiving *neuron.*

occipital lobe One of the four lobes of the *cerebral cortex*, mainly involved in visual processing.

opiate A substance derived from the opium poppy, such as heroin, morphine or codeine, that when smoked, ingested, injected or inhaled produces numbing of pain and a sense of well-being. Such substances are usually addictive.

paradoxical sleep The *REM sleep* state in which the mind seems alert but the body is virtually paralyzed.

parapraxis A term used by Freud for a meaningful mistake, such as a slip of the tongue.

parietal lobe One of the four lobes of the *cerebral cortex*, mainly involved in processing the information that comes from the skin and muscles.

perception The process by which what we sense with our *receptors* (eyes, ears and so on) is organized in the brain to become the experiences that we have.

peripheral nervous system The part of the nervous system made up of all the nerve cells of the body except those of the *central nervous system*. It relays information between the brain and the body.

phobia Excessive anxiety provoked by particular objects, events or situations, such as spiders or open spaces, in the absence of real danger.

photoreceptors *Rods* and *cones*: the structures in the *retina* that convert light energy into information that the *central nervous system* can analyze and process.

physiology The scientific study of the processes and functions of living organisms.

pitch The sensation of how high or low a sound is, created by the *frequency* of the sound waves.

plasticity The ability to modify and be flexible; in terms of the brain, this refers to the way one area can take over the functions of another if that area is damaged.

pons A structure in the *hindbrain* containing nerve cells that relay messages from one area of the brain to another. Also contains nerves connecting parts of the head and face.

psi phenomena Extrasensory phenomena that cannot be explained by conventional scientific means.

psychiatry The branch of medicine concerned with mental health and illness.

psychoanalysis A method of investigation and psychotherapy pioneered by Sigmund Freud, which traces the roots of mental illness and nervous disorders to unconscious concepts in the patient's mind formed during childhood, and attempts to treat the disorder by bringing these concepts and possible traumas to light.

psychodynamic theory A theory of human behaviour and motivations based on conflicting unconscious processes and the significance of childhood experience in determining adult behaviour.

psychology The scientific study of mind and behaviour.

reactive depression Depression with a plausible cause, such as divorce (see also *endogenous depression*).

receptors Physiological components of the nervous system that receive sensory information from "outside" (for example the *retina*). Also used more generally to refer to the organs containing these components, such as the ear or the eye.

REM sleep Sleep during which there is rapid eye movement that is usually, but not exclusively, associated with dreaming (see also *paradoxical sleep*).

reticular formation A network of *neurons* in the *midbrain* and *hindbrain* that regulates whether we are awake, asleep, alert or aroused, and also regulates heartbeat and breathing.

retina The structure at the back of the eye containing the *photoreceptors*.

retrograde amnesia A condition in which a person cannot remember events that occured before a traumatic experience.

right hemisphere One half of the *cerebral cortex* that controls the left side of the body and regulates spatial activity.

rods *Photoreceptors* for night-time and dark vision, incapable of colour vision. They are located on the periphery of the *retina* and are longer and more numerous than *cones*.

schema A term used by some psychologists to describe a cognitive framework for organizing associated concepts, based on previous experiences; used by Piaget in his theory of child development.

schizophrenia A group of mental disorders in which sufferers experience disturbances in perception, cognition, emotion and physical and social behaviour.

sensation A conscious experience that is aroused by any stimulus.

short-term memory (STM) Memory that lasts only a few minutes; it is organized separately from *long-term memory*.

spinal cord The bundle of nerves inside the spinal column starting at the brain and ending where it meets the parts of the peripheral nervous system in the legs.

stimulants Drugs such as caffeine, nicotine and cocaine that excite the level of functioning of the *central nervous system*, either by stimulating the heart or by inhibiting natural depressants. Problems of tolerance and addiction are linked with long-term use.

stimulus A specific energy that provokes a response in a *receptor*, or anything that causes an organism to respond.

suggestibility Being so open to influence that one denies what one either remembers or perceives. An important result of *hypnosis*.

superego Part of Freud's model of the mind, which comprises all the internalized norms and values of society acquired during early development through interaction with authority figures such as parents (see also *id* and *ego*).

synesthesia Confusions of *perceptions* and *sensations* so that colours, for example, seem to be linked to sounds.

synapse The gap between *neurons* into which *neurotransmitters* are released.

temporal lobe One of the four lobes of the *cerebral cortex*, mainly involved in auditory processing.

thalamus The two-lobed structure in the centre of the brain which helps to relay sensory information and control sleep patterns.

vesicles Little sacs in the *synapses* that hold and release *neurotransmitters*.

Brain-Imaging Techniques

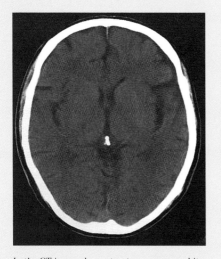

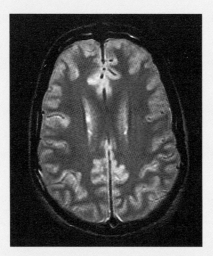

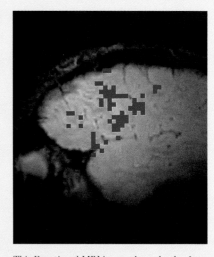

In the CT image, bony structures appear white and soft tissue appears in different shades of grey depending on its density.

An MRI image distinguishes between the grey and white matter of the brain in great detail.

This Functional MRI image shows levels of brain activity (coloured red) as the patient recalls words from memory.

Computed Tomography (CT or CAT)

CT scans produce images of "slices" through the brain, which show the layout and density of the tissues. The scanner is made up of a tube that produces a fan-like beam of x-ray radiation, opposite a bank of x-ray detectors. As the beam of radiation passes through the patient's head to the detectors, dense tissue absorbs more radiation than soft tissue. The beam is rotated to capture the image from all angles, and a computer combines these to produce an image of the "slice", showing the position and density of the tissues, with denser tissues appearing paler than the softer ones. The patient is then moved slightly to scan another "slice", and the computer combines images of all the slices to produce a three-dimensional view of the brain. Modern CT scanners produce images in a few seconds that can distinguish variations in density of about 1 per cent.

**Magnetic Resonance Imaging (MRI)
and Functional MRI**

MRI scans give a more detailed picture of the brain than CT scans, without using any potentially harmful radiation. The images show in great detail the density of the tissue, distinguishing clearly between grey and white matter and showing up even minute tumours. The largest component of an MRI scanner is a magnet: it must be large enough to enclose the patient, and it also must produce a very uniform magnetic field. Basically, an MRI scan is able to map the distribution of hydrogen atoms, because they respond more strongly to a magnetic field than other atoms in the brain do. Because water molecules contain two hydrogen atoms, MRI is an excellent method of imaging tissues with a high water content, such as the brain and the spinal cord. Functional MRIs image the functioning of the brain rather than just its struc-

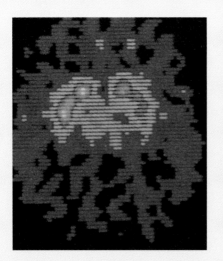 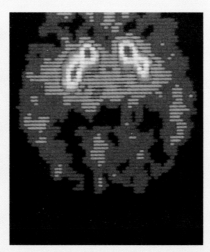

This PET scan of a patient under normal conditions shows areas of low activity in blue and areas of higher activity in green and yellow.

This PET scan shows unusually high levels of brain activity, coloured in red and yellow, because of the use of cocaine, a stimulant.

ture. As parts of the brain become active during different thought processes or body functions, the consumption of oxygen from the blood increases within that region. Functional MRI measures the change in blood oxygenation to that part of the brain. This can be accomplished because deoxygenated blood responds more strongly to magnetism than blood containing high levels of oxygen.

Positron Emission Tomography (PET)

Like the CT scans and MRIs, PET scans look at a "slice" through the brain, measuring the functioning of the brain in even more detail than Functional MRIs can. It does this by combining a radionuclide, which is a radioactive element, with another chemical that is easily absorbed by the body, such as a gas that can be inhaled, or a type of sugar that can be injected into the blood stream. The combination of the radionuclide and the other chemical is known as a radiopharmaceutical. This travels to the brain via the bloodstream, where it will concentrate in the most active areas of the brain, because increased mental activity demands an increased blood flow to the region or regions involved. As the radioactive element of the radiopharmaceutical decays, it produces positrons, which are identical to electrons but with positive charges; when the positrons encounter electrons, as they inevitably do, the two annihilate each other, in the process producing two gamma rays, which move out of the body in exactly opposite directions. They are measured by gamma ray detectors in the PET scanner, which compiles data on rays that arrive at the same time from opposite directions. This allows it to measure the distribution of the radiopharmaceutical in the brain, with the areas of highest concentration indicating high levels of mental activity.

Bibliography

Introduction

Kline, P. *Psychology Exposed*, 1990.

Mind and Matter

Chomsky, N. *Syntactic Structures*, 1957.

Churchland, P. and Sejnowski, T. *The Computational Brain*, 1992.

Darwin, C. *On the Origin of Species by Means of Natural Selection*, 1859.

Descartes, R. *Discourse on Method*, 1637.

Freud, S. *The Ego and the Id*, 1923.

Freud, S. *The Interpretation of Dreams*, 1899.

Freud, S. *Project for a Scientific Psychology*, 1895.

Locke, J. *An Essay Concerning Human Understanding*, 1690.

de la Mettrie, J. O. *L'homme machine*, 1747.

Skinner, B.F. *Beyond Freedom and Dignity*, 1972.

Skinner, B. F. *Walden Two*, 1948.

Wittgenstein, L. *Philosophical Investigations*, 1958.

Sensation and Perception

Grandin, T. *Thinking in Pictures*, 1995.

Gregory, R. *Eye and Brain*, 1966.

Melzack, R. and Wall, P.D. *The Challenge of Pain*, 1982.

Consciousness

Baddeley, A. *Working Memory*, 1986.

Bem, S. *The Lenses of Gender*, 1993.

Crick, F. *The Astonishing Hypothesis*, 1994.

Damasio, A. *Descartes' Error: Emotion, Reason and the Human Brain*, 1994.

Dennett, D. *Consciousness Explained*, 1994.

Eccles, J. *The Evolution of Human Nature*, 1985.

Firth, U. *Autism*, 1993

Gardner, H. *Multiple Intelligences*, 1995.

James, W. *The Principles of Psychology*, 1890.

Ornstein, R. *The Psychology of Consciousness*, 1976.

Ornstein, R. *Multiminds*, 1985.

Piaget, J. *Play, Dreams and Imitation in Childhood*, 1952.

Rogers, C. *Counselling and Psychotherapy*, 1942.

Sacks, O. *The Man who Mistook his Wife for a Hat*, 1985.

Sacks, O. *An Anthropologist on Mars*, 1995.

Sperry, R. (1974) "Lateral specialization in the surgically separated hemisphere" in F. Schmitt and F.G. Warden (eds), *The Neurosciences; Third Study Programme*.

Illusions, Delusions and Deceptions

Freud, S. *Jokes and their Relation to the Unconscious*, 1905.

Freud, S. *The Psychopathology of Everyday Life*, 1904.

Gombrich, E. *Art and Illusion*, 1961.

Gregory, R. *Odd Perceptions*, 1990.

Krafft-Ebing, R. *Psychopathia sexualis*, 1886.

Altered States

Darwin, C. *The Expression of the Emotions in Man and Animals*, 1872.

Ellenberger, H. *The Discovery of the Unconscious*, 1970.

Gauld, A. *A History of Hypnosis*, 1988.

Gurdieff, G. *Meetings with Remarkable Men*, 1921.

Gudjuddson, G. *The Psychology of Interrogations, Confessions and Testimony* , 1993.

Hacking, I. *Rewriting the Soul*, 1995.

Huxley, A. *The Doors of Perception*, 1954.

James, W. *The Variety of Religious Experience*, 1902.

Jaynes, J. *The Origins of Consciousness in the Breakdown of the Bicameral Mind*, 1976.

de Quincey, T. *Confessions of an English Opium Eater*, 1821.

The Mind under Siege

Clare, A. *Psychiatry in Dissent*, 1976.

Cohen, D. *Forgotten Millions*, 1988.

Cohen, D. and MacKeith, S. *The Development of the Imagination*, 1991.

Deutsch, A. *The Shame of the States*, 1948.

Eysenck, H. *The Decline and Fall of the Freudian Empire*, 1986.

Jung, C.G. *Archetypes and the Collective Unconscious*, 1954.

Klein, M. *Contributions to Psychoanalysis (1921-45)*, 1948.

Laing, R.D. *The Divided Self*, 1961.

Masson, J. *The Assault on Truth*, 1980.

Maslow, A. *Further Reaches of Human Nature*, 1973.

Orbach, S. *Fat is a Feminist Issue*, 1979.

Rogers, C. *The Clinical Treatment of the Problem Child*, 1939.

Rowan, J. *Subpersonalities*, 1988.

Rowan, J. *Discover Your Subpersonalities*, 1990.

Sizemore, C.C. and Pitillo, E. *I'm Eve*, 1977.

Sizemore, C.C. *A Mind of My Own*, 1989.

Szasz, T. *The Manufacture of Madness*, 1983.

Szasz, T. *Cruel Compassion*, 1994.

Thigpen, C.H. and Cleckley, H. (1954) "A case of multiple personality", *Journal of Abnormal and Social Psychology*, Vol. 49, pp. 135-51.

Thigpen, C.H. and Cleckley, H. *The Three Faces of Eve*, 1957.

The Ascent of the Mind

Eysenck, H. *Genius*, 1995.

Hudson, L. *Contrary Imaginations*, 1966.

Joynson, R. *The Burt Affair*, 1989

Picture Credits

p.5 (left): Science Photo Library; p.5 (right): Mary Evans Picture Library

p.6 (left): Werner Forman Archive; p.6 (right): Topham Picture Source

p.10: The Wellcome Institute

p.12 (background): Images Colour Library; p.12 (foreground): Mary Evans Picture Library

p.15: Science Photo Library

p.16: C.M. Dixon

p.17: Science Photo Library

p.20: Novosti / Science Photo Library

p.21: Novosti / Science Photo Library

p.22: Science Photo Library

p.23 (top and bottom): Science Photo Library

p.25 (top): Ann Ronan / Image Select; p.25 (bottom): Dept of Cognitive Neurology / Wellcome Institute / Science Photo Library

p.27 (background and foreground): CNRI / Science Photo Library

p.28: Science Photo Library

p.30: Mary Evans Picture Library

p.32: Dept of Cognitive Neurology / Wellcome Institute

p.33 (top right): Images Colour Library

p.34: Stephen Wiltshire / Margaret Hewson

p.35: William Kurelek / Bethlem Hospital Archive

p.36: Kobal Collection

p.41 (top): Mansell Collection; p.41 (bottom): Mary Evans Picture Library

p.42-43: Images Colour Library

p.45: The Royal Collection / Her Majesty Queen Elizabeth II

p.47: Images Colour Library

p.48: Science Photo Library

p.49: Michael Holford

p.55: Science Photo Library

p.61: Mary Evans Picture Library

p.62: BSP VEM / Science Photo Library

p.67: Images Colour Library

p.68 (top): Mary Evans Picture Library

p.70: Dept of Cognitive Neurology / Wellcome Institute / Science Photo Library

p.72: Science Photo Library

p.73 (top): Jean-Loup Charmet; p.73 (bottom): Science Photo Library

p.75: illustration by Stewart Clough

p.82: Werner Forman Archive

p.83: Ann Ronan / Image Select

p.87: Zefa Pictures

p.94: Mary Evans Picture Library

p.97: Escher Estate / Visual Arts Library

p.98: British Film Institute

p.100: Topham Picture Source

p.101: Zefa Pictures

p.103: Palazzo Ducale, Urbino / Scala

p.104: Tate Gallery / Visual Arts Library

p.108: Mary Evans Picture Library

p.111: Duncan Baird Publishers

p.112 (top): Bridgeman Art Library; p.112 (bottom): Bridgeman Art Library / Staatsmuseum, Berlin

p.113: e.t. archive / Kew Gardens Botanical Library

p.114: Bridgeman Art Library

p.117 (top): Bridgeman Art Library / Giraudon; p.117 (bottom): e.t. archive

p.119: Images Colour Library

p.120: Bridgeman Art Library / Victoria & Albert Museum

p.122: National Library of Medicine at the Wellcome Institute / Science Photo Library

p.124: e.t. archive

p.125: Ancient Art and Architecture; p.124-125: Eadweard Muybridge / Royal Photographic Society

p.126: e.t.archive

p.130: Mary Evans Picture Library

p.131: Adam Hart-Davies / Science Photo Library

p.134: NHPA

p.141: Wellcome Institute

p.142 (top): Science Photo Library; p.142 (right): Bruce Davidson / Magnum Photographers

p.143: David Chick / Bethlem Hospital Archive

p.146: Science Photo Library

p.147: Adam Hart-Davies / Science Photo Library

p.148: Topham Picture Source

p.151: Images Colour Library

p.154: Marek Walisiewicz

p.157: Images Colour Library

p.160: National Library of Medicine / Wellcome Institute

p.161: National Library of Medicine / Wellcome Institute

p.169: Topham Picture Source

p.182 (all): Michael Mooney at the Department of Medical Physics, University College, London

p.183 (left and right): Michael Mooney at the Department of Medical Physics, University College, London

Index

Real Questions

Reading and Writing Genres

Real Questions

Reading and Writing Genres

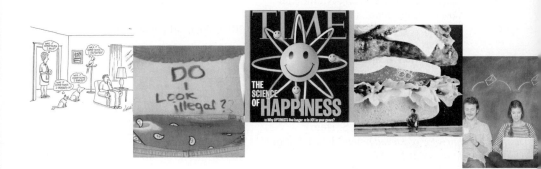

Kathryn Evans

Bridgewater State University

Bedford/St. Martin's

Boston ◆ New York

For Bedford/St. Martin's

Senior Executive Editor: Leasa Burton
Senior Developmental Editor: Adam Whitehurst
Production Editor: Jessica Gould
Assistant Production Manager: Joe Ford
Executive Marketing Manager: Molly Parke
Editorial Assistant: Nicholas McCarthy
Copy Editor: Jamie Thaman
Indexer: Melanie Belkin
Photo Researcher: Connie Gardner
Permissions Manager: Kalina K. Ingham
Art Director: Lucy Krikorian
Text Design: Claire Seng-Niemoeller
Cover Design: Donna Dennison
Cover Art: Question (Ask the Magic Box), 2010. Polaroid composite.
© Patrick Winfield.
Composition: Graphic World Inc.
Printing and Binding: RR Donnelley and Sons

President, Bedford/St. Martin's: Denise B. Wydra
Presidents, Macmillan Higher Education: Joan E. Feinberg and Tom Scotty
Editor in Chief: Karen S. Henry
Director of Development: Erica T. Appel
Director of Marketing: Karen R. Soeltz
Production Director: Susan W. Brown
Associate Production Director: Elise S. Kaiser
Managing Editor: Shuli Traub

Manufactured in the United States of America.

8   7   6   5   4   3
f   e   d   c   b   a

For information, write: Bedford/St. Martin's, 75 Arlington Street, Boston, MA 02116 (617-399-4000)

ISBN 978-0-312-60121-8

Acknowledgments

Acknowledgments and copyrights are continued at the back of the book on pages 701–704, which constitute an extension of the copyright page. It is a violation of the law to reproduce these selections by any means whatsoever without the written permission of the copyright holder.

To my parents, Beverly and Travis Evans,
who have always encouraged me to learn.